Herbs and Spices for Florida Gardens

How to grow and enjoy Florida plants with special uses

by Monica Moran Brandies

B.B. Mackey Books
P.O. Box 475
Wayne, PA 19087

Published by
B.B. MACKEY BOOKS
P.O. Box 475
Wayne, PA 19087-0475

Printed on
recycled paper

Printed in the United States of America
First Edition   10 9 8 7 6 5 4 3 2

Ink drawings by Betty Mackey   Art p. 204: All America Selections
Lithographs from antique sources
Cover photos by Betty Mackey and Monica Brandies

ISBN 0-9616338-6-7
Library of Congress Catalog Card Number   96-75721

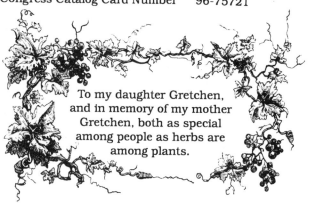

To my daughter Gretchen,
and in memory of my mother
Gretchen, both as special
among people as herbs are
among plants.

Acknowledgements:

Special thanks to God who did some of his finest works when he made herbs and the people who grow them, to my family, to Kaye Cude, Maryon and Mel Marsh, Terri Bikis, James Steele, Loretta Clements, Gene Joyner, Chef Hubert Des Marais (of the Grand Hotel), Billy Daniel, Chefs Rick Munroe and Dan Sullivan, the members of the Tampa Unit of the Herb Society of America, Peter and Betty O'Toole, Janice DiPaolo, the people at Great Outdoors Publishing, the people at ECHO, the staff and garden volunteers at the Hillsborough County Cooperative Extension Service, to Jean Mansmann for editorial work, and to all the other herb friends who have helped me. And especially to Betty Mackey who persuaded me to start this book and was a constantly encouraging partner.

TABLE OF CONTENTS

1. What is Different About Herbs in Florida?

You'll have a wonderful time growing herbs here in Florida, if you learn to make the best of our unique and challenging climate. Most kinds of herbs grown in northern climates will grow very well in Florida, but will need different schedules, exposures, or methods.

At first it may seem that a few herbs will not grow here at all because of the heat, but you'll soon learn when to plant what. Any herb that grows elsewhere in the United States will grow here for at least some part of the year, and that length of time is usually much longer than the more northern growing season.

Some herbs that come back reliably in northern states after hard winters will need replanting after our hot summers. But to balance that inconvenience, exciting semi-tropical herbs and spices like ginger and bay laurel will be perennial and easy.

Many delightful herbs actually grow wild here, and you will soon learn to recognize them and enjoy their leaves, blooms, fragrances, and fruit.

This book will give you cultural instructions specific not only to our state, but to northern, central, and southern Florida. You will not find this much herbal information keyed to your region anywhere else in print. Here you will learn how to adjust the herb growing advice found in other herb books to your own Florida conditions.

Although there are many herb books with intricate instructions for detailed herbal crafts, this one contains streamlined uses which fit into the busiest lifestyle. And although you can spend all your time and energy growing herbs as a business, or perhaps as an adjunct to another business such as a restaurant with a herb garden, you can also find satisfaction growing herbs on a much smaller scale. You will appreciate herbs in attractive garden beds that add to your landscape, in pots on your patio or windowsill, and even in a hanging basket over your kitchen sink.

Herbs have many delightful uses in gardens, in cooking, for wreath making and flower arranging, and in general for making life richer and more pleasant. Herbs can also serve practical functions: they'll repel moths, flies, and mosquitoes, serve as first aid in home remedies, and much more.

Herbs are not fussy plants. Most of them require only a minimum of care. Perhaps the ones that don't do well for you, or don't since you moved to Florida, will thrive by the time you finish reading this book.

HERBS AND SPICES DEFINED

A herb (yes, go ahead and pronounce the 'h;' both pronunciations are proper) by my definition is any plant with any part that has uses additional to being ornamental or producing food. These uses can be for flavor in cooking, for pleasing aromas, or even aromatherapy, in perfumes or cosmetics, to repel harmful insects, to attract butterflies or hummingbirds, or to make natural dyes.

With our subtropic Florida climate, we can grow many herbs and spices. While herbs are mostly, but not exclusively, herbaceous plants of which the leaves or flowers are most often used, spices are most often a vine, shrub, or tree grown in more tropical regions, more strongly flavored and aromatic, and the bark, root, berry, or pod is most often used.

Spices are not generally included in herb books intended for gardeners in the United States because they tend to be difficult to grow, especially in a cold climate. But conditions in Florida support many spices such as ginger, vanilla, allspice, bay, and neem, so they are covered in this book.

Herbs and spices include trees, shrubs, wildflowers, ornamentals, and vegetables, all with extra usefulness and fascinating history.

Throughout this book I pass along herbal lore, everything from uses mentioned in ancient herbals to recipes for seasoning foods and making cosmetics. But this information is for educational purposes and is not meant to prescribe any treatment for any ailment. Many herbs and spices contain powerful chemical compounds which affect differerent people in different ways and must be used with caution and common sense.

Do not continue using any herb or food if side effects appear. Use each herb or spice in moderation until you are sure that no one involved has an allergy to it, and do not let herbal treatment cause delay in seeing a medical doctor if someone is ill. Neither author nor publisher is responsible for any ill effects thought to be caused by herbs or spices mentioned in *Herbs and Spices for Florida Gardens*.

WHO AM I TO TELL YOU?

A long time ago, when I thought I knew little about growing herbs, I waited especially long at a county fair flower show to see what would show up in a class marked "Three Different Herbs." There were several combinations, and I was surprised to realize that I had most of the same plants growing in my garden. Parsley, nasturtiums, mint, calendula, roses: I already had more herbs than I knew to call by that name.

We are all living with herbs whether we know it or not. We probably eat them every day. A great percentage of our medicines contain herbs or derivatives from herbs. Herbs have probably been a part of every garden I've ever had, though I've only recently had a separate herb garden.

There were certainly herbs among the plants I brought into Florida in our van in the summer of '87 when we moved from Iowa. (I didn't learn that this is not allowed until a year or two later!) Nasturtiums were sprouting in peat pellets under the back seat even as we drove south. Lemon balm was in a pot. Mint and horseradish were in the bag of plants I'd dug and packed at the last minute.

I still shudder to remember how I sent a weekly column of garden advice back to Iowa newspapers that first summer while mint died in my Florida yard. The horseradish lived for about a year and then disappeared, as more than a few herbs have done for me here when I turned my back too long.

Those nasturtiums sat along the back porch wall (northwest side) and sulked for the entire first summer. It amazes me now to think that they survived at all, for I've since learned to expect them to disappear by mid June in all but the deepest shade. By fall I had picked up a few more herbs and the nasturtiums grew and bloomed bountifully all fall, winter, and spring. I was delighted with my success.

"Aha!" I was thinking, "Here is one form of gardening that is not so different here from what it was in the North."

It was spring when I first heard Kaye Cude give a talk about herbs. She had been professionally growing and selling herbs plus teaching and publishing a newsletter about growing herbs in Florida from her North Fort Myers farm for many years. I was captivated by both the subject and the speaker.

Kaye warned us that some of the herbs might die off in summer and some others would need special care to survive. And sure enough, the lemon balm that was almost a weed in Iowa slunk away from me that summer. I didn't know enough about Florida growing yet.

One of the great aspects of growing anything in Florida is that it grows fast, if it's going to die it usually dies fast, and the exper-ience teaches you much in a short span of time.

I presently have over 80 different herbs, counting the various lavenders and basils as one each, along with 42 different fruits, various cut flowers, and a few vegetables. I interviewed expert herb growers in northern, central, and southern Florida.

Perhaps now, after years of Florida research and experience, I can help you cut down on that "dies fast" part.

WHAT TO DO FIRST: IMPROVE THE SOIL

Soil in other places is a magic mix devised by nature to provide all that native plants need. That is somewhat true even of Florida soil, much of which looks like it would be great for filling sandboxes.

But we aren't dealing with native plants here, in most cases, and when we do, we have moved them away from their conditions in the wild. So we find that Florida soil mainly anchors the plant and we gardeners must provide most of whatever else is needed. This is primarily water and nutrients, and since these are valued resources, we want to make sure they are used as efficiently as possible, not poured through the sand, causing the nutrients to pollute the

ADD EXTRA NITROGEN

This is advice that I had most often ignored while I added mulch and humus in fairly large quantities to soil in other states and at first in Florida. And I never saw any signs of the nitrogen deficiency in the plants that was supposed to result from the nitrifying bacteria working first on the humus. But the fact that my bean leaves turned yellow after adding enzymes without additional nitrogen was proof to me that the nitrifying bacteria had abandoned the beans to work with the enzymes. After I added the nitrogen, good growth resumed and escalated.

underground water instead of feeding the plants.

The best way to make the most of all the water and fertilizer you use is to add plenty of organic matter to the soil.

The ideal soil preparation involves improving the entire bed. I'd like to add a truckload of Iowa topsoil, but since this isn't practical, I settle for adding as much organic matter as possible, either dug in or spread on as mulch. Organic mulch improves the soil below as it rots above.

I have also learned to add soil enzymes in the form of products like HELP (TM), Spray 'n Grow (TM), and Deep Root (TM), which are watered on. They contain soil bacteria, hormones, enzymes, amino acids, vitamins, and other minute ingredients. It seems they are naturally present in good soils, but largely depleted by heat and rain in our Florida soils. They would probably return on their own, as earthworms do, when we add enough humus to enrich the soil thoroughly, but since we may never quite achieve that, they can help make a difference.

See chapter 4 for more details on soil improvement. If you haven't already made a habit of adding humus liberally, do so. If you have, do it even more.

In the meantime, you can start your herbs, whether you have plants or seeds, in containers filled with a mix of approximately one part purchased top soil, one part humus such as purchased cow manure, peat moss, or homemade compost, and one part sand.

If you set bedding plants directly in the garden, dig generous holes and add ample compost or peat. This will improve the

water-holding abilities of the soil. Then add plenty of mulch around the plant and over an extended adjacent area.

Herbs are tough. Even in Florida, most kinds will grow, if mulched. Mulch improves the soil beneath while keeping moisture from evaporating too quickly. At the same time, it prevents weeds.

IN-GROUND VERSUS CONTAINER GROWING

In the long run, you will find that most herbs, once they pass the seedling stage, grow better with less constant care if they are planted in the ground rather than in containers. This is especially true from September until May.

However, it is wise to keep a few of the more sensitive plants in containers for convenience, for patio or porch decoration, or for winter or summer protection or backup.

WHAT TIME OF YEAR CAN YOU START HERBS?

For every disadvantage you face in Florida growing, there are several advantages. The greatest of these is our year-round good weather. You can start herbs from seed, cuttings, or purchased plants at any time of the year.

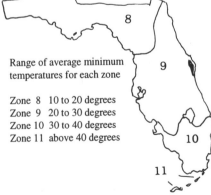

Range of average minimum temperatures for each zone

Zone 8 10 to 20 degrees
Zone 9 20 to 30 degrees
Zone 10 30 to 40 degrees
Zone 11 above 40 degrees

If you start in fall or winter in northern Florida (N), you may want to start in containers indoors, on a porch or patio, or outdoors in a spot that is easy to cover in case of frost. In central (C) and southern (S) Florida, protection is needed for frost-tender species only when temperatures are predicted to dip close to that 32 degree mark.

Spring and fall are ideal times for sowing seeds and taking cuttings in most of the state, especially in C and S, for then you have the longest growing time for annuals or summer-sensitive herbs.

There is no reason why you can't start a herb garden in the summer. But you can't plant the same plants or plant in quite the same way as growers do in the northern states, especially in summer. Summer there is comparable to Florida's April and May.

The intensity of the June-to-September sun in Florida along with the frequent heavy rains and high humidity make summer the most difficult time for growing certain of the most common herbs like lavender, sage, and thyme. Read on for more details and solutions.

START ANNUALS IN AUTUMN

Some annual herbs like dill, borage, calendula, marjoram, fennel, and chamomile will usually die out in Florida summers. By then they have given you many productive months of good growth.

Keep them going as long as you can or want when the hot and soggy summer days return. Then let them go without grief or guilt, and start them over from seeds or buy plants in the fall.

After losing the nasturtiums the second summer, I put one in a pot in deep shade and brought it

through the third summer. The next August, and every August since, volunteers have come up in a color range limited to yellows and oranges. So every few years I introduce seeds of new colors to grow with the others.

TAKE SOME LOSSES IN STRIDE

Most herb growers, even expert ones, admit to losing a few herbs through the summer. I find the first to go for me are the low, creeping herbs like marjoram and thyme. Using stone or pebbles as mulch will help.

SUMMER-SENSITIVE HERBS

Most difficult to save through summer:
lamb's ears, savory, tarragon
May live but will look bad for a time:
catnip, costmary, lemon balm, mint (some) lavender, parsley, santolina, scented geranium, sorrel, thyme, watercress
Difficult but you'll soon get the knack or find the resistant variety: artemisia, curry plant, feverfew, rue, salad burnet

---

All herbs, but these in particular, need excellent drainage. I suspect that what seems adequate the rest of the year proves just too soggy in summer rains. Some people keep these very herbs growing all summer in raised beds or containers, and I just saw some thriving in an in-ground bed on the side of a house where they get only about four hours of sunlight a day.

Some herbs will thrive in the conditions of one spot (the climate and soil plus the care-versus-neglect pattern of the gardener), and some will not. For those difficult varieties that do not, we might adjust the care or move the plant to a better spot. But why fret? There are dozens of other choices that grow more easily.

TOUGH SUMMER SURVIVORS

Here is my own list of 30 tough herbs that are summer survivors.

aloe	full sun
anise hyssop	partial shade
basil	full sun or partial shade
bugleweed	partial shade
butterflyweed	full sun or partial shade
cardamon	full sun or partial shade
chicory	full sun or partial shade
chive	partial shade
comfrey	partial shade
culantro	full sun, partial shade
elderberry	full sun partial shade
eucalpytus	full sun
garlic chive	full sun or partial shade
ginger	partial shade
goldenrod	full sun or partial shade
gotu kola	full sun or partial shade
grapefruit sage	partial shade
horseradish	full sun or partial shade
hydrangea	partial shade
juniper	full sun or partial shade
lemon grass	full sun or partial shade
lemon verbena	full sun or partial shade
mint	full sun or partial shade
nicandra	full sun or partial shade
tropical oregano	full sun or partial shade
passion flower	full sun or partial shade
pepper	full sun or partial shade
periwinkle	full sun or partial shade
pineapple sage	full sun or partial shade
pokeweed	full sun or partial shade
rose	full sun or partial shade
rosemary	full sun or partial shade
sage	full sun or partial shade
summer tarragon	full sun or partial shade
Vick's salve plant	full sun or partial shade
winter savory	partial shade

Other herb growers would have other names to add to this list.

BRINGING SENSITIVE PLANTS
THROUGH FROST AND HEAT

You'll select most herbs for your garden from among those that thrive in your area without coddling. In this book, you'll find an evaluation of the suitability of each kind for growth in N, C, or S in the plant-by-plant directory at the end of, and more information in the three chapters on herb growing in these regions. But most of us cannot resist trying herbs that are borderline in our area. Here are ways to increase chances for their success.

1. Make the most of the microclimates of your yard. Put marginally hardy plants on the south or west side of buildings for the most warmth. The south and east have the least wind as a rule. High spots may get less frost than low pockets. Plants in containers can be turned on their sides and rolled under the deck or more easily covered with leaves or blankets. I use our above-ground pool for protection, for its water stores heat. Plants growing around its edges are often killed on the front edge but survive at the back.

2. A healthy plant withstands more cold or heat than a stressed one. Water well before a frost or at the beginning of winter in N. Cover loosely with mulch to reduce frost damage. Floating row covers will help plants stay a few degrees warmer.

3. Resist pruning or heavily harvesting marginal plants in the fall. Leave plenty of vegetative growth for winter protection. If frost damages some of the foliage, leave it there. It will provide some protection if there is another frost. Don't be concerned with neatness until all danger of frost is past.

4. Many herbs that like full sun in Florida winters will benefit from partial to heavy shade in the afternoons in summer. For permanent in-ground plantings, take advantage of deciduous trees and shrubs, place potted plants or plant quick growers like pigeon peas or sunflowers to provide shade.

5. Raised beds or containers will help summer-fussy herbs make it through. Often it is not the heat but the moisture that kills them. What seems like fine drainage the rest of the year may not be sufficient during the summer rains.

6. For ultimate insurance, take cuttings of tender plants, or bring them indoors in containers if they aren't too large. Make the going out and coming in gradual during the period of adjustment.

PLANTS TO PROTECT FROM FROST

Tender perennials: scented geraniums, lemon verbena, marjoram, patchouli, pineapple sage, rosemary, and tropical oregano.

Tender annuals: basils, nasturtium, perilla.

Tropicals: allspice, bixa, cardamon, clove, cinnamon, ginger, mace, nutmeg. The tender perennials ginger and allspice (the only tropicals I've had have come through the last several winters in the Tampa area, but would be the first I'd bring in, cover, or back up with cuttings in a severe frost.

Maryon Marsh, who grows herbs at The Misting Shed in Durant, Florida, says she brings most of her herbs through the summer, but they often look worse for the wear by August. She uses misting and shading that home gardeners may not be able to match, but if you grow herbs in pots on screened porches you can get pretty close, especailly if you give them a light spray of water now and then.

I had thought I must lose parsley every summer, but some growers assured me theirs lasts as long as four years. Some claim lemon balm as a summer survivor, but it has been iffy for me. In containers or shade it can make it through. It is easier to grow farther north, and harder farther south.

SOLUTIONS FOR SAVING SUMMER-SENSITIVE HERBS

1. Take cuttings of doubtful plants, put them in containers, and move them into more shade for the summer. If you lose your parent plant, you can start over from the cutting.

2. Use light soil mixtures, plus styrofoam peanuts on the bottom for better drainage, and none of the moisture retaining gels or products you might add to other container soil mixes.

3. Use peat, perlite, or vermiculite. These help retain moisture, but they also aid drainage and hold some air in the soil.

4. Sprinkle plants with water daily in the heat of the day to cool them off, and also to wash off any insects or disease spores.

5. Remove saucers from under containers during the season of summer rains.

6. Put some containers of herbs inside the screened pool or porch area: screening filters direct sunshine and lessens stress.

WINTER PROTECTION IN FLORIDA

Most perennial herbs are hardy in northern winters, so Florida's worst winter is a lark to them. They may go dormant in northern Florida, but they come back soon. One year my hydrangea lost its leaves in frost at the end of December and started putting out new spring leaves before January was over.

Some of the more
tropical herbs and
spices like ginger,
cardamon, and bixa need winter
protection. Grow them in containers so you can move them indoors as needed.

In central and southern Florida, some herbs may need covering
during certain frosts. Even plants
that would take an Iowa winter are
stressed (stunned is more accur-
ate!), when a warm spell suddenly
becomes a freezing night. In such
a case, cover any herbs you have
lost in previous winters or any you
treasure most. Also, take cuttings
and bring them indoors for material
with which to start over.

TIMING CAN BE CRUCIAL

While people in C and S will
want to start annuals, seeds, and
most new plants in the fall, growers
in N may want to wait until early
spring. Even then they may need
to cover some tender seedlings if an
unexpectedly late frost comes. For
most Florida plant growers, the
new season starts officially at either of these two times but never
quite stops altogether.

I used to think I might miss
having a time of dormancy if winter
didn't give me one. I don't. I find
that now I can take off a few days
at a time as needed and still grow
more over the year than I could in
the Midwest. I am happy to assure
you that herbs are patient plants.

SEED SOWING CAN BE MORE
DIFFICULT

Starting from seed can be
much more difficult in Florida than
it was in northern states. For one
thing, seed doesn't last as long in
this hot and humid climate as it
did in Ohio or Iowa. There, some

packets stayed viable for five or six
years. Here they may be dead by
the second year. So now I keep all
my seed, new or used, in the freezer
until time for planting. I put many
packets into a zipper bag, plastic
container, or coffee can and keep
them on or near the door so they
don't get lost. This sounds like a
way to kill seed for sure, but not so.
Freezing preserves the viability.

Sometimes I leave several
packets out for a few days in the
spring or fall during peak planting
times, and even that I shouldn't do.
Plant what you need and put the
seed back in the freezer.

Also, in the north I always
asked for untreated seed because I
didn't want to use any more poisons than necessary. Here I am
glad enough for treated seed (usually covered with pink powder, a fungicide) for it is more resistant to rot
during germination. I have not gone
so far as to treat seed in other packets, but you can do that by adding a
pinch of fungicide and shaking.

In Florida I find that even
good, treated seed too often disap-
pears in the ground before I ever see
it germinate. I now plant most
herbs in peat pellets or containers
first and transfer to the ground only
when the plants are large enough to
stand up to some opposition. I raise
seedlings outdoors in a shady spot
and on the screened porch under
artificial light, checking them and
watering daily (see chapter 4 for
more on planting).

The time of adjustment or settling in after transplanting is more

crucial in Florida. Even the most drought resistant plant needs regular watering for the first few weeks until it is off and growing.

It is easier to buy a healthy plant in a small pack or pot than it is to start from seed. From this new plant I can take cuttings (see chapter 4) with little trouble and have several plants in a few weeks.

On the other hand, Mother Nature doesn't have nearly the trouble with seeds that I do. Once I get most plants started, I find volunteers aplenty. But even they are not as certain as they were in northern gardens.

SELF-SOWING IS LESS RELIABLE

Herbs that usually self-sow, such as borage, calendula, and California poppy, may well do so in Florida. But if they are in an area that gets only occasional watering and they sprout at the wrong time, we may never notice them. Or our year round growing season leads us to plant something else there and they get lost in other growth.

A site where there is automatic watering and limited planting is the best bet for germination, and this can serve us even if we have no intention of letting the plants continue to grow there. Just take off the ripe seed pods or spent flowers of plants that might self sow and spread these among the mulch in an uncrowded spot in your oasis or most frequentquently watered growing area. Watch for the seedlings and, when they are large enough,transplant them where you want them to grow. Or save seeds and carefully start and nurture them in containers.

SELF FEEDING DOES NOT HAPPEN HERE

In Iowa many farm animals were on self-feeding equipment. So were many of the plants, for the soil was rich. Farmers added plenty of fertilizer to get top numbers of bushels per acre, but in the home garden, fertilizer was almost optional. There you could grow herbs for a lifetime without feeding them.

You can't do that in Florida, where fertilizing is a necessary, though not difficult, task. If a plant shows signs of nutrient deficiency: poor leaf color, lighter green color between leaf veins, or just poor growth that cannot be blamed on the weather, then foliar feeding with a water soluble plant food will help most quickly. Use the finest spray possible, from a pump sprayer if you have one, and apply the solution to both sides of the leaves in the early morning or late evening.

Otherwise spread dry fertilizer over the herb bed or the soil around isolated plants. Feed as often as every three weeks in summer when growth is active, to every six or eight weeks in winter when it is slower. Wash or brush fertilizer from leaf surfaces. If you use a slow release fertilizer like Osmocote (TM) or any of the organic fertilizers, you may need to apply them only every few months. Feeding is necessary, but use any kind of fertilizer you prefer. How you feed is not as important as that you feed.

MOTHER NATURE DOESN'T PROVIDE THE WATER

This is still a shock to me after gardening for 40-some years in the Midwest, starting when I was seven. I am still appalled to see how it can pour for four days straight in the summer and yet the plants can be panting for a drink when it hasn't rained again four days later.

More rain falls in the summer in Florida than falls all year in seven other states, and as much as falls in four years in some places. Only other coastal states and Hawaii receive this much rain. Nevertheless, even in Florida summers there are times when watering will be needed, for sandy soils dry out quickly and plants used to deluges don't always tolerate thirst in between.

I catch rainwater in three garbage-can rain barrels set under the downspouts and dip this out to water sensitive or newly set plants between rains. One rain barrel has a faucet inserted into the bottom and a soaker hose attached.

SHORTER DAYS MEAN SLOWER GROWTH

Most herbs grow very well from September until June, but these include the shortest days of the year, so expect growth to be somewhat to very much slower than it was in a northern summer. Even in Iowa I could tell a definite difference in "days to maturity" between the first beans of summer and later ones grown during the shorter days of August. This is not as apparent with herbs as with vegetables because we can start to use foliage very early, but it is a definite factor in any kind of Florida growing.

SUN AND SHADE

As important as sun and shade are to gardening anywhere, they take on new meaning in Florida, where herbs are grown year round. Because the angle of the sun is so much lower in the winter and the shadows are so much longer, parts of your yard that are sun baked in the summer may be sun starved in the winter. This is increasingly true as your trees grow larger, so keep in mind this side effect of successful landscaping. It's amazing how fast trees grow here.

Average Rainfall by Months in Florida (in inches)		
(N) Tallahassee	(C) Orlando	(S) Miami
JAN 3.2	2.2	2.2
FEB 4.4	3	2
MAR 5.6	3.2	2
APR 4.2	2.8	3.4
MAY 4	3	6
JUN 6.4	7	9
JUL 8.6	8.2	7
AUG 6.8	6.8	6.4
SEP 6.4	7.2	8.6
OCT 3	4	8.2
NOV 2.8	1.8	2.6
DEC 4.2	2	1.6

From *Water Resources Atlas of Florida*

Even after eight years in the same yard, I am constantly being surprised by the changing amounts of sun and shade and where they fall.

Added to the scarcity of sunshine in winter is the intensity of its summer performance. Especially for herbs, summer shade is helpful. So I let big plants like bush spinach and pigeon peas grow tall and my herb garden is then not nearly as neat in the summer, but it has some shade to see it through. I remove these temporary shade plants when the weather gets cooler and the days get shorter.

I keep tender fruit trees like black sapote, tamarind, and rose apple in containers so I can bring them inside in winter frosts. In summer they sit in the herb garden to provide shade as needed. I also plant some summer-fussy herbs like lemon balm at their base or set pots on the soil around the trunk of the fruit trees in the containers. Many of the summer-sensitive herbs like lavender, thyme, wormwood, and parsley get moved to deep shade or the screened porch until September.

All microclimates are more significant in Florida, where year-round growing is possible. Wind can be a problem, especially along the coasts. Hurricanes can be felt fairly far inland as well. Nooks that are sheltered from wide temperature fluctuations will save some herbs from flash freezing.

SALT TOLERANCE IS IMPORTANT ON THE COAST

People who live on the coastline in Florida soon learn that some plants tolerate salt spray, but many will not. This is also true of herbs. In stormy weather, the wind along the coast blows salt spray much farther inland than usual while its turbulence causes additional damage.

I have seen two fine herb gardens placed in protected areas on the inland side of waterfront property. Anyone living on the water can position the herb garden this way.

The first, the chef's herb garden at the Grand Hotel in Palm Beach, is separated from the Atlantic Ocean only by the beach and the building. See chapter 8 for a description of the many herbs being grown there.

In the second, Mary Alice Harley grows herbs near the beach in St. Petersburg. Salt spray is a problem when there is a windy storm, but does not harm the rampant ground cover of wild oregano. By the way, Harley mulches her herbs and roses with seaweed with no ill effects.

There are a few salt tolerant native herbs that will grow near the water's edge: aloe, agave or century plant, hibiscus, lantana, junipers (especially *Juniperus chinensis* and *J. conferta* or shore juniper), *Myrica pusilla* or dwarf wax myrtle, and portulaca.

But for growing the culinary and more common herbs, the landside of your beach house is a much safer place. Or grow your parsley and thyme on an indoor window sill.

PROBLEMS WITH PESTS

There are not necessarily more insects in Florida than elsewhere, but they are different. My herbs seemed immune to pests in other places. Here even mint can disappear overnight if some bug pounces. This is especially true of herbs that are fighting for their lives against summer humidity.

Last summer I had a delightfully fragrant grapefruit sage that was eaten down to its stems and veins where I first planted it. Luckily, I had taken a cutting and put that across the garden where the insects did not find it. And now that I think of it, I'd better take more cuttings just in case.

A daily shower will help keep some insects in check. So will your being there with your eyes open. Most insects respond to simple measures like insecticidal soap, but I'd go as far as to use Sevin(TM) in an emergency. Read and follow label directions and do not use treated leaves or flowers for cooking until the specified time is past. Kaye Cude finds that a simple foliar feeding (page 14) often deters the insects.

Nematodes, invisible underground organisms that attack roots, can be a problem to Florida plants. Herbs in general are not particularly sensitive, calendula and sun-flowers being exceptions. Adding plenty of organic matter and humus to the soil is the best

preventative and sufficient in most cases. If not, treat the soil with *Soil Fungi* from United Agricultural Services in Hudson, Florida, or *Prosper Nema* from Circle One, Inc. (16209 Flight Path Drive, Brooksville, FL 34602). Nematode problems may well diminish in importance in Florida growing now that such non-poisonous and effective means of treating them are available.

Diseases are more insidious, often resulting from uncontrollable summer weather. For my part, I feel the use of fungicide is usually not worth the effort, but others are free to disagree. On vulnerable plants I may use some of Vince Sims'* Insect and Disease Prevention recipe:

To your 20 gallon size hose-end sprayer (the standard size for this small appliance that mixes substances such as fertilizer with 20 gallons of water) simply add:

1 cup liquid dish soap
1/2 cup Listerine
6 Tablespoons copper sulfate
6 Tablespoons alcohol

Fill the remainder with water. I try to spray my fruit trees with this once a month, after 6:30 p.m., from March to October. If some of the herbs look bad, this won't hurt them, but don't eat them for several days after treatment.

* Robert Vincent Sims' publication, *Old Fashioned Garden Rebel Recipes*, a small booklet of useful information, can be purchased from author and radio Rebel Gardener, P.O. Box 1390, Mt. Dora, FL 32757.

BETTER LIVING WITH HERBS

The problems we face in herb gardening in Florida are minor, especially when balanced against our ability to enjoy nearly or fully year-round interest, fragrance, and harvest. When we see news clips of snarled traffic on snowy highways, who cares whether herbs grow more slowly in Florida, or even if we must replant some of them in September.

Herbal annuals, perennials, trees, shrubs, and container plants contribute to the use and enjoyment of our landscapes. We can harvest or appreciate them outdoors as well as indoors almost every day of the year.

There are herbs and spices for sun and for shade, for cooking or just for looking. The lists in the landscaping chapter that follows will help you select the right ones for your site and purpose.

As the scope of the lists shows, Florida gardeners have such a broad choice among herbs and spices from around the world that your herbal landscape is bound to be very exciting.

2. Easy Ways with Herbs and Spices

 Our busy lives can be enriched by using herbs in many quick and simple ways. These, over the years, have become part of my life, like breathing, washing, or walking in the yard to see what is sprouting or blooming. Using herbs for scent, ornament, beauty, and health are as important to me as cooking with herbs (chapter 3).

The more we learn about them the more we use herbs. Bringing them indoors allows us to spotlight their interesting colors, textures, blossoms, and aromas. This multiplies our own appreciation while it introduces these simple delights and comforts to family members and visitors who might never get to the garden. Putting herbs at tabletop, counter, windowsill, or mantle level makes them easier to see, touch, and sniff.

It is only natural to want to share something we so enjoy with others. Herbs plants, seeds, bouquets, crafts, or cosmetics make unique and special gifts. Tuck a sprig of rosemary into a card or letter or the bow of a present.

HERBS IN FRESH BOUQUETS

From November until June, my favorite household bouquet is a handful of nasturtiums in a little brown pottery jar. It takes two minutes to pick and set in the flowers, two more to replace them a few days later when they start to fade. The colors are like jewels and if I place the flowers on the table near the pillow of the couch, I can smell the fragrance whenever I rest and read.

Other herbs that do well in Florida and offer colorful flowers include calendulas, borage, butterfly weed, elderberry, feverfew, goldenrod, nicandra, passionflower, purple coneflower, roses, sunflowers, and yarrow. Elderberry berries are great in arrangement at all stages from their green youth until their purple ripeness.

Hibiscus is one of my favorite indoor decorations because the bushes yield them so abundantly, the flowers need no water, and a single bloom makes a bright focal point in a ceramic hibiscus holder, adorning the foliage of a houseplant, or tucked among the other flowers in a bouquet.

Most last only one day, but for no more effort than the picking, that is a good return. I have one bush with a soothing shade of pink flowers that will last two days if I pick the new blooms. The best way to do this is to go out between 8 and 9 in the morning. Then I can tell that the flowers that are closing are gone, the ones still open are on their second day, and the ones just starting to unfurl are the newest. Picked at this stage, the buds open fully indoors within an hour and last well into the second day.

It is cheating a bit, but I've plucked nasturtiums, rose petals, and hibiscus from such bouquets and added them to the supper salad. All are edible and colorful, and I am more apt to use them if they are near at hand at this busy time of day. It takes only a few petals to add that appealing touch of color.

DON'T FORGET THE FOLIAGE

Many of the herbs with less showy flowers make excellent fillers or foliage for bouquets. In fact, herbs are so interesting that they don't require much arranging. Choose more mature foliage rather than what appears tender. Pick a handful of basil, beebalm, eucalyptus, lemon balm, mint, boxwood, juniper, parsley, sage, scented geranium leaves, rosemary, tarragon, thyme, or yarrow. Bring them in and wash the leaves and stems because you might decide to eat them or pull a stem for iced tea. If stems are woody, split the ends with pruning snips for about two inches so they will take up more water.

Take off any leaves that will be below the water level and set them aside for cooking, drying, or potpourri. A piece of paper towel on the warm top of the refrigerator hardly shows and can be a tidy place to dry extra herb leaves.

Put stems in plenty of water, just as you would to condition cut flowers. But don't set this container in the cool or dark. You can put it on the table as is because it is already decorative. A misting with cool water once a day will keep leaves fresh longer. Experiment with various foliages, flowers, and seedpods cut at different stages.

Of course, you can arrange herbs just as you would any cut flowers or use them for foliage in any arrangements. They bring their properties of bug and germ repelling, air freshening, and soul uplifting subtly into the room even if no one notices them in the bouquet. Most herbs will keep better than most cut foliages.

I almost always add mint, pineapple sage, or silver dollar eucalyptus to bouquets because these are always available in ample supply and benefit from the pruning. The eucalyptus lends an elegance that makes three rose buds into a bouquet. The others fill in with foliage and some color, but most of all they add fragrance.

basil

HERBS MAKE GREAT DRIED BOUQUETS

Many herb leaves are excellent in dried arrangements and can be air dried by hanging loose bunches upside down in a dark, well ventilated place: eucalpytus, lamb's ears, horehound, sage, mints, and oregano are but a few. These will wilt somewhat, but this only changes their beauty.

If you wish foliage to remain in the same shape as when fresh, give it the glycerin and water treatment (p.23). This is especially good for leaves with a little more thickness and substance, but you can experiment with your material. Glycerin treatment works well for bay, bayberry, boxwood (which turns a golden yellow), broom, hops, linden (flowers and bracts as well as leaves), magnolia, rosemary, rue, and willow. Do not use glycerin on most flowers.

The resulting foliage is more pliable than fresh and can be used in dry or fresh arrangements since the water will not hurt the stems.

Foliage can also be dried by pressing it between layers of newspaper with heavy books on top, or inside the pages of an old telephone book.

Use the seedpods of dill, fennel, nicandra, nigella, feverfew, coneflowers, chamomile, juniper, elderberry, and rose hips in arrangements. Many fine sages do very well in Florida and the spires of flowers can be hung to dry or simply allowed to dry standing in bouquets with fresh flowers. The same is true of goldenrod and yarrow. If you use them with other flowers, the water will not hurt. Many stems need to absorb about an inch of water as they dry to keep from wilting. When you throw away an old bouquet, including those from the florist, keep the stems that have dried and still look good. A thin coating of hair spray keeps them from shedding.

Other flowers, especially those with soft petals, are best hung to dry so they keep their shapes, or can be dried in silica gel or clean sand so they keep their color as well. Follow the directions on the can of silica gel.

It is often necessary to take stems off and later replace them with a stem of florist wire and tape or dried stems of grasses or daylilies. In sand, borax, or cornmeal, bury flowers, upside down for flat ones like daisies, but right side up for marigolds and geraniums and anything else that needs to have the sand filled gently into its empty spaces.

The beauty of working with sand is that timing is not so important. Most flowers dry well in two weeks or less, but if you forget them until you need them, they will not overdry.

Florida Style Herb Wands

Other herb books will show you how to make lavender wands, but it's not easy to get that much bloom from lavender in Florida, although herbalists like Billy Daniel have mastered it.

I often use Mexican sage, *Salvia leucantha*, instead, because it grows easily and blooms abundantly here. It is almost the same color. The stems are not quite as supple, and I am not quite as patient as I should be, so I just bent mine back, didn't worry when a few stems broke instead of bending, and wrapped the wand with lavender ribbon. It hangs in my kitchen. If you want one with lavender fragrance, dab on drops of lavender essential oil occasionally.

HERB WREATHS

I brought home a cutting of my friend Betty's hydrangea from Pennsylvania last year. The following spring it was about a foot tall and I was amazed to have three flower buds. I cut one off early to keep the plant from blooming itself to death, but the other two grew into large papery flowerheads and turned from pink to tan as they decorated the growing bush for months. In late summer when they became leathery I cut them off and hung them upside down to dry. Then I took them out and added them as a new focal point to the grapevine wreath already beside my door.

Dried herb foliage, seedpods, or flowers can be used in or as a wreath by wiring bunches to any wreath frame. Whatever you have

(continued on page 25)

CUTTING AND KEEPING HERBS

-For most fresh herbs, pick, wash, strip off lower leaves as described on page 20, and put in an ample container of cold water.

-For artemisia or wormwood flowers, cut when only half the spike is open. Cut foliage anytime after true leaves develop. Split base of woody stems (mashing doesn't work quite as well). Condition for 24 hours in deep cold water or submerge entirely for 6 hours. If foliage wilts, recut and use warm water, 80-100 degrees F. Wormwood will last 5 to 10 days fresh, indefinitely dried.

-Some herbs, like the flowers of various sages, will dry rather than wilt in a bouquet. Remove these to waterless containers as they do and wire or replace stems if needed. Other herb flowers and foliages like wormwood and perilla should be hung upside down in loose bunches to air dry with straight stems. Soft flowers like calendula will need to be buried in sand, borax, or silica gel.

-For beebalm flowers, cut when 1/4 of the blooms on each stem are half open. They will continue to open in water. Condition overnight, using warm water to start. Flowers last 5 to 7 days, buds and foliage up to 10 days.

-Butterfly weed blossoms should be cut when clusters are 1/2 to 3/4 open. Sometimes searing is not necessary, but if the flowers begin to wilt, recut the stems and put in hot water, 100 degrees F. If all else fails, recut and burn up to an inch of the milky ends with match or candle flame. Flowers will revive quickly and last 5 to 8 days.

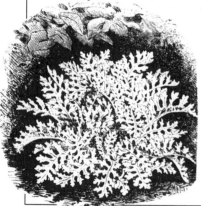

-Dusty miller adds a lovely silver touch to bouquets, whether used fresh or dried. The plants last so long in Florida that they often need pruning to keep new growth coming. To use fresh (great with pink roses), split stems and condition overnight in hot water, 100 degrees, to start. Recut and put again in hot water if the foliage is not crisp and firm. To dry, hang upside down in bunches.

CUTTING AND KEEPING HERBS

-Eucalyptus needs stems split and put in cold water. Dry like sage or **treat with glycerin,** one part glycerine to 2 parts water, with stems at least 6 inches into solution. Add food coloring if you want a special color like blue. Recut stems once a week and leave in solution until they have a pliable feel and the color desired. Then they will last indefinitely with no water needed. Sometimes the color does not change until sunlight hits the foliage. Also it is sometimes necessary to cut off tender new growth from the ends as this does not seem to take the treatment or wilts first in fresh bouquets.

-For needled evergreens, wash to remove dust or dirt. Use soapy water if needed and rinse in cold. Split woody stems for 2 to 3 inches and condition in warm water overnight or longer or submerge completely for several hours. Tie them in desired curves while conditioning if you wish. When using evergreens for Christmas decoration, spraying with an antitranspirant spray (Wiltpruf (TM), Forevergreen(TM)) will cut water loss, make greens last longer, and reduce the worry about fire.

-Cut goldenrod spires at any stage to use fresh. To dry them, cut when open. Condition in cold water. Fresh, these last 1 to 3 weeks, then dry nicely.

-Cut lavender for fresh bouquets when half the flowers on the spire are open. Cut foliage separately. Split stems and condition overnight in warm water and flowers will last 10 days. Cut when 3/4 are open for drying and spread on newspaper. Save any flowers that fall off for potpourri.

-Cut lemon verbena panicles when 1/4 to 1/2 open, split stems, and condition overnight in hot water. Mist with cold water and remove some leaves to make them last 7 days or more.

-Nasturtiums last a bit longer if you recut and mash stems ends when you get them inside. Condition flowers in cold water, leaves in warm to start. Flowers will only last 1 to 3 days on the plant or in the vase. Foliage lasts longer.

-Passion flowers last only one day. Cut well-developed buds showing color in late afternoon and condition overnight in cold water or cut as they are about to open, split stems, and condition 1 to 4 hours. Or float just the flowers.

CUTTING AND KEEPING HERBS

-Condition perilla foliage, flowers, fruits, or a branch with some of each in warm water to start.

-Cut periwinkle flowers when 2 or 3 are open and buds will continue to open for a week. Split stems. Put in cold water. Remove extra foliage and spent flowers if they are noticeable.

-Cut roses with sharp shears when outer petals begin to unfold. Make a slanting cut just above an outside, 5-leaved leaflet for the good of the plant. Then recut just below a node and put in deep, cold water overnight. Rose experts make it a practice to cut stems underwater so no air can enter and block the open cells. Roses should open gradually over 5 to 7 days. If blooms wilt, recut and give hot water treatment. Dry small, half-opened buds in sand, borax, or silica gel.

-Cut rosemary foliage, split stems, and put in cold water. Give hot water treatment if it wilts. Bend branches as desired with warm hands.

-Cut sage spires when half open or let dry on the plant. Split stems and condition in warm water. These will dry in the vase and last for years.

-Cut sunflowers when outer petals are open but centers are tight and they will last 6 to 10 days. Or cut a branch with several flowers when at least half are open. Remove unneeded leaves. Split stems and put in warm water. Wire stems if the bloom is too heavy.

-Violets and johnny jump-up buds do not open after picking. Submerge blooms in cold water for 1 hour and keep pushing down gently. Remove carefully, put stems in cold water. Wrap violet bunches loosely in wax paper until you want the fragrance to escape. Flowers will last 4 to 7 days.

-Cut yarrow when more than half the flowers are open. Add 2 tablespoons of salt per quart of cold water. They will last 3 to 15 days. Cut when fully open and hang upside down to dry.

in abundance, pick for drying. Do this especially at the end of spring. Summer may claim some of your herbs in any case.

Until you gain experience, dry your foliage before using it to make a wreath. Later you can learn to weave fresh materials into wreaths and let them dry in shape. Your wreath frame can be a purchased wire, styrofoam, or straw one, or one you weave yourself from prunings of grapevine, privet, or other pliable wood. If necessary, soak the wood in a bucket or in the rain barrel for a few hours until you can weave it into a circle, heart, or bow.

Use bunches of herbs, 3 to 4 inches in length. Mixed bunches of several kinds of herbs are interesting and make less of a dent in any one plant, or you can use all one kind if you have plenty of eucalyptus or wormwood, or want more uniformity.

You can buy wired wood picks from any florist or florist supplier. Wire each bunch of herbs separately, and punch the picks into a wreath frame of straw, ribbon-covered styrofoam, or grapevine, in whatever pattern pleases your eye. This works well when some or much of the frame is meant to show.

Spool wire (flexible wire on a spool) is easier for a full wreath. Just cut your herbs and bunch them as you wrap the wire around and around the frame. Add a new bunch with every wrap, turning herbs to the front or sides to cover a wire or styrofoam frame completely.

POTPOURRI THE EASY WAY

My daughters save all the roses they get in corsages whether they are fragrant or not, for the memories are more important. Perhaps you'd like to start a potpourri jar for a young girl in your family. Find a decorative but tightly sealed container and start her off with a few dried herbs. When she accumulates a cup or two of dried rose petals, give her some fixative like orris root, oakmoss, sandalwood, patchouli, or sweet flag root. These are available from craft shops or herb shops as powders or small pieces that absorb and hold the other scents. Your gift might also include a vial of essential oil. My favorite is called Arabian wild rose.

Any rose petals add bulk and color as well as fragrance to potpourris, sachets, or herbal pillows. So gather them on your daily walk around the garden and keep a good supply on hand. Those from flowers just about to open often increase in perfume as they dry, but I hate to miss the bloom. I'd rather wait and then peel the petals off just before they'd fall from the plant or the bouquet. You can even gather them from the ground before they fade.

BASIC RECIPE FOR DRY POTPOURRI

Use this easy basic recipe and adapt it for the scents and materials you prefer: Just mix and use:

* 1 quart dried herb flowers and leaves
* Up to 3 tablespoons of spices such as cinnamon or clove
* 1 to 3 tablespoons of fixative to which a few drops of essential oil may be added

If you collect herb leaves whenever you make cuttings or bouquets or prune, or save the petals whenever you throw away a bouquet of roses, you will soon have enough to make sachets or potpourri at any time.

Until you are ready to stir your dried herbs into potpourri, you will preserve the most scent by storing them in an airtight container: tupperware or well sealed plastic containers, canning jars with lids, zip-lock freezer bags. Once they are mixed into proper potpourri, you can use any decorative container. My mother had a lovely, painted jar, made for that very purpose, and there are many possibilities to be found in attics, antique shops, garage sales, and housewares stores.

The idea is to take the lid off when you want the fragrance to pervade the room. Many places put out potpourri in open baskets or dishes, coordinating the colors with the interior decor. These should be revived with essential oils whenever the fragrance fades.

At the medical complex where I take my daughter Teresa, one clinician has a cloth bag of potpourri that he uses as a door stop, and his is the most pleasant room in the place. He must have a rock in there with the potpourri to give it enough weight.

Potpourri Sachets

Sachets can be as simple as a few dried rosemary leaves or orange blossoms tied up in a handkerchief, pressed into the teabag papers sold in health food stores, or scooped into plain or fancy sachet holders. While unpacking, one lady found lavender sachets that were six years old and still very fragrant.

Infinite variations are possible. Try different ingredients until you find several combinations that you like especially and make note of these. Two ingredients I have learned to save and cherish: all rose petals and a supply of citrus peels. These are abundant enough in Florida. Save the best when you are cutting up grapefruit, oranges, limes, or tangerines whether they come from your own trees or from the market.

Dry them on a plate in the oven or cupboard, but faster by putting them in the microwave and heating at full power for enough 30-

SPECIAL ROSES

In the midst of writing this book my beloved Mama was called to heaven. At her funeral there was a spray of gorgeous red roses and white fuji mums. After the prayers at the cemetery, the funeral director asked if anyone would like a rose from the spray. I would not have replied myself, but my grandchildren had no such inhibitions. Before long the rest of us decided this was a very nice idea. It didn't hurt the spray at all and Mama would have wanted to share her roses even if it did. Each rose was in a pick tube of water, so it made a lovely keepsake. On the way to luncheon at church, someone said her daughter had hung such roses in a dark closet and had them dry beautifully. So that is what I did with mine. They dried a rich, red-black without shattering, and are now in an arrangement with other sentimental treasures.

second segments to make them just crisp. Microwave drying also emits a delightful fragrance into the kitchen, so you may want to save the actual drying for just before company comes.

Fixatives are few and specific from such plants as clary sage, orrisroot, patchouli, and sweet flag root. The last time I ordered herb plants from a catalog (before I realized how well patchouli grows here) I also bought a half pound of oakmoss for potpourri. That was over a year ago and I expect it to last me the rest of my life. I bought a few vials of essential oils. I use a few drops of lavender on my pillowcase to help me sleep and of roses as perfume. These, too, will last me for years.

Spices can be dried orange peels, whole cloves, pieces of cinnamon stick, cedar or sandalwood shaving or chips (found among pet supplies), or crushed leaves from an allspice or cinnamon plant. You can buy most at a grocery, health food, or craft store.

I have everything on hand. If you don't, you can buy the ingredients at most craft stores or buy ready-made potpourri. Sachets and such variations as herbal pillows and covered hangers make lovely, fragrant, unique gifts for yourself or for others.

It doesn't take me long to crochet a little heart, bell, or clover leaf. When I have four ready for stuffing, I mix my dried petals, oakmoss, and a few drops of old rose and rosemary essential oil. The result has a delightful fragrance.

There are easier ways to make little cloth pockets. I just enjoy crocheting. You can cut squares of fabric with pinking

shears, stitch up three sides, fill them with potpourri, and tie them with a bit of satin ribbon.

Or you can make them eight at a time out of old handkerchiefs, either men's white linen ones or quaintly printed ladies' hankies.

Wash and iron the handkerchief. Cut off the hem all around, if you wish. Fold it in half and stitch around the sides, top, and bottom with a single line of machine or tightly done hand stitch-

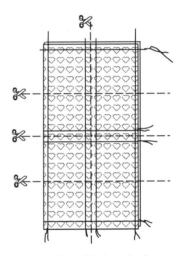

handkerchief sachets

ing a half inch from the outer edge. Make a double line of stitching (parallel lines half an inch apart) down the center, in each direction, as in the illustration above. Cut squares apart as shown. Use pinking shears or finish the edges with a zig-zag stitch. Eight sachets are ready to fill and use.

Scented Hangers

You can keep a closet fresh with sachets simply hung around the hanger or put in the pocket of the winter coat you only wear when traveling north. But scented hangers combine the freshening of herbs with the padding that keeps garments in good shape. These can also be quite decorative and lovely gifts and are fun to make in any of the following ways.

1. Sew and stuff with potpourri a strip of cloth 1 inch wide and as long as the upper two triangular parts of the wire or plastic hanger. Pin or baste this in place. Cover it with decorative yarn or ribbon.

2. Or wrap the herbs in place around the hanger, round and round, with strips of muslin, plain or patterned.

3. For crocheted covers, use matching or contrasting color. Start with a chain as long as the underside of the strip and covering plus four inches. Turn and double crochet (DC), in third stitch from the end. Work DC across. Chain three, turn, add as many rows as necessary to fit around the hanger and herbs. Then connect lengthwise edges with a row of single crochet that will leave a decorative ridge at the top edge of the hanger. Close ends. Add additional crocheted edging or embroidery decoration as desired.

4. Or knit or crochet two tubes to fit, closing them at the ends and joining them in the middle, after stuffing them with potpourri.

5. For fabric-covered wooden hangers, cut strips of material 6 1/2 x 24 inches. Round out both ends with two 3 1/4 inch semicircles. Bind the edges with ribbon or seam binding. Make a line of gathering stitched 3/4 inch from the outside of the material all the way around. Gather up and fit it around the coat hanger. Then add sachet mixture. Even out the gathers and close the bag with the ribbon over the top of the hanger either by hand with back stitches or by machine with a zipper foot.

6. Or simply pink two rectangles of fabric or use wide satin ribbon with rounded ends to fit over the hanger and herbs, stitch one set of edges together. Fit over the hanger, stuff with potpourri blend, and stitch the other edge.

KEEPING INSECTS IN THEIR PLACE

Instead of powerful pesticides, we can use gentle, fragrant herbs that are safe, non-poison-

ous, and often keep pests from appearing. Try these methods:

Moth protection. One of the main uses for herbs in days not so long gone by was to keep moths out of clothing, much of which was pure wool. This was a serious responsibility for the housekeeper. Both our lives and our clothing have changed considerably. Wools these days are often blends that are unappetizing to moths. Now moth-chasing herbs serve mostly to freshen closets and drawers.

The best of these for clothes or linens are lavender, southernwood, tansy, wormwood, basil, eucalyptus, rue, santolina, thyme, rosemary, pennyroyal, and most mints. Secondary scents can come from citrus peel, lemon verbena, tansy, bay leaves, fennel, cedar shavings, tobacco leaves, or peppercorns.

Use a combination of herbs for best results and most pleasant fragrances. If you have several choices, let your nose decide since the scent will cling to your clothes. Pick, dry, and crumble the herbs almost to a powder. Mix 1 tablespoon of ground cloves for every 4 tablespoons of herbs and pack into sachets or tea bag envelopes, available at health food stores.

Some experts advise using the most aromatic herbs with no fixative. Others say for the most lasting and effective moth chasers, use chipped orris root as a fixative and half again as much essential oil as you would for a plain potpourri. The best oils to use are those that are also insect repelling: cedar, lemon, lavender, pennyroyal, peppermint, eucalyptus, or bayberry.

Use at least 1/2 cup of the mixture in each bag or sachet for spreading scent. Put one bag in every bureau drawer, in the knitting basket, in the dog's bed, and several in every closet. Replace them once a year.

Cedar chests. Cedar loses its moth-chasing fragrance over the years, so renew your cedar chest by sanding the wood periodically or by rubbing it with fresh cedar oil. It is natural for the oils near the surface to evaporate.

Flies. Shoofly (*Nicandra physaloides*) grows well in Florida and works for the flies in stables or kennels or wherever needed (refer to the plant-by-plant directory).

Ants indoors and out. I'd have to call these the worst insects Florida offers. Outdoors, I've tried everything, herbal and chemical, and found no ready solution for fire ants. So I wear sensible work-shoes, never sandals, in the yard and white socks to better see the invaders approach. And I console myself with the fact that ant hills are one of the first stages in soil improvement. Ants prepare the sand for earthworms.

You can help that preparation and discourage the ants somewhat by (carefully! with a long hoe) burying in their hills any extra citrus peels or by pouring on any juice that gets too strong to drink.

Herbal solutions for indoor ants include:

-planting tansy around the foundation of the house.

-sprinkling catnip along any ant path.

-making a decoction of four

cups of walnut leaves to three cups of water, simmering for 20 to 30 minutes, then painting this around floor, counter cracks, and work surfaces.

-squeezing lemon juice into the places ants could enter. Then put the lemon peelings in likely spots for residual control.

-spreading hot red pepper on shelves or counters or making it into a spray to use as needed. Of course, ant traps from the hardware store can be effective, too.

Mosquitoes and gnats. I find these no worse and sometimes bet-

ter in Florida than they were in other places I've lived. The best mosquito prevention is to eliminate standing water and encourage birds and toads. To my rain barrels I add a tablespoon of vegetable oil or dishwashing soap or Mosquito Dunks(TM) so they don't become breeding spots for the mosquitoes. It also helps, especially in the rainy summer, to work early in the day rather than in the evening, wear long pants rather than shorts, and rub exposed skin with elderberry leaves. If all else fails, apply whatever repellant will protect you.

UNDER-THE-CARPET HERBS:
    Children have dreams of living in a castle, but if you've ever seen one, or even if you visualize honest-

HERBS FOR MANY PURPOSES:

To repel flies
Shoofly (*Nicandra physaloides*), mints, especially var. Eau-de-cologne, pennyroyal, elder leaves and flowers, lavender leaves and flowers, rue, thyme, tansy

To repel mosquitoes
Elder, chamomile, mosquito bush, cedronella (*Agastache cana*), mosquito shoo geranium (*Pelargonium citrosum van Leeni*)

To repel ants
Tansy, catnip, lemon peel or juice, cayenne pepper, dried or in an infusion, walnut leaves, dried or in infusion

To repel fleas
Society garlic, pennyroyal, tansy

To repel mice or rats
Mint, sassafras, dog fennel (*Matricaria inodora*), tansy, catnip

To repel moths
Lavender, most mints, pennyroyal, rosemary, rue, santolina, southernwood, thymes, wormwood

To repel garden predators
Marigolds, nasturtiums, peppers

ly, you know castles were long on protection but short on comfort.

Luckily, centuries ahead of modern sanitation or conveniences, wise housekeepers knew the benefits of strewing herbs. Without advertising to stir up desires for what they could not afford, they found in nature, grew in their gardens, and spread in their cottages or castles what would make their lives more pleasant and less painful. Lavender was strewn on hospital floors to cut down on contagion long before people knew about germs.

Housewives tucked fragrant herbs under carpets or spread them among the rushes on the floor to release their oils underfoot.

Strewing Today

Spring cleaning no longer means taking out all the rugs, beating the dirt out, and tacking them back down over a padding of straw and strewing herbs. But we can still use sprigs of herbs from the wild or from pruning or extras from the potpourri box. Put these under the welcome mat to send up their soothing, pleasing fragrances. This works well both outside and in during the dry months, perhaps only indoors during Florida's rainy season. A vase of fresh herbs beside the umbrella rack or near the door is inviting. You might make these the insect repellent herbs along with the fragrant. Mint offers both in one.

Put herbal bouquets where you will brush them to release more fragrance. Keep a vase of elderberry leaves handy so you can grab a few to rub on your skin as you go out and prevent the mosquito bites you would otherwise

have gotten between the door and the elder bush.

Scent Your Furniture with Herbs

Have you ever thought of putting herbs under the cushions on the couch? Herbs in the furniture may help to banish fleas or moths. They definitely replace musty odors with pleasant ones. Put herbs in stored away suitcases, picnic coolers, and purses. Put them in the glove compartment of the car or under the floor mat.

Mosquitoes used to get into our cars whenever we left the windows open a crack. Strewing stems of elderberry or scented geraniums discourages them. By the way, the car is also a good place for drying herbs like mint and lavender, and the residual fragrance is pleasant to people but not to bugs or germs.

Mix Herbs in the Mulch

Plant herbs like lantana, scented geraniums, rosemary, mints, or low junipers, or taller plants like gingers, bayberry, or cardamon along the driveway or garden walk. You and your visitors will enjoy the pleasant sights and smells, and this placement makes it easy to brush against them as you pass, releasing even more fragrance.

Don't throw away extra herb prunings. Use them in or under the mulch in beds along garden paths, or in and under mulched paths. Plant herbs among the flowers and vegetables. They give off fragrance wherever you step and make weeding and harvesting more enjoyable for the fragrance while helping with insect control.

BEAUTY CARE WITH HERBS

I pretty much outgrew the obsession with outer beauty during the years of tending children and milking cows, when I was lucky to get time to wash my face. Still there is no sense in blowing good points one has or allowing age to make deeper marks than necessary. The fact is, I probably use as many herbal cosmetics as I do the other kind. You, too, can find quick but delightful uses for the herbs on hand. Try the following to soothe and bring out the best in body and spirit.

-Add a few stems of mint or lemon balm to your bath. Hang them under the faucet and let the water pass over them. Or put them in a net bag and hang them from the showerhead. They will remind you to relax and enjoy as well as scrub.

-Use a herbal tea bag in your bath if you are too rushed, or if it is cold, rainy, or dark, or you are undressed and can't run out to the garden. Use up to four at a time for stronger fragrance.

-Put a gardenia or magnolia flower in a bowl or brandy snifter in the bathroom. Better yet, let it float on your bath water. Get a lift of luxury from a corsage you weren't going to wear again or a bush or tree that is overflowing with fragrant bloom.

-Save cucumber ends when you make salad and after dinner sit back with them on your eyelids to rest and refresh yourself.

-Treat a child's hurt, or your own, with aloe, and then rub the rest of the juice on your face. You can feel it tightening and cleansing the skin.

-Use a mint or sage leaf for a toothbrush. Put some in a glass beside your bed and pluck a leaf first thing in the morning.

-Hang a wreath of eucalyptus or put a basket of potpourri in the bathroom where steam from every shower will release the scent.

-Put a potted herb plant on your bathroom counter and make a habit of rubbing it as you pass. The humidity of a bathroom makes it good for growing plants. If the light is bad, revolve plants as needed from there to a shady spot outdoors or onto a windowsill and back to bathroom service when revived.

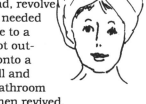

STEAM FACIALS

My steam facials started as a beauty treatment that immediately enlisted the interest of my teenage daughters. Then someone got a cold, so we added Vick's salve plant and eucalyptus and opened the sinuses as well as the pores. One daughter was also facing exams at the time. Into the pot went basil, mint, and bayleaf and she felt sure it helped her think more clearly that day.

For a steam treatment, pick a time when you have 20 minutes to half an hour and will not have to go outdoors for a few hours afterward. Put a kettle with 4 to 6 cups of water on to boil. Then start your steam treatment with a walk in the garden to gather the desired herbs. You could use dried or frozen ones if you want, but digging in the cupboard isn't as much fun. As little as three tablespoon of dried herbs will do, but gather two large handfuls of fresh herbs if you can. Return to the house and wash your herbs. Then wash or cleanse your face in your usual way. Take a large towel and bowl to a place where you can sit and comfortably lean over with your face 12 to 18 inches above the bowl. A counter and stool, table and chair, or easy chair with the bowl in a pillow on your lap will do. You can listen to your favorite music or TV show or say your prayers and savor the silence while you relax.

Put the herbs into the bowl and pour the boiling water over them. Stir and immerse them to begin the infusion. Yes, you are making tea, but this time you will use the steam first. Close your eyes and slowly lower your face into the steam, staying at least a foot above the hot water. Drape the towel over your head to make a tent and keep in steam, but open a corner whenever you need fresh air. Your face will perspire as the steam opens the pores. Herbal properties will penetrate and help soften the skin.

The steam also draws out impurities, increases the circulation, and eliminates toxins.

Stay in there for 10 to 15 minutes. Finish with a tepid and then a cool rinse and an astringent to close and tighten the pores. Or proceed to a facial pack. Try to avoid changes in temperature for an hour or more.

Facials are good once a week for normal skin, up to three times a week for oily skin, and every two to three weeks for dry skin. Avoid them if you have thread veins or any serious skin, breathing, or heart problems.

Use the leftover scented water in your bath, as a hair rinse, or for other cosmetic purposes.

HEALING WITH HERBS

Neither the author nor the publisher of this book advocates ever using herbs instead when consultation with a doctor is indicated. We take no responsibility for the effectiveness of any uses or for

---

HERBS FOR FACIALS

Good base for all: comfrey, fennel

For normal to dry skins: borage, comfrey, parsley, salad burnet, sorrel, violet flowers or leaves.

For oily to normal skins: comfrey, fennel, lemon peel, lemon grass, lavender, rose petals, sage, witch hazel.

For cleansing and calming: applemint, chamomile, chervil, lavender, lemon balm, rose petals, linden, spearmint, thyme.

To increase circulation and stimulate: pansy leaves, rosemary, peach leaves.

To tighten and stimulate mature skin: aniseed, dandelion, comfrey, elderflowers, lemon verbena, lavender, peppermint, tansy leaves or flowers.

For astringent at the end: elderflowers, yarrow, witch hazel, herbal vinegars.

possible mistaken identification
of herbs.

I am glad to pass along this
herbal lore showing how herbs and
spices have been used through history. I also mention my own experiences using herbs.

For many centuries herbs
were principal medications and
they remain so today for many
people in many places.

HERBS: EARLY HELP WITH HEALTH PROBLEMS

I find the best thing about medicinal herbs, after all the interesting stories and history that make
growing them so much fun, is their
sheer availability. When something
first hurts, or when you get that
uneasy feeling that a cold or sore
throat may be coming on, you can
do something about it right away.

This gives us the feeling of more
control over life, and there is great
strength in the resulting thoughts
and feelings. Sometimes the satisfaction of having done something,
anything, is enough to ward off
worse.

With herbs on hand, we can
often help ourselves or members of
our family long before a minor
problem develops to the doctor
stage.

I've joked that aloe and such
herbs were ideal first aid because I
always knew where they were, and I
never run out. The leaf I use grows
back. Drugstore medicine eventually dries up, gets lost, or loses
its potency. What is more, herbs
are available for a hurt that starts
at midnight or on a holiday when
the doctor is hard to find and the
patient or parent is less inclined to
call.

I try to keep aloe and mint,
my most often used herbs, either in

pots indoors or close to the door
where I can get them in my night-
gown if I have to.

Though some strong herbs are
dangerous, most herbs are fairly
safe. Even if they do not help
much, at least they do not hurt.
They also do not cost $50 and an
afternoon in the waiting room. And
when something does progress to
the stage when a doctor is needed,
herbs may already have eased the
pain and hurried the cure.

I have a dear friend who was
making jelly when it boiled over
onto her hands. Her husband
slathered them with aloe juice
before he rushed her to the emergency room. She had second and
third degree burns, and everyone
remarked that she must be in pain.
But she said her hands hardly hurt
at all. She credited the quick healing and absence of pain to the aloe,
which even doctors will agree has
an anesthetic and a slight antiseptic quality.

HERBAL PREPARATIONS

In its simplest form, preparing herbs for use in pain relief is a
matter of placing a leaf on a hurt or
sting.

A more advanced form of
treatment is preparing an INFU-
SION or tea. For this, boil the water, remove it from the heat, and
pour over the herbs. Steep longer
to make it stronger, a few minutes
to several hours. Make a day's dose
at once and take it hot or warm, or
else cold after keeping it in the

refrigerator. Distilled water is best but tap water does fine. Glass, pottery, or unchipped enamel containers are better than metals that can leach into the tea. Cover the container to capture all the herbal properties except in the case of steam facials (page 32).

A TISANE is actually one cup of tea brewed at a time and steeped briefly, as with a tea bag or tea ball. For therapeutic use, use more of the herb to strengthen the tea.

A DECOCTION is used to extract the properties of bark, seeds, and roots, or any plant part that is hard and woody. Mash or grind these into small pieces. Add water in a glass or enamel pan with a lid and bring slowly to a boil. Then reduce heat and simmer from 15 minutes to an hour, and let steep with the lid on until cool. These are best made fresh daily but will keep in the refrigerator for three days.

Make a COMPRESS by soaking a cloth in a tea, tisane, or decoction, not too hot to touch, wringing the cloth, and placing it on the skin or muscle problem. Cover this with a dry towel to hold in the heat and redip when the warmth is gone. Repeat for up to 30 minutes.

POULTICES are made of dry, powdered, or blended herbs mixed with just enough water or herbal tea to make a paste. Add oatmeal or flour to bind. Spread this over the ache or wound, cover with a warm cloth or bandage.

PLASTERS are almost the same except that, since they are made with hot herbs like mustard and garlic, the paste is best spread between two layers of porous cloth and then laid or bandaged in place

To make a TINCTURE, mix 1 ounce of finely chopped herb with 5 ounces of alcohol (brandy, gin, or vodka, never poisonous rubbing or wood alcohol) or vinegar. Put in a closed container and shake occasionally to extract the herbal properties. Then strain if you wish and store in a cool place. Tinctures stay more potent longer. Use them with caution. The usual dose is several drops to 1 tablespoon

WHICH HEALING PLANTS SHOULD YOU GROW?

(For further information, look these herbs up individually in chapter 9, the plant-by-plant directory.)

Aloe. Absolutely the first plant I'd choose for a garden, container, or both would be an aloe. This grows easily and blooms attractively in Florida.

By breaking off a leaf you expose the fresh jelly inside. It soothes everything from diaper rash and mosquito bites to serious burns. It can ease hundreds of little hurts you would never take to a doctor.

The plant also heals itself. You can rub off the brown edge of the broken leaf. Select an inconspicuous leaf growing on the underside of the plant, Break off a piece of the same leaf each time to keep the plant looking tidy.

Comfrey. This herb, also called knit-bone, has been essential in our garden, home, and our barn when we had one. We fed it to our animals fresh and made a tea for them when they were sick.

Comfrey is famous for its healing powers, but can have side effects. See warnings on p.116 in the plant directory entry, and use comfrey in moderation, only externally if you want.

But in my house, comfrey tea is the next step toward healing, after aloe. I ate a bit of leaf every day while my broken arm was mending. Research shows that comfrey contains allantoin, which promotes the growth of cells and connective tissue of bone and cartilage. A slurry of leaves that dried as a cast was once used to set bones. Never boil comfrey, for high temperatures can destroy the allantoin.

Fennel. This was a sacred herb in ancient Greece and supposed to cure all ills. Bulbs of fennel are sold in grocery stores and eaten as a vegetable.

Fennel is still considered good for soothing tired and sore eyes and improving sight, and a tea of fennel is used as a mild eyewash. Greek athletes ate it to give them stamina and guard against overweight. It is supposed to increase mother's milk, and a poultice of this relieves the swelling of engorged breasts.

Small amounts of the tea are fed to babies for colic and a decoction of seeds is said to work for worms. Fennel is also advised for colds, sore throats, congestion, and digestion. Put it in your garden, use it in cooking or in salads, or enjoy it as a butterfly plant.

For Nervous Obesity and To Improve The Figure

Put a plastic or glass container of water in the microwave or set the tea kettle to boil. Go out and gather at least a teaspoon each of fennel, anise, thyme, marjoram, and mint. If you don't have all of these herbs, use whichever ones you have. Wash and steep for an infusion. Drink 2 to 3 cupfuls a day, no more.

Garlic. Pharmacologists consider garlic one of the safest herbs for home remedies as long as it is used in moderation and not given to very small children. The component allicin gives it both its odor and its antibiotic qualities. It is unstable and cooking reduces its effectiveness.

Warning: Some individuals are allergic to garlic, so avoid it if you are.

You can buy bulbs at the grocery store. Keep them on hand in the cupboard, not the refrigerator. Apply a whole clove to a toothache or mouth sore. Mash into hot water for an infusion, into honey for cough medicine, and into olive or sweet oil (highly refined olive oil, sold in drugstores) for an earache.

The year our Teresa had the fewest ear problems was the year her Italian-born teacher taught by cooking and she came home redolent of garlic at least once a week. This odor can be somewhat controlled by eating parsley, fennel, or celery with or after the garlic.

Odorless garlic, available at health food stores, is not quite as effective. Some people find garlic improves the immune system and relieves symptoms. Most of us won't want to eat a clove a day for any reason, but there is ample reason beyond the flavor for using it lavishly.

Plant a few cloves of garlic in your garden. They may not form bulbs in Florida, but the green foliage that results will add both flavor (milder than the bulb) and nutrition to foods. Mince and add it to salads.

Ginger. This is a safe and effective spice that grows easily in Florida. Try candied ginger for motion sickness on car or boat trips. Or get empty capsules at the health food store and fill them with powdered ginger. Studies show it can be effective and does not make one sleepy. For nausea from chemotherapy, make ginger tea from the roots or from powdered ginger from your spice shelf, 2 teaspoons to a cup of boiled water, steep 10 minutes. Gingerale and gingerbread started as digestive aids. However, pregnant women should avoid ginger.

Mints. Mint has as many uses as it has varieties and it grows abundantly all over Florida. Be careful if you gather it in the wild, for roadsides may have been sprayed. Mint makes a good tasting tea that will help digestion and nausea, morning sickness, insomnia, coughs and respiratory ailments, flu and viruses, toothache, and gum troubles. Use mint as a compress for aches and wounds, or to simply increase energy.

You can be sure of fresh breath by having mint in your tea or by chewing a sprig. It has antiseptic, anesthetic, and antispasmodic properties. A noted herbalist makes a tea of 3 teaspoons dried mint and 1 teaspoon of rosemary to 3 cups of water to put bicycle champions in peak condition for racing in the Tour de France.

Parsley. This most common herb has been called "essentially worthless" by one modern herbalist and "a major medicinal plant" by another. You can take your pick. But we already know it is easy to grow here in Florida except in summer, so it won't hurt to use it. We also know that it is rich in vitamins A, B, and C, calcium, and iron. The

Romans fed it to gladiators to increase their cunning, strength, and agility. As author Ruth Stout said,, "That may be too much to ask of a plant." But she also told of using it so lavishly in her cooking that her husband Fred once said,""Please pass the parsley" when he wanted the potatoes.

One of the most active and successful Florida gardeners I know plants parsley among her prize-winning camellias and eats it to relieve her arthritis.

Besides adding color and nutrition to cooking, add parsley to tea. Or make a tea of parsley and whatever other herbs you have handy. It is said to ease coughs, asthma, problems of menopause, and painful periods.

The leftover tea can be used for compresses to relieve burning eyes, swollen breasts, for a hair rinse, or to clean the pores of the skin. One study shows that it has an antihistamine effect that may inhibit allergy symptoms. Mothers find it increases milk and tones the birthing muscles, but it should be used in moderation when pregnant or it may irritate the kidneys.

Roses. Plant the most fragrant kinds for herbal uses. Petals picked just after the dew dries and before the flower opens, dried quickly and stored in a covered container, have the most therapeutic value, which lasts for three or four months. After that they can go into potpourri. An infusion of rose petals in water or wine is used as a sweet, safe, gentle strengthener, especially for people who live or work in much pollution and for convalescents, young children, or the elderly. Rose petals in the bath seem to help rheumatism and arthritis. Rose hips are known to be rich in vitamin C.

It is easy to gather and wash rose hips, add a cupful each to several quart canning jars, and fill with boiling water. Seal jars with safe canning methods or when cool, pour contents into plastic containers and freeze. Use the liquid in soups, stew, tea, or other foods as part of the daily diet. I always keep this on hand, and when we moved I decided to take my canned rose hips along. No matter that one mover couldn't figure out what in the world I had in those jars. I figured anything that was free, easy, and promised to keep my kids healthy was worth doing. And all nine of our kids have been remarkably healthy.

HERBS TO HELP WARD OFF COLDS

-To warm a chilled body, drink tea to which you add a pinch of cayenne pepper, no more than a fourth of a teaspoon to 3 cups of water. Soak cold feet in an infusion of mustard seeds. Both of these are on your spice shelf and stimulate circulation.

-Ground ginger and honey also make a warming drink and ease coughs. Slice fresh ginger and put it in a glass jar, covering it with vinegar. Put it in the refrigerator. After it steeps for a week or so, add a spoonful or two of the ginger-flavored vinegar to a drink of cold or hot water or tea. Use the ginger pieces for seasoning.

-Tobasco sauce in tomato juice is good for a sore throat as well as a hangover and the vitamin C will also help. Use it as a gargle as well as a drink. Start with 1/4 teaspoon tobasco to 1 cup juice and increase to 1/2 teaspoon only after you test your tolerance.

-Soak pods of hot pepper in hot water and add a little of this to orange juice, with sugar if you need it, and drink freely for fever. The pepper adds vitamins C and A, iron, potassium, and niacin and induces sweating.

-Make a tea with elderflowers to soothe the throat and quiet a cough. Dry some when they are plentiful and keep them on hand.

-All alliums (onions, garlic, chives) are good for colds and coughs but the leek is best. Cook, puree, add honey to taste, and take by the spoonful as needed.

FOR BEE AND OTHER STINGS

Remain calm. Though a sting is a terrible shock, it only feels like but is not a serious problem for most people, and the pain is short-lived. Carefully remove the stinger by scraping. Never squeeze it. Then quickly apply crushed fresh leaves of basil, betony, borage, comfrey, plantain, lemon balm, calendula, marsh mallow, parsley, or any mint. A slice of onion will draw and soothe. So will a dampened aspirin. Extract of witch hazel or oil of thyme or eucalyptus will also reduce the pain and swelling. Do not be unduly upset if a large area of redness develops. It will pass quickly. If swelling of the throat and difficult breathing occur, get to the nearest doctor at once and thereafter always keep on hand whatever antidote your doctor recommends. People who are critically allergic should always carry their prescription.

3. Cooking with Homegrown Herbs

Family members who seldom notice the garden are sure to compliment you on the way herbs enhance flavors, fill the house with delicious aromas, and make everything you cook taste wonderful. Wherever you live in Florida, you can grow wonderful culinary herbs, so you'll always have them at hand, and your growing season is much longer than that of people in northern states.

Chefs in great restaurants buy and use herbs lavishly. Homegrown herbs are fresher than those most chefs buy and use.

HAVING HERBS HANDY

You can plant herbs and spices around your home, so that there is always something thriving, something you can share with visitors and use to make even your easiest cooking zestfully elegant.

You can make more difference in your family's diet by growing herbs than with any other garden venture. 16 to 20 kinds of herbs will fit into a bed measuring only 4 by 5 feet. Half a dozen kinds fit into a window box 8 by 30 inches, and more will fit into a strawberry jar or tiered flower pot. Others, including herbal trees and shrubs, can be used in your landscape.

You'll want to place your beds or pots of herbs near the kitchen door to make adding fresh garnishes and seasonings more convenient. Or grow them in a hanging basket above the sink, or in planters on the deck, windowsill, or patio. I now have herbs growing around my front door as well, because there is more light there for gathering them at cooking time in the winter.

Take advantage of the Florida climate by planting two identical herb planters. Bring one indoors and use it as long as it thrives. The length of time depends on how much and how often you cut the herbs, whether or not and how powerfully the air conditioner is running, how much light you get in your kitchen, etc. When the one inside looks straggly, exchange it for the outdoor one, and let the one you've been using grow back in ideal conditions outside.

If you don't have time to pick herbs when it's time to cook, just harvest herbs you'll need when you are working in the garden, plunging them into a bucket or jar of cool water. Rinse them off when you come in and store them in a jar or plastic bag in the refrigerator with a bit of water in the bottom for the stems.

Or you can freeze them. I do this with tropical oregano when I take cuttings. Then I not only have the leaves on hand, but I save chopping because they break up easily: just crush them in the bag while they are still frozen.

BUYING WHAT YOU DO NOT GROW

Even ardent herb growers will not be able to grow all the herbs they would like to use. No climate is right for all of them all of the time, though Florida comes close. No problem. You can buy everything you need.

Start with the salt and spice section of the grocery store for individual dried herbs or special combinations. Check the produce section for fresh herbs. Farmers markets, ethnic groceries, and local herb growers are especially good sources of fresh herbs. By the way, it's easy to start plants from roots of lemon grass, ginger roots, rosemary cuttings, dried coriander seeds, and certain other herbs right from the store.

Health food stores may well have a large selection of herbs at low prices and allow you to buy smaller amounts. Many catalogs that sell herb plants also sell dried herbs, some in special combinations. These may be less expensive than those in the grocery. But put those that come in bags into jars or cans once you get them home. I've had cumin all over the cupboard when my good intentions met with long delay.

GARNISHES MAKE IT GREAT

Magazine photographers and restaurant chefs know the value of garnishes and use one or more on every plate. They recognize the importance of eye appeal. A sprig of parsley, the face of a pansy, or a bit of any fresh herb enhances a plate or platter. Use herbs that don't wilt readily: lemon balm, dill, rosemary, scented geranium, mint, or fennel, or flowered stems of nasturtium, chive, or pineapple sage.

You can pick herb sprigs for garnishes in the morning or whenever you pick fresh flowers. Wash them and put them into a glass or into the vase with the flowers, and pluck them from there at dinner-

---

COMMON SENSE GUIDE FOR USING HERBS

* At first use small amounts and only a few herbs at a time so you'll know which ones to repeat or delete to suit individual tastes.

* Keep in mind that fresh and newly dried herbs have the most flavor, usually more intense than the ones you've been buying. Adjust the amounts by adding a little at a time. You can always add more. Let the herbs bring out flavors, not overwhelm them.

* Start with a pinch to one fourth of a teaspoon of dried herbs or a teaspoon of fresh leaves for a dish serving four, a pound of meat, or a cup of sauce.

* Use herbs in only one or two dishes per meal. If your family resists change, add them gradually to recipes they already know and like rather than springing too much too new at once.

* Add herbs to cold foods ahead of time and let them absorb the flavors for several hours or overnight.

* Add herbs to hot foods only at the end of cooking, for flavor and nutrients can be destroyed by heat. For a roast or stew that cooks 2 hours or more, add them in the last half hour. For vegetables, fish, and sauces, add herbs in the last few minutes.

* As you add fresh herbs, crush or bruise them with a wooden spoon or your fingers to release the oils.

* When you make herbal blends, let one herb dominate and add others that complement it.

WHOOPS! HOW TO HANDLE TOO MUCH OF A GOOD THING

If you get carried away and overdo in your enthusiasm for herbs, or have a spill, there are ways to save the supper.

1) Spoon or strain out as much of the herb as you can.

2) Add half a teaspoon of sugar to cut too much salt.

3) Add more of the bland ingredients to absorb the stronger flavor. In some cases you can make a second batch of the recipe, leaving out the seasoning, and add it to the first. Then freeze half the dish and you'll come out ahead from your mistake.

4) Add a whole raw potato, peeled, to soak up some of the excess flavor. Remove it just before serving if it seems inappropriate.

5) Some dishes can be served cold and the taste of the overseasoning will not be as obvious.

6) After making your best effort to correct the seasoning, provided that the dish is edible, present it as if it were fine. With luck, everyone will think that it is.

time when you are too busy to rush outside. You can let guests choose their own from a centerpiece composed of herb sprigs, or from individual cups or salt cellars containing mixed herbs, next to each plate.

Most people never eat garnishes. My son Tom, who was head waiter in a French restaurant, says, "Some people eat them and some people leave them, but Mom is the only one I've known who took them home to root."

I've gotten watercress that way. One time I thought I was rooting watercress. When it turned out to be the most healthy and thriving watercress I'd ever had, I realized it was really pennyroyal, but that was fine. Mine had died out over summer and I was happy to get a free replacement.

Our parents come to dinner every Sunday, and that reminds me to put mint or lemon balm in the tea or water, or an herbal garnish on the plate. That simple addition seems to make the food taste better, even if no one so much as crushes the mint against the glass.

Be creative. Use any edible part of any plant (see the list on p. 55). Then add some nasturtium flowers as well as leaves beside the pork chops and put a pink hibiscus flowers on the ham platter.

Leaf garnishes are wonderful, but edible flowers are spectacular. As long as you've washed the roses and not used pesticide in your garden, there is no reason you can't surround or decorate a cake with real rose petals or buds. Use an open rose in the center. Or put a cluster of three rosebuds beside the name on the birthday cake.

One couple was preparing for a banquet and trying to think of table favors. I led them to my garden where they easily found enough branches of pineapple sage and mint to make 50 cuttings that would be rooted by the time of the dinner. Such herbs provide the table decoration and give each person something to take home and keep. The cutting can sit in water or in moist vermiculite in a cute little cup.

Save sprigs of whichever herbs you are using in your cooking to use as a garnish. Use fennel, dill, or rosemary for garnish with a different texture and color or mince them to sprinkle on the top of the fish or the soup. Minced basil over a plate of sliced tomatoes makes a salad. Sprinkle dill and lemon juice over the green beans. Freeze edible flowers like violets or borage in ice cubes and use them in drinks. Or candy them and save them for special occasions.

Before you even plan the menu for a special meal, check the herb garden for possibilities and go from there. Garnish family meals until it becomes a gracious habit.

USE MORE HERBS IN COOKING

Creative herbal cooking wins you praise from everyone who dines at your table. Just the eye appeal of a scattering of bits of green on top of the soup or sauce can make a marked difference. They do as much for flavor as salt, but herbs have good side effects and increase nutrition as well. Some herbs will not alter the taste much, others are pronounced.

Fresh herbs are better than dried. But your own herbs, dried, have richer flavor and cost less than any you could buy. It is a good idea to harvest and dry some of the culinary herbs you have in quantity, especially in the spring when they are thriving. Then you will have them on hand whenever you need them or find a new use for them.

As you use up the dried herbs in your cupboard, save and wash their containers. When your own herb garden is growing well, refill them with homegrown, dried garden herbs, packaging them either plain or in mixtures. It's instructive to read the ingredients of prepackaged spice mixtures -- they are listed in order of quantity, with the first ones mentioned used in the greatest amounts. Dry and try your own mixtures. Label them with contents and approximate amounts so you can increase or delete next time.

Don't worry about exact recipes. Experiment with what you have. You might want to record the most successful dishes in your recipe book or file.

Here are some herbal combinations for quickly adding spice to your cooking. It's inspiring to think of automatic refills growing outdoors.

Basic Herbal Seasoning
Combine these dried herbs in a small bowl and then funnel them into labeled herb jars:
> 4 tablespoons parsley
> 3 tablespoons marjoram
> 3 tablespoons oregano
> 3 tablespoons onion, garlic,
> or garlic chive
> (use dried leaves)

Chili Powder
Combine and bottle these dried herbs and spices:
> 6 tablespoons powdered dry
> chile (ancho chile is good)
> 1 tablespoon oregano
> 1 tablespoon garlic
> 1 tablespoon cumin seed
> 1 teaspoon clove

Bouquets Garni

These are small bundles of fresh herbs tied together inside a square of muslin or cheesecloth, with string long enough to tie around the pot handle for easy removal when the flavors but not the flecks have spread through the dish. Herbs most often used are parsley, thyme, and bay leaf, but you can add whole peppercorns, cloves, allspice, chives, celery leaves or seed, rosemary, garlic, true or 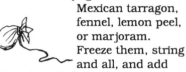 Mexican tarragon, fennel, lemon peel, or marjoram. Freeze them, string and all, and add them directly from the freezer to the pot. Or make them of dried herbs. They are nice as gifts. At home, try mixed herbs in a tea ball (remove it before serving).

Fines Herbes

This term is often used in French cooking and refers to a combination of fresh herbs finely minced and added at the end of the cooking or as a garnish. This mixture usually includes three or four herbs: parsley, chervil, and thyme, plus basil, chives, or salad burnet. You can also make a dried version of this, which is not quite as good but much more convenient.

Poultry Seasoning

Mix dried sage, thyme, and marjoram, plus small amounts of rosemary, celery or lovage leaves, parsley, and perhaps a touch of basil.

Hot Pizza Spice

Mix crumbled, dried spices in a bowl and funnel into labeled jars, preferably fitted with shaker lids under the caps:

6 tablespoons oregano
4 tablespoons basil
1 tablespoon rosemary
1 tablespoon celery leaves
3 tablespoons hot pepper
1 tablespoon garlic powder

Herbes de Provence

Mix these dried herbs and store in small herb jars. Use with roast chicken or steamed vegetables for a subtly different flavor.

2 tablespoons lavender
  flowers
2 tablespoons thyme
2 teaspoons sage
1 tablespoon rosemary
1 tablespoon marjoram
1 tablespoon fennel leaves

Curry Powder

Mix these dried, ground spices and store in a jar:

3 tablespoons coriander
5 tablespoons ground
  turmeric
2 tablespoons cumin
1 tablespoon black pepper
1 tablespoon ginger
1 teaspoon clove
1 teaspoon cardamom seed
  (if available)
2 tablespoons cayenne pepper
1 tablespoon garlic powder
2 teaspoons cinnamon
1 teaspoon nutmeg

HARVESTING, USING, AND STORING HERBS

NAME	BEGIN HARVEST	HOW AND WHEN TO USE	HOW TO PRESERVE
Basil	In 4 to 6 weeks	Use often, prevent flowers from forming	Dry in bunches. Store in opaque jars. Blanch before freezing.
Borage	8 weeks after sprouting	Use tender young leaves raw, mature leaves cooked or in tea or vinegar. Use flowers in ice cubes, as garnish, or candy.	Leaves lose flavor when dried or frozen.
Calendula	When in bloom	Dry the flowers or petals and use like saffron, or use petals fresh for color.	Keep moisture out, store dry. Grind into powder.
Caraway	When seeds turn brown	Snip clusters into bowl before seeds scatter.	Dry 2-3 weeks, store in airtight, opaque jars. Do not freeze.
Catnip	When in full bloom	Dry in shade	Does not freeze well.
Chervil	Six weeks after sowing	Use fresh. Mince and use like parsley.	Make frequent sowings.
Chives	When six or more inches tall.	Use fresh. Snip often to stimulate growth.	Do not freeze or dry well. Use flowers in vinegar
Chives, garlic	When six or more inches tall	Use fresh. Divide bulbs, use extras in soups or salads.	Good in vinegar
Coriander	Use leaves anytime or seeds when brown	Hang seed clusters to dry, seeds are bitter until dried.	Store dry seeds in airtight jars, use leaves fresh.

HARVESTING, USING, AND STORING HERBS

NAME	BEGIN HARVEST	HOW AND WHEN TO USE	HOW TO PRESERVE
Dill	When 6" tall, snip green leaves of young plants.	Let other plants grow for seeds, collect when light brown, before they scatter.	Hang clusters of seeds in a dark place, inside a paper bag. Flavor of leaves partly lost when dried.
Fennel	When 8" tall Use tender leaves and stems.	Best when in bud. Use bulbs when plants mature	Collect and dry seeds as for dill.
Garlic	When plant can spare leaves use them.	When bulbs mature, dig, dry, and store like onions.	Do not dry or freeze. Preserve diced fresh garlic in small jar of olive oil, refrigerate.
Ginger	After 3 months, use small piece of root.	After 8 to 13 months, dig and use whole root, save some to replant.	Do not dry or freeze, store in jar of wine or vinegar, refrigerate.
Goldenrod	When in bloom	Use in crafts, fresh or dry.	Hang in small bunches to dry
Lavender	When in bloom.	Hang and dry flowers before summer. Cut back and dry foliage when 6" high.	Dries well, do not freeze.
Lemon Balm	Best before flowering.	Use before summer heat. Cut back to 1/3 of foliage.	Dry quickly or it will turn black.
Lemon-grass	When 12" tall.	Cut and use often	Hang in bunches to dry, do not freeze.
Lemon verbena	When well established.	Hang to dry in fall before it goes dormant.	Dries well. Store in airtight jars.
Loquat	When fruits are soft and orange.	Taste for sweetness, eat or use fresh in jellies, jams, or wine.	Delicious dried or frozen.

HARVESTING, USING, AND STORING HERBS

NAME	BEGIN TO HARVEST	HOW AND WHEN TO USE	HOW TO PRESERVE
Lovage	When leaves are ample	Best used fresh, yellows quickly.	Blanch to freeze, dry seeds and roots.
Marjoram	4 to 6 weeks after transplanting.	Cut and use often. Dry spring abundance.	Dry away from sunlight, freezes well, store airtight.
Mint	When leaves are plentiful.	Best used when young and fresh or when in bloom	Dries and freezes well.
Nasturtium	When leaves are plentiful.	Flowers and leaves Best used fresh. Refrigerate until needed.	Does not dry or freeze well. Store seeds or leaves in vinegar.
Onions and Alliums	When leaves are ample.	Cut leaves for salad. Harvest bulbs when foliage yellows.	Hang and dry bulbs in cool dry area.
Oregano	When 6" tall	Cut and use often. Hang to dry in bunches before summer.	Dries well, store in airtight containers. Do not freeze.
Parsley	When leaves are ample	Cut and use often. Dry before summer.	Dry in cool dark place. Freezes well.
Passion Fruit	When fruits are ripe	Ripe when ready to drop. Cut in half. Scoop out centers, Strain out seeds.	Freeze as juice.
Rose	Before petals fade or as hips.	Add boiling water to hips and seal in jars. Dry or store in vinegars or jams. Use petals in jelly.	Petals and hips dry well in sun. Freezing not recommended.

HARVESTING, USING, AND STORING HERBS

NAME	BEGIN HARVEST	HOW AND WHEN TO USE	HOW TO PRESERVE
Rosemary	When leaves are plentiful.	Cut no more than 1/5 of foliage at a time.	Dries well, does not freeze as well.
Rue	When leaves are plentiful.	Cut and dry before summer.	Dries well, does not freeze as well.
Sage	When leaves are plentiful and plant vigorous.	Harvest regular sage before summer, Pineapple sage does not dry well, use fresh.	Freeze flowers of pineapple sage in ice cubes. Most sage dries well.
Salad Burnet	When leaves are plentiful.	Use fresh and often, before summer.	Does not dry or freeze well.
Savory	When 6" tall.	Use or harvest before flowering or summer.	Dries well. Does not freeze as well.
Scented Geranium	When leaves are plentiful.	For maximum fragrance, cut when flowering begins.	Dry in shade. Store in airtight containers.
Sorrel	When 4 to 6" tall.	Cut off individual leaves or cut whole plant back, it will come back.	Do not dry. Freeze in small packets.
Tarragon	When leaves are plentiful.	Harvest spring growth before summerkill.	Dries well, freezes even better.
Tarragon, Mexican	When leaves are plentiful.	Cut flowers off to encourage foliage.	Dries and freezes well.
Thyme	When leaves are plentiful.	Use and harvest in spring before summer.	Dries and freezes well.

GOOD HERBAL COMBINATIONS

Here are groups of herbs with flavors that go well together. Try some of the following combinations in seasoned flours, sugars, salts, cheeses, mustards, vinegars, oil, honeys, or butters.

lemon rind, dill, and garlic

oregano, garlic chive, and thyme

tarragon, chive, and chervil

tarragon, peppercorn, and thyme

ginger, cardamon, and coriander

garlic and dill

garlic chive, parsley, red flowers of pineapple sage

Seasoned Flour: Add 2 teaspoons of your favorite mixed dried herbs and spices plus 1/2 teaspoon of salt and a dash of pepper to 3 cups of flour. Mix well and put in a container that seals tightly. Use this right away in gravies, sauces, biscuits, pizza or quiche crusts, or to dip food for browning or frying. Make larger batches or several kinds and store in the freezer. Increase herbs for a stronger flavor if you like.

You might want to add
-sesame or poppy seeds or bits of dried garlic chives or garlic or onion leaves to flours for breads and pizza crust,
-dried Aztec sweet shrub or stevia to flour for anything sweet from cornbread to cake.
-marjoram and a bit of tar-ragon and rosemary to flour for gravies and sauces,
-powdered sage and a bit of ground cayenne pepper to flour for fried chicken.

Seasoned Sugar: Chop 2 tablespoons of rose petals, lemon balm, mint, pineapple sage, or rose geranium into each cup of granulated or powdered sugar, depending on how you want to use it. Mix, seal, and let set for six weeks until flavors blend. Then sift out herbs or leave in. Use for teas, as a topping for cakes, cookies, or French toast, or to sweeten fruits. For gifts, put in decorative jars and label with suggested uses.

Herbed Stuffing Mix: see recipe for Scalloped Vegetable Casserole, p. 58. Use these seasoned bread cubes also as croutons in soup or salad.

Bread molds so quickly in Florida that you need to replace a loaf every few days no matter how much is left. We used to use 14 loaves a week when our sons were home, so it was hard for me to adjust to this. Now I split each loaf in half and freeze one part so I only have to shop once a week. Mid week, I take anything left of the old loaf and put it in the freezer. When enough stale bread collects, I use it for stuffing.

Cut 4 cups of stale bread into cubes or break into small pieces. Finely mince one medium onion and saute in 1/4 cup of olive oil, salad oil, or melted butter in a large skillet or dutch oven. Add bread bits and saute until brown and crisp, stirring often and watching heat to prevent scorching. Add minced fresh herbs to taste, or dried ones, or some of each, as you stir. Add salt and pep-

CUSTOMARY COMPLEMENTS:
FAVORITE FOODS AND HERBS

Poultry or Pork

Sage
Thyme
Bay leaf
  or substitutes
Coriander
Garlic or garlic
  chives
Ginger
Marjoram
Orange or lemon
  peel
Parsley
Rosemary

Lamb

Mints
Parsley
Bay leaf
  or substitutes
Garlic and onion
Chervil
Cinnamon
Coriander
Dill
Lemon, sour orange
Marjoram
Rosemary
Thyme

Yellow Vegetables

Beebalm
Celery or lovage
Cinnamon
Garlic
Ginger
Nutmeg
Orange peel
Parsley

Beef and Veal

Basil
Bay leaf
  or substitutes
Caraway
Chervil
Garlic or onion
powder
Marjoram
Orange or lemon
  peel
Oregano
Parsley
Rosemary
Sage
Tropical tarragon
Tarragon
Thyme

Salad

Arugula, roquette
Basil
Calendula
Chickweed
Chives
Fennel
Garlic chives
Lovage
Nasturtium
Parsley
Purslane
Rose petals
Salad burnet
Sorrel
Sweet cicely
Violets, pansies

Green Vegetables

Basil
Bay leaf
  or substitutes
Caraway
Chervil
Chives, onions
Garlic chives
Marjoram
Mints
Parsley
Sage
Tropical tarragon
Tarragon
Thyme

Rice, Beans, Pasta

Caraway seed
Chiles and peppers
Cumin seed
Garlic
Good King Henry
Lemon peel
Oregano
Parsley
Mint

Fines Herbes

Chervil
Chives
Parsley
Tarragon or tagetes

Bouquet Garni

Bay
Marjoram
Parsley
Thyme

Fish

Basil
Bay or substitutes
Dill
Fennel
Lemon balm
Orange, lime, or
  lemon juice
Pickling spices
Rosemary
Sorrel
Tarragon

Eggs and Cheese

Basil
Chervil
Chives, garlic
chives
Coriander
Dill
Fennel
Mustard, dry
Oregano
Parsley
Sorrel
Tarragon, Mexican
Thyme, especially
  lemon thyme

per to taste. After all ingredients are browned and mixed, the stuffing mix is ready to use or freeze. To store in tins or jars, bake in the oven at 200 degrees F for another half hour, until completely dry. Cool, pack, and store.

When herbs are plentiful, blend dry leaves of parsley, sage, rosemary, thyme, marjoram, celery leaves or lovage, oregano, fennel, leaves of onion, garlic, or chives.

Or stop at a day-old bread store when you have all the fresh herbs. Make plenty of stuffing and keep some on hand in airtight containers or in the freezer for croutons, stuffing, or casseroles. If you want finer crumbs, just whirl them in the blender.

Herbed salts: These are easy to make and let you enhance flavor with less salt. Used noniodized salt or sea salt with up to equal parts of fresh herbs. If you like you can replace some or all of the salt with a salt substitute. Chop herbs well or whirl in the blender. Then spread on a cookie sheet and dry in a 200 degree oven for an hour, stirring often to break up lumps. Or mix 8 tablespoon of dried herbs per cup. Herbed salts will keep indefinitely.

Herbed Mustards: People worldwide use 400 million pounds of mustard a year and the jars keep fresh on our shelves because the herb is so antiseptic. To make your own mustards with special flavors, blend together 1/2 cup dry mustard, 1/2 cup white or whole wheat flour, 1/4 cup sugar, and 1 cup liquid (water, wine, plain or herbed vinegar, or beer) until lump free. Add herbs and spices to the entire amount, or separate into small portions and experiment with com-

binations of garlic, basil, thyme, parsley, marjoram, rosemary, or other favored culinary herbs. Use about 1 tablespoon of dried herbs or 2 tablespoons of fresh ones to the entire amount or divide accordingly. Let stand overnight, then stir again and add more flour if the mixture is too thin. You can also mix your own herbs, chopped and combined to your taste, with prepared mustard. Pack this into covered containers and store in the refrigerator for several months. Spread this with mayonnaise and a bit of horseradish on chicken before baking or broiling. Use with herbal vinegar in deviled eggs. Add to pasta or potato salads, vegetables,or dips.

Herbed Vinegars: These are easy and fun to make when herbs are plentiful. Save, wash, and sterilize attractive bottles or buy them from a wine makers' supplier. Wash and dry fresh herbs well. Water will cause cloudiness that affects eye appeal but not taste. Bruise seeds with a mortar and pestle. Fill the jars with any combination of herb leaves, flowers, or seeds and use approximately 4 ounces or 1 cup of fresh herbs for each quart. This is much more than most pictures suggest. Bruise leaves with a wooden spoon and then cover with vinegar to within an inch of the top. Push down and bruise the herbs further and shake the jar to remove bubbles. Cover with an acid-proof lid, label, and place on a sunny windowsill. Shake every few days. If the vinegar does not cover the herbs after a few days, add more vinegar. Taste after two to four weeks. When you like the flavor or after a month, strain out the herbs with a coffee filter and then put back only a decorative and identifying sprig of leaves or flowers. Cap and use in salad dressings or cooking, give as gifts, or use in cosmetics. Store at room temperature. Most will last up to 18 months.

Herbed Wines and Brandies: Make these exactly the same as you would vinegar, but use smaller containers because wines are more perishable. Airtight sealing is important with these, so cover any questionable seals with melted wax. Glue a short length of ribbon up and over the neck before dipping the cap or cork. This gives you a professional look and an easy way to lift the wax.

Herbed Butters: This is one of the easiest way to add herbs and reduce calories, because half the amount of butter will carry twice the flavor. Save little containers. Just soften the butter by creaming, microwaving, or melting and mix it with chopped herbs or flower petals of your choice. You need 1 to 2 tablespoons of fresh herbs, 1 1/2 teaspoons of dried, or 1/2 teaspoon of seeds for each stick or 1/4 pound of butter or whatever spread you use. Fresh herbs work best for these. Use parsley, rosemary, garlic, fennel, dill, ginger, chives, tarragon, basil, peppers, thyme, or any of the lemon herbs. A bit of lemon juice, vinegar, or Worcestershire sauce mixed in can help bring out the herbal flavors, especially if you must use dried herbs. It is best to use unsalted butter and a wooden spoon. If you don't have containers, roll your butters into balls or logs and decorate each with a leaf to indicate its ingredients. Allow at least three hours for

flavors to blend. Then use within a few days or weeks. Freeze to keep longer. Add as you would add butter to any dish: vegetables, eggs, pasta, baked potatoes. Serve homemade bread with a choice of butters and a salad for a delicious luncheon.

Herbed Honeys or Oils: You can add herbs to honey or oils. Use any vegetable or olive oil or almond oil with scented flowers for a sweet oil for baking. These should sit on the windowsill for two weeks to blend flavors and then will keep in a dark cupboard.

Herbed Breads: Add minced herbs to any bread, muffin, or biscuit dough, stirring or kneading them in until they are distributed. A tablespoon of minced herbs will strongly flavor two cups of raw dough. *Fine herbes* in bread go well with any kind of food.

HERBAL TEAS

Many people are quite familiar with the wide variety of herbal teas sold first in health food stores and now in groceries. Both coffee and regular tea are actually herbal drinks. They come from plants. But most people think of herbal teas as the aromatic, less addictive mixtures. Many of these started as medicines and contain little or no caffeine.

Use any edible herb or herb part to make tea. Chamomile, sage, rosemary, and mint are the most popular. Borage, catnip, dill, scented geraniums, lemon grass, lemon verbena, lemon balm, marjoram, savory, thyme, and sweet woodruff are also good. So are calendula, chamomile, hibiscus or

RECOMMENDED HERBAL TEA BLENDS	
* any lemony herb and borage * pennyroyal, peppermint, and ginger * fennel and goldenrod * mint, elderberry leaves or flowers, and lemon balm * lemon grass and scented geranium * jasmine, sage, and orange peel * rosemary, thyme, and lemon balm	Combine rose petals or rose buds, if you have enough to spare, to make teas such as: * rose petals, rose hips, and raspberry leaves * elderberry, rose hips, and bay leaves * lemon grass, rose petals, and rose geranium * lemon balm, rose petals, and orange blossoms

rose of Sharon flowers, citrus blossoms, marigold petals, pineapple and other sages, roses, and thyme. Float a flower or two on the top for garnish. Citrus peel also gives good flavor.

If you want certain herbs for health that are not your favorite flavors, add mint, lemon balm or others to make them taste good. Most herbal teas are made by steeping the fresh or dried herbs in boiled water until the tea reaches desired strength. A ceramic teapot gives the truest flavor, but you can easily make a cup at a time. I often use a pint or quart jar with a lid. You can put the herbs in a tea ball or in empty tea bags from a health food store. Or just add the herbs and strain them out when you pour.

Use 1 to 2 teaspoons of dry leaves or 2 to 3 tablespoons of fresh or thawed frozen ones per cup. Soon this will translate to so many fresh sprigs of each as you develop your favorite combinations. Seeds or roots should be ground or bruised in mortar with pestle and then made into a decoction. Use up to a heaping teaspoon of seeds for each cup of water.

Add herbs when you make sun tea, or use them instead of regular or herbal tea bags. Place needed amounts in a clear jar to absorb the most rays and set out in the sun for several hours to all day. Once made, you can enjoy tea hot, iced, or at room temperature. Make teas to be iced up to half again as strong since the melting ice will dilute them.

Sweeten herbal tea any way you would sweeten regular tea, but taste it first and then decide if you want any sweetener at all. Add lemon if you wish or a slice of star fruit.

Teas that are left over after a day or two can be frozen as ice cubes for flavoring drinks later. Or use the tea as a hair rinse, herbal bath, or for other cosmetic purposes.

OTHER HERBAL DRINKS

Herbs have long been used to flavor wines and liqueurs. My father used to make a famous mint julep from wild mint, until we brought home mint transplants to have it handy. I remember how frosty and delicious they looked and how festive any occasion became the minute we brought in the mint.

For quenching thirst, try adding yogurt to herbal teas. Or make a hock cup with a bottle of dry white wine, 6 cups of club soda, and the finely grated rind of 1 lemon and 1 orange plus a sprinkling of calendula petals.

Or add mint or mint tea to any combination of lemonade, citrus juice, and ginger ale and serve with crushed ice and a garnish of orange slice and mint sprig. Try any fruits that your family doesn't favor fresh as a drink. I used to make rhubarb punch as a treat for birthdays when children wouldn't touch it any other way. Now I have more exotic fruits to celebrate and sometimes camouflage.

Make a modern switchel (medieval herb drink) with a pint of boiling water, 1 to 2 tablespoons honey, and 2 tablespoons herb vinegar. Serve hot or cold for quick energy. It is high in potassium and serves as a diuretic.

EDIBLE FLOWERS

Eating flowers goes back at least to the Romans. Although this practice is colorful, healthful, and delicious, you may find that it goes against the grain for some people. Introduce them to it and they will soon be charmed.

> Never spray what you are going to eat or eat what may have been sprayed.

Pesticide-free flowers from your own or a friend's garden are best. Nasturtium petals add a tasty tang to salads. Calendulas and rose petals add color and a little sweetness. A dusting of elderflowers will add great beauty but little flavor.

Chop edible flowers into cheese spreads, herb butters, biscuits, and pancake or crepe batter. Stuff larger ones like squash blossoms. Dip these into cornmeal or flour batter and fry, or add elderflowers to fritter batter.

PAPA'S MINT JULEPS

Put 3 to 4 4-inch sprigs of mint in bottom of glass with 1 tablespoon powdered sugar. Bruise well, until syrupy with pestle or handle of wooden spoon.

Add 1 ounce whiskey and crushed ice to fill glass halfway. Add one more ounce of whiskey, crushed ice, and 1 teaspoon powdered sugar. Stir. Fill glass with crushed ice. Stir again.

Set aside for 10 to 15 minutes or in the freezer for 1 to 2 hours until the glass is frosted. Add a sprig of mint to each glass. The making of juleps is more a ceremony than a process. SIP for the whole afternoon. This is not a thirst quencher to be downed quickly. To make a julep for drinking, replace half or more of the whiskey with club soda.

EDIBLE FLOWERS

HERB	COLOR
anise hyssop	dark blue
bachelor's button	blue, white, pink, burgundy
beebalm	red, white, lavender, pink
borage	blue edged with pink
calendula petals	yellow, orange, cream
carnations	pink, white, red, yellow, orange
chamomile	white and yellow
chive	lavender, pink
chrysanthemum petals	yellow, bronze, white, lavender, red
citrus blossoms	white
coriander	white
dandelion petals	bright yellow
daylily	yellow, orange, red, violet, pink, cream
elderflowers	white
garlic chive	white
geranium (*Pelargonium* species)	pink, red, white
gladiolus	white, pink, yellow, lavender, red
hibiscus	yellow, orange, white, pink, lavender
honeysuckle	white, yellow, pink
hyssop	white, pink, blue
impatiens	pink, white, red, purple, orange
lavender	lavender
lemon thyme	pale lavender
marigold	yellow, orange, reddish bronze
mint	white, pink
myrtle	white (remove green part)
nasturtium	cream, yellow, orange, red
pansy	white, pink, yellow, purple, blue
pink	pink, purple, red, white
pineapple sage	red
portulaca or purslane	yellow, orange, pink, white
redbud	lavender
rose	all colors but blue
snapdragon	all colors but blue
squash and pumpkin	yellow (avoid white)
sunflower (petals)	yellow, gold, orange, cream, rust
violas (violets and pansies)	lavender, white, yellow
winter savory	white
yucca	cream

* Blooms of all culinary herbs are edible. The flowers listed above are also edible, but others may be unappetizing or even poisonous.

* As with any edibles, try new types cautiously, in small amounts, in case you are allergic to them or find the taste disagreeable.

Add flower petals such as calendula, nasturtium, sunflower, marigold, and hibiscus to tossed salads for a distinctive lift of color and fragrance, Use herb blossoms such as sage, rosemary, viola, beebalm, coriander, and borage in salads or as delicate garnishes.

When making a molded salad, mix the gelatin and chill it all until it is thick and syrupy. Then chill a thin layer in the bottom of the mold until firm while leaving the rest out of the refrigerator. Arrange the flowers (nasturtiums, pansies, or johnny-jump-ups are lovely) face down on this layer. Pour in enough gelatin to cover the flowers and chill this until firm. Then mix whatever you want with the remaining gelatin and add it to the mold for the final chilling.

HORSERADISH

Horseradish is great to accent meat or fish. Fresh horseradish makes the best sauce, and it will keep for months in the refrigerator. Be careful not to touch your face or eyes while working with it, for like hot pepper, it is so hot that it can cause pain.

The simplest horseradish sauce is made of peeled, grated horseradish, packed into a small jar and covered with vinegar. This can be mixed with catsup for seafood cocktail sauce, one spoon of horseradish for three or four of catsup, or to your taste.

A creamier, more subtle horseradish sauce is wonderful with roast beef, hot or cold, or other hot meats. Here is my recipe:

Creamy Horseradish Sauce
Whip one cup of cream until very stiff while adding:
1/2 teaspoon minced garlic
1 teaspoon salt
2 to 4 tablepoons (to taste) of freshly ground horseradish, or use grated horseradish that was frozen or bottled in vinegar
1 tablespoon lemon, lime, or sour orange juice

Keep the sauce cold until just before time to serve it.

HERBS IN SALAD

Many herbs are tender enough to be used in salads, where they add wonderful flavors, shapes, colors, nutrients, and, sometimes, therapeutic properties.

When I was a young bride I had a garden rich in kale and other greens but a thin purse. I sometimes made tossed salads without any lettuce at all after that crop bolted in the summer heat. Once at a potluck dinner I was embarrassed for not conforming to what seemed like the honeymoon special (lettuce alone) until several of the men wondered aloud why their wives never made such interesting salads. After that I took pride in the variety of colors and flavors in the bowl.

Such variety was much more unusual then than it is now, with today's fashion for *mesclun* and other interesting mixes of greens, herbs, and edible flowers for salads.

With milder flavors, add any that you have or like. With stronger, more distinctive flavors, go easy. A little will go a long way, and too many flavors at once will be confusing. Taste your herbs before including them, for a tender dandelion leaf in late winter is much less bitter than the same leaf a few weeks later when the weather starts getting hot, and a big, soft leaf of lettuce-leaf basil may be mild enough to tear up into the salad, while an older leaf or a stronger-flavored variety could be too strong.

For a crowd, try a salad bar approach with many bowls and dishes of different salad greens, sliced salad vegetables, minced herbs, toppings, and edible flowers, with a cruet of *vinaigrette* salad dressing on the side.

Vinaigrette Dressing

Add the following ingredients to an empty 16 oz jar with a tightly fitting screw-on lid:

1 1/4 cup olive oil or a mixture of olive oil and salad oil
1/2 cup wine vinegar
2 cloves garlic, finely minced, or leaves of garlic chive
2 tablespoons minced chervil, tarragon, or fennel leaves
2 tablespoons dry mustard powder
2 tablespoons minced parsley
1 tablespoon salt
1 tablespoon freshly ground pepper

Shake vigorously before each use. Add minced onion and other herbs if you wish.

Arugula-Orange Salad

Adding one or two leaves of arugula to a tossed salad livens it up so much that it would seem that a salad of mostly arugula would be too much. It isn't. It is surprisingly delicious.

Mix 2 cups arugula greens (roquette), washed and chopped into bite sized pieces, with an orange, tangerine, or papaya, or a combination of these, peeled, sectioned, seeded, and cut up, and 2 tablespoons almonds, walnuts, or pecans. Toss with celery seed dressing and serve.

Celery Seed Dressing

Combine the following ingredients in your blender or food processor.

2/3 cup sugar
1 teaspoon dry mustard
1 teaspoon salt
1 small onion, grated
1/2 cup vinegar

Blend, then add 1 cup salad oil. Mix well. Add 1 teaspoon celery seed. Stir before each use. This is also good on any fruit or tossed salad.

HERBS WITH VEGETABLES

A sprinkling of herbs makes a serving of vegetables look more finished and interesting. Mince parsley for your potatoes (parsley has more flavor than people give it credit for), marjoram for squash, and dill for green beans, along with a squirt of lemon juice and a dab of butter. Any herbal cookbook will give you many ideas.

Here is one of my family's favorite vegetable dishes, which uses the stuffing/crouton recipe given earlier in this chapter (p.48). I often make this dish with green papayas.

Scalloped Vegetable Casserole

Cut up and cook in saucepan with a small amount of water, until tender:
  4 cups of vegetables such as zucchini, green papayas, chayotes, carrots, eggplant, squash, broccoli, cauliflower, lima beans, or corn. Or combine two or three that go well together. Drain.

In a large, ovenproof frying pan, saute half a cup of chopped onion in 6 tablespoons butter or margarine. Stir in 2 1/4 cups herbed stuffing mix. When crisp and light brown, remove 1 cup of crumb/onion mix to cover the top of the casserole.

To the rest of the crumb/ onion mix add 1 10 3/4 oz. can cream of chicken soup and 1/2 cup sour cream or cream cheese. Mix the vegetables with the other ingredients in the frying pan. Top with the reserved crisp bread crumbs. Bake 30 to 40 minutes at 350 degrees F. Serves 6.

COLORING WITH HERBS

Commercial food packers know that color makes a big difference. You can use the same wisdom at home. A sprinkling of minced orange zest on a dab of whipped cream over dessert looks special. Roselle tea is a delightful pink. Yellow rice (colored with turmeric) looks great with the chicken.

If the children want their macaroni and cheese to be orange, like the kind that comes out of the box, add some calendula petals, or add paprika and tumeric in small amounts. They add color with very little change in flavor.

Green Noodles

Pick and wash edible greens and herbs in any combination: mustard, spinach, tampala, cress, chard, or turnip or radish tops. Add sprigs of basil or oregano if you wish, without using woody parts. Put three eggs into the blender. Add a handful of leaves and puree. Add more, pureeing each time, until the color is a little darker than desired. The flour will make it less intense. Almost any food (carrots or beets, for instance) can go into the blender with the eggs for noodles, making them more interesting and nutritious.

Add enough flour to make the egg mixture kneadable, roughly three cups. Turn it out onto a floured pastry cloth or tablecloth. (After use, I freeze my pastry cloths in plastic bags to keep from having to wash them each time they are used.) Knead in enough more flour so it will roll easily. Sprinkle flour over the mixture as you roll if needed. Roll uniformly thin. Let dry until the edges just begin to curl.

Rub a thin layer of flour over all. Then cut strips of dough about 3 inches wide. Pile these on top of each other and cut into noodles of desired width. Use at once or spread them out to dry. If dried overnight in an oven with a pilot light, they will keep for months on the cupboard shelf. Otherwise, put them in bags in the freezer to be sure of keeping.

Noodles will dry a lighter color but cook up a lovely green, and children who would never touch spinach or mustard in recognizable form will gobble up these delicious green noodles.

Yellow Noodles

Use two eggs for the average family, up to seven if you have two pastry cloths and want to make a lasting supply. Add, if desired, yellow or orange calendula petals, well ground or pureed with one of the eggs. Mix enough flour in the slightly beaten eggs to make a dough you can roll. Proceed as for green noodles.

ROSES IN THE KITCHEN

Rose petals, as long as they've not been sprayed or dusted with poisons, are edible and good in salads or added to fruit pies. Pick freshly opened roses as soon as the dew is dry in the mornings.

Damask roses do not have the bitter white base to the petal. If using other rose petals, take as many petals as you can hold between your finger and thumb. Pull them from the rose all at once and cut the white bases from all of them with just one clip of the kitchen shears.

You can candy them to use as a garnish or on cakes. Pickle the rosebuds or add with young leaves to tea.

Candied Rose Petals

This also works for violets, violas, johnny jump-ups, geraniums, pineapple sage, and other edible flowers or herb leaves.

* Wash and gently dry petals, flowers, or leaves.

* Make ready small bowls of superfine granulated sugar. Use the sugar white, or color it by putting one drop of food color per 1/4 cup of sugar into a tightly covered jar. Shake until color is evenly distributed. Use colors only to deepen natural shades, not to change.

* Beat one egg white until slightly frothy. Hold the petal or flower in your left hand and use a camel's hair paintbrush to cover all surfaces with the egg white.

* Then gently spoon the sugar over the petal, leaf, or flower to cover all surfaces, letting the sugar that does not stick fall back into the small bowl.

* Spread the sugar-coated petals on waxed paper to dry for two days.

* Use immediately or store by refrigerating in an airtight container with waxed paper between the layers. Use within four to six months.

* Candied flowers, leaves, or petals may be used for decorating cakes, as a candy, or for garnishing fruit salads, parfaits, or other desserts.

Rose hips or fruits are very rich in vitamin C, organic acids, and pectin. Some roses are bred especially to produce many large hips for easy gathering, but all rose hips are edible. Puree, sweeten, and add lemon juice for a meat sauce. Or collect and wash rose hips, add a cupful to a clean canning jar, and pour the jar full of boiling water. The resulting tea has a rather sharp, pleasant taste with a hint of sweetness. Add it to juices, fruits, soups, or any other dish.

GETTING THE MOST FROM YOUR CITRUS

Although we eat much of the fruit our yard produces right off the tree or out of hand, I find that the easiest way to get the family to use it in great quantities is in drinks. I have an electric juicer that makes this quickly and simply. Various combinations of fruit, two sweet tangerines to three grapefruit, for instance, make delicious drinks. Adding a sprig of mint, lemon balm, or pineapple sage adds color, that subtle bit of flavor, and a few different nutrients as well.

Most juices and fruit drinks need no sugar, only the right combinations. However, when faced with my tree full of sour oranges (it was grapefruit before the '89 freeze killed it to the rootstock) I resort to a little sugar mixed with the juice to make a great drink. Native Floridians assure me that they were raised on such orangeade, and that a sour orange can do anything a lemon can do, including making a pie according to any Key lime recipe.

Orangeade

Mix:

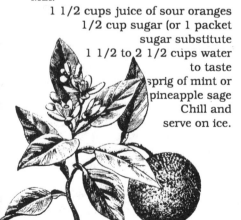

1 1/2 cups juice of sour oranges
1/2 cup sugar (or 1 packet sugar substitute
1 1/2 to 2 1/2 cups water to taste
sprig of mint or pineapple sage
Chill and serve on ice.

Lemon, Lime, or Orangeade Concentrate

* Use equal parts of water and lemon, lime, or sour orange juice. Use an equal amount of sugar, or use artificial sweetener as part or all of the sweetening. Have a sprig of mint, lemon balm, or pineapple sage for each container.

* Combine water and sugar. Chop up the entire rinds from several of the fruits, or add sweet Miowa kumquats for sweeter taste. Boil for 6 to 8 minutes. Let cool. Remove and discard rind.

* Add juice. Label and freeze in portions of 1 1/3 cups.

* Thaw as needed and add 2 2/3 cups of water to make a quart of lemonade or juice drink.

From 3 cups of juice I get 4 portions of concentrate to freeze, about 1 1/3 cups each. This is not as nutritious as pure juice, but more so than many purchased drinks, and much less expensive, which is a big help for families with thirsty children.

Freezing Citrus

There are various ways to save citrus for summer use. One of the easiest is to freeze the juice in the amounts you are likely to use.

Freeze it in ice cube trays for enough for seasoning. Pop out the cubes as soon as they are firm, put them in a freezer bag and label so they can be used one or several at a time.

Or freeze one cup each in doubled paper cups with foil on top. When they are frozen solid, fit as many as possible into a freezer bag, label, and use as needed. You can freeze citrus fruits whole for summer use, but you may find it is more convenient in the long run to do a little processing first.

Using Citrus Peel

Minced citrus peel or zest is a fragrant, colorful garnish. Orange zest on whipped cream is a classic topping for pecan pie. Lemon zest may be sprinkled on lemon flavored desserts or used with many meats. Mixed with minced parsley, anchovy, and garlic, it is called *gremolada* and used with *osso buco* and other Italian dishes.

I find that the best way to dry citrus peel for cooking is to thinly pare it off the whole, clean fruit with a carrot peeler or small, sharp knife. You can also use a small cheese cutter or grater, which works especially well on the firm, pointed end of a lemon.

Spread peel on plates to dry. This will take 3 to 5 days at room temperature. Or dry in the microwave in as many 30-second segments as necessary.

Store the pieces in an airtight container. When you are ready to use them, chop them finer or powder them by whirling them in the blender or grinding them with a mortar and pestle. Use the powder with tea blends or in place of extract in baking, or to flavor sugar, honey, or barbecue sauce.

Citrus As Garnish

Pick and use branches of citrus blossoms or of kumquats, lemons, or calamondin oranges as garnish. They also look and smell wonderful in flower arrangements. Or follow the example of Florida restaurants and put a slice of orange or lemon on every plate. Round slices of lemon can also be dried for use in garnishing. The skin retains its color but the pulp turns dark brown or black.

DELICIOUS FRUIT SHAKE

Put into blender:

1 cup apple juice or 4 tablespoons apple juice concentrate and 3/4 cup water

1/3 cup or so of fresh orange or tangerine pieces or the equivalent amount of juice

1 large or 2 small frozen bananas

1/2 cup or more frozen strawberries

3 leaves of mint, lemon balm, or pineapple sage

Blend the ingredients until smooth. If necessary, add a little more juice or water so that it is not too thick to whirl.

Substitute mild fruits to taste. So far I've found only grapefruit and ripe papaya too dominating. Peaches, plums, pineapple, loquats, and a few surinam cherries are great. If the fruits you have need more sweetening, use sugar or honey.

Serves one to four people, depending on appetite and demand. This can be a fruity breakfast or a great snack or dessert.

PASSION FRUIT JUICE

My friend Charles Novak of Plant City grows his passion fruit right up into an oak tree where he never has to trim it and it cannot take over. He picks the fruits off the ground, about 1000 a year, and freezes the juice by the gallon, without sugar. Later he adds it to juices or makes a syrup, as needed. He just scoops the insides into the blender, hits puree for the second it takes to separate the seeds from the pulp, and strains the pulp and juice to remove the seeds.

HERB CLUBS

Share your culinary herbs with other cooks in exchange for ideas and recipes. This is easily and happily done by joining a herb club, and there are excellent and active ones throughout the state. The County Extension Service can probably tell you if there are any in your area. If not, or if the existing one meets on the wrong day or had a different emphasis from what you want, form your own. Call the garden editor of the local paper and put in a meeting notice or a phone contact to start. Enthusiasm, information, encouragement, plants, and enjoyment

will multiply in such a sharing group.

OTHER SOURCES OF INSPIRATION

This is really a garden book, not a cookbook, so I have barely touched on the subject of herbal cooking. The range of herbs one can grow or buy fresh in Florida is really amazing. Authentic international, American, ethnic, and regional dishes can be made without a difficult search for ingredients. Be sure to check your bookstore and library for herbal cookbooks about the kinds of cuisine you are most interested in.

One of the most complete resources is *The Encyclopedia of Herbs, Spices, and Flavorings: A Cook's Compendium*, by Elizabeth Lambert Ortiz (Dorling Kindersley, Inc., 1992, London. This beautiful book is a major reference on the flavorings of the world. With color photographs throughout, Ms. Ortiz completely explores each herb, spice, and technique, and explains regional influences as well. As she says in the introduction, "the flavors of the world are yours to discover, they are just waiting for you to try them..."

4. Cultivating Herbs Throughout Florida

I'd grown herbs for years in the Midwest and Florida before I read with some surprise that herbs are among the easiest of plants to grow. And I had to agree that in most cases they certainly are. I only wish I had realized it sooner, for it would have added a measure of relaxation to some of my earlier efforts.

PLANNING YOUR HERB GARDEN

I have a friend who always said, "Someday I am going to have a herb garden." He said it with the same seriousness that one would say, "Someday I want to have another child." And all the while, I was experimenting with herbs in my flower and vegetable garden, chives beside the roses, sages with the shrubbery. I did not want a proper herb garden at the time.

My friend got his and it is lovely. And in spite of myself, I got mine not long ago. It is by the back door where I can quickly pick a handful of sprigs for seasoning or garnish. It is handy to my hose and work area, but in soil still so bad, despite several years of adding humus, that I've never managed to get a good crop of green beans from it.

Nevertheless, the herbs are growing better there because their needs are simple, and I watch them more closely. Yet I manage to neglect them enough not to kill them with overcare, which is possible in some cases. Also, there is some shade there that helps them through the summer.

In Florida, you can grow herbs and spices either casually, as I do, or formally, as my friend does. I am a learn-as-I-go person and I encourage all who would like to grow herbs to start right away. But if you want a certain type of herb garden, a knot garden, a Shakespearean garden, a moonlight garden of silver foliage and white flowers, a butterfly garden, or a formal or a kitchen garden, study herb books and plant lists and make your plans accordingly.

Always keep in mind the peculiarities of Florida growing. Move certain plants into the shade for summer or into the kitchen or onto a porch for winter. Plan to add some temporary shade to a permanent garden to get it through the summer.

Rick Munroe, executive chef at a nearby restaurant, studied herb books thoroughly and laid out a lovely herb garden near the restaurant's kitchen door, within view of the hotel rooms. It was a success from the start. But the start was in the autumn and the books were not specifically for Florida, and I feared summer was going to give him problems. It gives all Florida herb growers problems (see chapter 1).

Rick's garden remained nearly perfect until mid-August, when summer made it look more like mine. Even then it was wonderful to visit and see that the lavender and sage were still doing fairly well and that even professionals had a few weeds in the summer when it was too hot and they were too busy to care.

SELECTING THE SITE

Which should come first, the planning of the garden or the selection of the site? It depends.

There are usually several possible places for every plant in every yard.

Most herbs need at least five or six hours of sunlight a day, a bit more in winter, less in summer. You cannot change the shadows of buildings or large trees, but you can come to understand them better by taking note of them in every season, and position your garden OR decide what to grow with these factors in mind.

Exposure is very important in all of Florida because gardening year round, or almost so in N, means different shade and sun patterns on the same site at different times of year. Luckily, most herbs are adaptable to variation. Others can be planted in two or more places at first and eventually remanded to wherever they do best.

Consider the wind. In most of inland Florida it is not a major factor most of the time. But on the coast, it is very important to give a herb garden protection from high winds and salt spray by planting in a protected spot or putting up or planting protection in the form of fences, screens, or windbreak plants. Such enclosures add to your enjoyment of the herb garden in other ways, providing privacy and a sense of seclusion, blocking out noise and undesirable views, and confining herbal fragrances for ultimate enjoyment.

CHECKING DRAINAGE

Herbs will tolerate a much wider range of soil structure and fertility than most plants, but they are with the majority when it comes to drainage. Let them stand with constantly wet roots and they will perish either from root rot or from other fungal diseases that multiply in soggy soil.

To test drainage, dig a hole big enough to pour in two or three gallons of water. Then watch to see how long it takes to drain away. It should go down as you watch, and will in most of Florida during most of the year because of the high percentage of sand in the soil (about 98 percent in mine). Repeating this test in the midst of the summer rainy season can be enlightening. What seems like adequate drainage for most of the year may not prove good enough in the summer.

If the water does not sink into the surrounding soil in an hour, you must improve the drainage or find a different spot with better drainage for your plants.

To improve drainage, you can drill through the hardpan with a post hole digger or power augur or such, put in drainage tiles, or use other drastic measures that are beyond the strength and equipment of the average gardener.

Chances are that another spot in your yard, where there was never any compaction from building equipment or inferior fill dirt added, will not have the same problem and you can put your herb garden there with no trouble. Otherwise, you can plant in containers or in raised beds.

ENRICHING THE SOIL

In one of his books about his Malabar Farm, Louis Bromfield emphasizes the importance of being stewards of the land. Stewards put back, he says, and improve soil as they use it. Miners, on the other hand, use and take without putting anything back until all the good is gone, leaving only ruin in their wake. American soil has seen too many miners and too few stewards. As a result, much of our country's rich soil has washed away in the few hundred years of our greedy use, whereas European soils have supported crops for centuries.

Nature enriches soil so slowly that Florida's heat and rain have never allowed for much of a build-up of humus or loam. But as stewards we can accelerate the enrichment process. How do we do this? As stated in chapter 1, by adding as much organic matter as we can as often as possible. This organic matter can be in any form. Use plenty of grass clippings and every last banana peel.

Kitchen and garden wastes that are a problem for city trash collection and landfills are a solution for our soil. Get into the habit of recycling every product you can: leaves, kitchen scraps, newspapers, cat litter, and so forth.

We used to joke about garbage husbandry when I was in college. My children teased me about it, but they also grasped serious import from the time they were big enough to pick up and throw away. Anything that rots goes on the garden or into the compost pile. We all developed this habit for our Ohio clay and continued it for our already rich Iowa loam. There is no such thing as too much humus.

Florida's sand has taught us to intensify the effort. As this organic matter breaks down and becomes humus, which looks much like dark, rich soil, it makes either sand or clay more easily workable. The humus slows down the percolation of the water and dissolved nutrients through the root zone. It also allows for plenty of air so there

is no danger of rot. And since humus breaks down and is used up in any soil, but more quickly with warm temperatures, the process of renewal must be continuous.

Most of my accomplishments in life are questionable, but if I faced St. Peter today, at least I could say I left behind my share of enriched soil and happy earthworms.

New gardeners will have plenty of questions about this. I did when I first read Ruth Stout's books on mulching and organic gardening (see bibliography). But the following pages should answer most of them for you and the bibliography will give you sources for further study.

COVER CROPS

These are crops grown only to be turned under to add humus and nutrients to the soil. They are also called green manure crops and will allow you to produce more humus on the spot than you would ever care to carry.

The strawberry fields of Florida spend their summers growing sudan grass, sorghum, or cowpeas as cover crops to add quantities of organic matter to the soil when they are plowed down, before the strawberry plants are set in each autumn.

Herb growers can learn a lesson here. We can even plant dual purpose plants like southern or cowpeas, peanuts, or beans, harvest some, and turn under the rest. You can't go wrong in planting a cover crop in the area designated for your herb garden. Plant the entire area and grow your herbs in pots for the first two months. Or plant a small garden in herbs and an area for enlargement in cover crops.

If you don't have or can't find cover crop seeds (check the resource list), buy seeds for sprouting in a health food store or plant bird seed for an interesting mix.

Water and feed your cover crop plants and be aware that they will grow more lush as you improve the soil.

If you don't have a tiller, you may want to rent or borrow one to till in your cover crop. Or mow it off and leave the green leaves in place as mulch. Then put news-

papers over the top and proceed as described under Spreading On (page 67). It is best to wait two to three weeks after tilling or covering to give the soil microbes a good start on turning the green manure into humus.

HOMEGROWN HUMUS

Save anything that will rot and return it to the soil. Use natural grass clippings, leaves, kitchen scraps, newspapers (made from wood fiber, you know), cardboard, garden trimmings, non-seedy weeds, sod from places you no longer want in turf, clumps from lawn aeration or verticutting, ashes from a fireplace, and whatever else you have. The rare exceptions are diseased plants or plant parts, weeds that have gone to seed, grass clippings from a lawn recently treated with herbicide, and meat or grease that might draw animals.

COVER CROPS FOR FLORIDA

TO SOW IN SUMMER

beggarweed (a legume)
cowpeas (a legume)
crotalaria (a legume)
hairy indigo (a legume)
peanuts (a legume)
millet (not a legume)
sorghum (not a legume)
soybeans (a legume)
sudan grass (not a legume)
velvet beans (a legume)

TO SOW WINTER THROUGH SPRING

snap beans (a legume)
oats (not a legume)
amaranth (not a legume)
buckwheat (not a legume)
hairy vetch (a legume)
millet (not a legume)
peanuts (a legume)
rye (not a legume)
soybeans (a legume)

Legumes add the most nitrogen. Weeds can be a cover crop, but cut them before they go to seed.

I pile up woody trimmings behind shrubbery where they won't show as they rot down. This brush also offers cover for wildlife in your garden. You can use a shredder to change these into instant mulch or humus. One of my friends has two shredders and considers them a good investment.

NEIGHBORHOOD HUMUS

My ultimate success as a garden writer will come the day that everyone uses their own leaves and grass clippings, but that seems unlikely to happen. Even new laws have not yet limited amounts put out for trash collection, which fill our landfills. My only consolation for that is my son Mike's conviction that all that humus will help the synthetic trash rot faster there.

The city employees must pick up every bag and pile, every time, and I am amazed at their strength and endurance. As the neighborhood "bag lady," I go out only on days when I need and have time to handle more organic material. I bypass any bags that are too heavy or are too few to make it worthwhile to stop. I usually go on a Monday morning after workers and school children have left the area almost empty, though I have gone on the weekend when bags are lighter and drier and homeowners have often happily helped me load.

My easiest-to-handle source of humus is the neighbor who sends her handsome sons for my garden cart, puts all their grass clippings and leaves right in so neither of us has to bother with bags, and brings the cart back full every week.

SPREADING ON

There are several ways to get this organic matter into your soil.

The usual way is to spread the material, rotted or fresh, on top of an entire area and then spade or till it in. The former is hard work and the latter requires heavy equipment.

I mulch instead of tilling. I was skeptical at first, but this method has been working well for me for several years. Spread newspapers, about a section thick, over the area you wish to plant, even over turf, overlapping the edges, and doing a small section at a time so the papers won't blow away. Cover this with a thick layer, 6 to 12 inches, of grass clipping, leaves, or other mulch. Mixed layers of green and brown material work best. Water everything well. You can pour on soapy water to act as a wetting agent and hasten the breakdown of the organic matter into humus.

I usually plant at this point. But Kaye Cude states correctly that this is an ideal place for weeds to grow, so she spreads another layer of newspapers over the top of all that and covers it with a thin layer of attractive mulch.

In either case, plant by pulling the mulch back to the top (or only) layer of newspapers. Add enough good garden or potting soil to cover the seeds or plant roots. Water well, then pull up the mulch around the plants. Or wait until the seedlings sprout and grow tall enough before adding mulch. In either case, the roots will eventually grow down through the damp newspapers.

In the meantime, the papers tend to keep the moisture and nutrients up where the roots can get them and the nematodes down where they can't do harm. You can dig through the layers of paper and sod to plant trees or shrubs.

MULCHING

Mulching is one of the best and easiest things you can do for your garden. It is the simplest way to incorporate organic matter: just spread it over the ground around and between plants. Mulch keeps the ground a more even temperature, cooler in summer and warmer in winter. If the layer is thick enough, it prevents germination of weeds. Even a thin layer makes weed pulling easier. Mulch discourages nematodes. As it rots, and it does that quickly in Florida, it adds to the humus in the soil.

Soon you will see those great garden helpers, earthworms, where none had been before. The invisible microbial life of the soil also improves and benefits your plants.

Ground-hugging, spreading herbs such as thyme do better if mulched with gravel or small rocks. This keeps low leaves from getting soggy in the rain.

New grass clippings can heat up enough to burn or at least overheat your plants instead of cooling them, especially if they are spread too thickly. They can also pack down and get mushy or pull nitrogen from the soil. This does not mean that you can't use them. It only means that they are better if mixed with shredded leaves or some other material. Pull them back far enough not to touch any plant parts. Add nitrogen fertilizer as needed.

COMPOST

One easy way to get humus into your soil without delay is to add compost or well rotted material in any planting hole you dig. One part humus to two parts soil is a good rule, but you can hardly get too much humus for annual or perennial plants. With a tree you might make the roots too happy in the hole to ever spread into the surrounding soil.

Making Compost. There are many books about composting and many methods, aids, and containers. All such information can be helpful, but don't be intimidated. Composting is only an accelerated form of natural decomposition. Do it any way you want. You can't do it wrong, only more slowly.

A hot, quick compost pile destroys many weed seeds, insect eggs, and disease organisms. It gives you finished compost in as little as 14 days, with maximum nutrient retention. A slow pile takes much longer, months to break down some substances like egg shells and pine needles. The resulting compost may have more weed seeds and such, and the rain may leach out more nutrients, but it is still good stuff.

Mulching is composting on the spot, and the simplest way to go about the job. Since I've been gardening in Florida, I've found, to my surprise, that it is possible to grow plants in 100% compost or even in uncomposted mulch if you add the needed nutrients and water. But most of us will do better if we have a pile of compost to mix with soil for containers or mix with soil in planting holes in the ground.

Until your compost is ready, just buy compost or decomposed cow manure for plantings you are making now. This will not be redundant but a good investment.

COMPOSTING MADE EASY

1. Collect fodder for your compost pile by putting a large container on the side of your sink, preferably an attractive one with a lid and a handle, such as an old copper pot. Put in vegetable peelings, non-meat scraps from the plates, water poured off cooked vegetables, faded bouquets, banana peels, and such. Once a day take it out to the compost pile or dump it under the most deserving tree or shrub. Camouflage it with grass clipping, leaves, or pine needles, especially if you want to discourage wildlife.

2. Cut the waste material into reasonably small bits before composting it, because a pile made of small pieces breaks down faster and looks neater. Some people puree their scraps in a blender. I'm not about to go that far, but I sometimes chop a water-melon rind into smaller sections.

When I cut down a banana stalk, I saw and snip the stem and leaves into sections small enough to pile up under the plant. When I have a large pile of weeds or large discarded leaves, I take the lawn mower and raise it up and down on the pile until it chops everything into little pieces.

3. If you have a pile, you can turn it every few days to speed the decomposition process. Of you can just put a spading fork into it and loosen it up some to let in more air.

4. A good compost pile should be one third plant material and soil, one third air, and one third water. So remember to add water when you have the hose out except during the rainy season.

5. There are not so many nutrients in compost, but we might as well save all there are. A lid or plastic sheet over the pile in the rainy season will do this job.

6. Compost barrels and drums that turn are an excellent idea, but try them before buying. I bought a used one that was difficult to turn, and it soon rusted to the impossible stage. Now I roll it on the ground.

7. A compost pile with separate bins for new, partly decomposed, and ready-to-use compost is ideal and easy to build with cement blocks piled into shape with plenty of air space between them. Add new material at one end and fork it from bin to bin until you reach the other end.

8. Add amendments to the pile. A layer of soil every foot or so will add natural enzymes that activate the pile, increasing temperature and speeding decomposition. Prepackaged compost activators are available. A layer of cottonseed meal will do this too, as will a layer of inexpensive dry dogfood. Other ingredients that improve the quality and speed of the compost include rock dust, wood ashes, milled oyster shell, bone meal, and dolomitic limestone. These add minerals to the soil and aid beneficial organisms. Lime may be needed for this even where it is not needed to change pH.

PLANTING YOUR HERB GARDEN

Now comes the exciting part, even some instant harvest. It's time to fill the herb garden.

I've gotten herbs from many sources: planted seed, bought herb plants from nurseries and grocery stores, started cuttings from wherever I can beg or find them, even rooting herbal garnishes brought home from restaurants. The most fun of all is to share cuttings, seedlings, or divisions with other herb enthusiasts.

STARTING WITH SEED

Planting seed is usually the least expensive way to get large numbers of plants. But seeding in Florida can be risky. At first I wondered why many seeds never came up or only grew for a time and then just disappeared. I had always favored untreated seed before, since I don't like to use any more poisons than necessary. But, in Florida, soil rot is a problem. So buy seed pretreated with fungicide (these are often stained pink inside the packet) or treat them yourself by adding half a teaspoon of fungicide (or Rootone (TM) which contains fungicide) to the packet and shaking to cover the seeds.

Also, it took me some time to realize that leftover seeds I had always saved were not staying viable in storage as they did in the North. Florida's heat and humidity take a toll. Now I try to keep all unplanted seed in a zipper bag in the freezer until I'm ready to plant, and I get much better germination. But still it is not what I got before.

I plant many seeds in containers instead of in the ground directly, more than I did up north. There are several ways to do this. Gather everything you'll need before you start: seeds, clean containers, sterile potting soil or other seed starting medium like milled sphagnum moss or vermiculite, water, plastic bags, flat pans for watering, and labels. Spread newspapers or plastic to keep your worktable clean in the kitchen or on the porch. Or work outdoors on a bench or shelf.

Wash recycled containers in hot water containing a bit of soap and bleach. For most seeds, containers should be about three inches deep. Use recycled pots or market packs from annuals, margarine dishes, 4 inch pots, or milk cartons cut down to size. Or save those clear plastic containers from the deli. Stab drainage holes in the bottom with a paring knife or an ice pick warmed over a flame.

Fill the container to within half an inch of the top with soil or medium that is fairly moist but not soggy. Level it off and press it down gently. Then sprinkle seeds evenly over the surface. Small seeds like marjoram need only be pressed in, not covered. Larger seeds should be barely covered.

Plant one kind to a small, 1 to 2 inch pot or several kinds in rows in larger containers such as seed flats.

Water each container well. The best way is to let it soak in a pan of water until the soil surface is moist. If watering from the top, use only the gentlest spray that will not dislodge the seeds or wash too much soil over some and expose others.

To hasten the germination of certain seeds with hard seedcoats, like parsley and some of the other carrot cousins, water them with boiling water. This does not hurt them and hastens germination as much as several weeks.

Label the containers with the name of the plant and the date planted. Write on plastic labels with a pencil or indelible horticultural or laundry marker. (You can easily scrub off old markings with a soapy steel wool pad.) Close the top of deli containers, but watch carefully. If too much condensation forms, open the top occasionally, wipe it off, and let air in, or make air slits in the top. Put other pots or trays into plastic bags, but do not close tightly. This should prevent drying out for a week or more and many seedlings will sprout by then.

Most seedlings germinate best if the soil temperature is 75 degrees F. During the cold months, set containers on top of the TV, refriger- ator, dryer, warming tray, or heat pipes. Or run a heating cable under the flats. Only a few kinds need light to germinate, see sidebar.

Another easy way to start seedlings is to use peat pellets which come as flat disks and swell in water to become little pots. They give a nice feeling of magic. If I can grow a pot, certainly I can grow a plant. I buy these by the hundred, line them up in deli containers, and water until swelled. Then I scratch the top enough to plant one to three seeds in each. I often do two containers, close them, and stack them on the kitchen counter where I can watch them carefully. I love to watch seeds sprout. Each day I move the ones that have germina- ted, using a spoon to lift them to another container that goes into brighter light, either outside to sun or under the fluorescent light on the porch.

CARING FOR SEEDLINGS
Watch carefully. As soon as seedlings begin to sprout, remove

---

PREFERRED TREATMENT FOR HERB SEED GERMINATION

Difficult to transplant. Sow in the ground, in peat pellets, or in individual pots.	Need cool period, 55 degrees. Plant and refrigerate containers for a week, then move. to a warmer site.	Presoak overnight or water once with boiling water.
anise dill artemisia fennel arugula nasturtium borage parsley caraway sesame chervil poppy coriander cumin	chamomile lavender rosemary thyme	nasturtium parsley and any other member of the carrot family (anise,chervil cumin, caraway, dill, and fennel)
	Need light to germinate: dill yarrow ornamental pepper	

GUIDE TO GERMINATING HERB SEEDS IN 4-INCH POTS

Billy Daniel, the owner of Sweet William Herb Farm in Lutz, gives his list for germinating herb seeds, gained from Florida experience. He recommends a loosely packed seed germinating soil such as LG3 or Sunshine Mix.

thyme	6 to 8 seeds	barely cover
marjoram	6 to 8 seeds	do not cover
lemon balm	5 to 6 seeds	do not cover
catnip	6 to 8 seeds	barely cover
hyssop	5 to 6 seeds	barely cover
anise	5 to 6 seeds	barely cover
caraway	5 to 6 seeds	barely cover
cumin	5 to 6 seeds	barely cover
oregano	5 to 6 seeds	do not cover
winter savory	5 to 6 seeds	do not cover
wormwood	5 to 6 seeds	do not cover
tansy	5 to 6 seeds	do not cover
lavender	3 to 5 seeds	cover 1/8 in.
sage	5 to 6 seeds	cover 1/4 in.
upland cress	6 to 8 seeds	cover 1/4 in.
dill	10 to 15 seeds	cover 1/8 in.
cilantro	10 to 15 seeds	cover 1/4 in.
sorrel	8 to 10 seeds	cover 1/4 in.
parsley	10 to 15 seeds	cover 1/4 in.
watercress	8 to 10 seeds	cover 1/4 in.
perilla or shiso	8 to 10 seeds	do not cover
salad burnet	8 to 10 seeds	cover 1/8 in.

TIPS ON SEEDS FROM BILLY DANIEL

"Seeds will germinate best if gathered and sown while fresh. Take them off the plants when they are ripened but not yet dropped."

"For minimum damage during frost, mulch well with oak leaves, seed-free hay, or something that allows the air to circulate and hold in moisture."

the plastic covering, and move containers into brighter light and cooler temperatures. If the overhead light is not bright enough to make a strong shadow, put trays of seedlings on shelves just a few inches below fluorescent lights and they will grow almost as well as in a greenhouse.

For much of the year, Florida IS a greenhouse, so new seedlings can grow outdoors as long as the snails and insects can't get to them. They do best in partial to full sun and humid air and then need no hardening off.

Water carefully. Never allow the seed containers to dry out. But also do not overwater or damping-off disease will cause seedlings to rot at the soil line. It is best to cover containers of seedlings during summer rains so they are not beaten down or drowned. If you use clear plastic containers from the deli you can just close the lid or bend it down enough to stem the rainfall, but be sure to add drainage holes in case water gets inside.

Fertilize seedlings with a weak liquid solution of any plant food such as Peters(TM), Miracle-Gro(TM), or Schultz's Instant (TM), beginning when the first true leaves are open. Repeat every few weeks to keep growth constant.

When seedlings in flats or crowded containers show four to six leaves, transplant them directly to the garden if it is warm enough, or to individual pots or into large containers of mixed herbs. Fill pots with damp fertile soil. Then use a table knife or spoon to lift plants and a pencil to make a new hole. Hold seedlings by the leaves, not the fragile stems, as you firm soil gently around the roots.

PLANTING SEEDS OUTDOORS

One often reads that some herbs resent transplanting and do better if sown directly in the garden where they will grow. This is true for most of the country, true in theory in Florida, but not always true in reality in Florida because of pests and extreme conditions.

Planting in place outdoors assures good light, room for roots, better air circulation, and no transplanting shock. But if you provide all of the above, you will be even more successful planting most herbs in a better controlled place: in containers inside, on a porch, or in an intensive care area outside. I sow arugula directly and find it does much better that way than from transplants, but it is about the only herb for which I am convinced direct sowing is best. Calendula, dill, coriander, and borage have done fairly well for me when sown in place.

On the other hand, God sows many seeds casually with the help of the birds, the winds, and simple gravity. Plants like perilla and butterfly weed pop up automatically in surprise places in my garden. See chapter 1 for more on self sowing. Transplant volunteers to garden spots as needed.

If you decide to plant right in the garden, prepare the soil well. Plan the arrangement of the plants with tall varieties toward the back, shorter ones farther front, and colors and textures in harmony. Leave walkways or place stepping stones so you can get to all parts of the bed.

Decide whether you want to plant in rows or in patches or drifts. Drifts look more artistic, but in rows it is easier to tell weeds from herbs. This is important when sowing new plants you may not recognize in the seedling state. In either case, measure out the spots for seeds, rake the patches of soil, and label.

Then plant your seeds according to packet directions except for depth. In Florida, plant seeds no deeper than their largest dimension. Pat down. Unless it is raining, water seeded areas twice a day or oftener with a gentle spray to keep the soil evenly moist at all times. The top layer of soil, where most seeds are germinating, can dry out quickly on a hot or windy day. A hard rain, on the other hand, may wash out smaller seeds. If it does, replant as soon as possible.

STARTING WITH HERB PLANTS

In Florida, you may find it much saner and safer to buy herb plants already well started. Culinary herbs are often offered in the produce section of the grocery. More and more nurseries carry herb plants as demand grows. If yours doesn't, ask them if they could. Or ask if you can order a kind or variety that they don't have. If you are planning to buy a number of plants, it can't hurt to ask about buying wholesale.

I made such a purchase in April, not the best time to buy herbs in light of the coming of summer. But by June I had lost only one plant and that was because we were away, and after I

had already taken cuttings. I lost a few more, chamomile for one, over a very rainy summer, but the other plants multiplied and I also learned quite enough to make me feel the initial purchase well worth the price and time.

Some plants I try once and not again if they die. But others, like lavender, that I want badly, I try again and again until we learn to coexist, and I enjoy every day that they live in the meantime.

Some successes are only a matter of patience and determination. I tried several times to start butterfly weed with no results, but ever since someone gave me plants, I have them coming up all over.

If you are buying from the grower, pay close attention to any suggestions he or she may have. Often they have grown many varieties and found some to be superior for that particular climate. That is how I finally found a lavender that is thriving for me.

Choose healthy looking plants with compact rather than leggy growth, and good color in the leaves rather than yellow or brown. Avoid any with signs of disease and look carefully for insects. But also remember that the more summer-sensitive plants may look less than perfect in the fall. Their very survival of summer is a good sign. They will soon look much better.

TRANSPLANTING HERBS

Hardening off or gradually acclimating a plant to its new environment is not often necessary, since most Florida plants are grown or shown outdoors. If yours are going into a great deal more sun and wind than they grew in, move them there gradually by going from porch to protected spot in the garden to their permanent place. Or plant them at once but protect them for a few days with a bottomless plastic milk jug, a cover of Reemay, or some other form of shade and shelter. The only way I've ever killed an aloe was by moving it too suddenly into full sun. It could not adjust that fast.

In a shaded area you can protect new plants or even root cuttings under overturned glass jars. But if it is hot or sunny, plants under glass can quickly cook in their own juice.

When possible, transplant late in the day or on a cloudy day to give plants the longest possible time to readjust. Cloudy days, let alone a spell of them, are rare in Florida, so we have to compensate with extra shade and watering until plants are established, especially during the hotter months.

Cut back foliage to reduce transpiration and stress on the roots. This seems wasteful with other plants, but with herbs this can be an immediate harvest, so use, freeze, or dry the extra leaves.

Herbalist Kaye Cude says to slice off the bottom half inch of root growth from well-rooted plants in 4-inch pots like the ones she grows, to encourage new growth. Otherwise, massage the sides of the root ball gently to start roots out of their perfect soil mix and into the real world.

If there are several plants in a pot, you can separate them or plant them in a clump. Unless they pull apart easily, cutting the root ball instead of pulling it into sections usually damages fewer roots. Plants that have been divided or separated will need more care during the next few weeks.

New plants, even ones that will be drought resistant later, need constant moisture when first transplanted. Make a doughnut-like depression around the plant and then water well and slowly. The foliage may also need sprinkling or misting. If so, the plant shows this by wilting, and should be watered right away.

If some foliage does dry up, clip it off and use it just as if you'd dried it on purpose to use for potpourri, mulch, or on the fireplace or grill.

MAKING MORE PLANTS WITH CUTTINGS

It is prudent to start many kinds of herbs from cuttings, and not at all difficult. Certain herbs, like true French tarragon and horseradish, do not produce seeds, so cuttings or divisions are required. Others are grown from cuttings for quality control. Since all seedlings have a genetic mix from two parents, there can be variations of flavor or flower color. Cuttings or divisions give the exact variety or cultivar of plant and grow more quickly and surely.

New plants from cuttings can sometimes be made by simply breaking off a piece of a plant and sticking it in the ground in a new place. I've done that with geraniums in Florida's humidity.

Most of the time, more care is best expended, and the rooting still seems like magic to me. Fill a clean container with a sterile medium like vermiculite, perlite, or sand that is wet but not soggy.

I bought old dishpans at the Good Will store and put drainage slits in the bottoms (very important during summer rains). I keep four of them full of cuttings most of the time on top of the rabbit cages, shaded under the oak tree. You can also use plastic flats from the garden center, recycled or new, but they are not as deep as the dishpans.

You can also mark off a certain area in partial shade and use the soil there for cuttings if it is mostly sand (creating a shaded sand bed). However you may have too many problems from insects, snails, cats, and so on, and it may become waterlogged in summer rains. I prefer using a container filled with sterile medium. Having it above ground level improves drainage and also makes for less stooping.

Some of my friends have mist beds with nozzles on a timer to release a fine mist for say 10 second intervals every 20 minutes. This works well, but is not necesary for the average herb grower.

Softwood Cuttings. To make softwood cuttings, cut off 4 to 8 inches of tip growth, cutting just above a node so no unsightly stubs on the parent plant will attract insects and diseases. Then, on the cutting, make a sharp new slanting cut just below a node and remove the lower leaves. A one-sided razor or sharp knife is good for this job.

To use powdered rooting hormone like Rootone(TM), dip the stem ends in water and then in the hormone. This also has some fungicide in it to guard against rot, so it can be even more helpful in Florida than elsewhere. Never-

theless, I often root cuttings in vermiculite without it.

One grower told me to cover the ends with saliva, that it contains disease killing properties. That may or may not be so. If you try it, put the saliva on your finger or a dish and dip the cut ends in it. Don't put cuttings into your mouth unless you are sure that they are harmless and don't taste bad.

Next make a hole in the medium and insert the cutting deep enough to cover at least one node. Firm the medium around the stem. Cuttings can go fairly close to one another in the container with the leaf tips just touching. Keep cuttings out of direct light and keep humidity high. Remove any dead foliage or leaves that fall from overhead trees. After about two weeks, pull one stem to test. If it comes right up, see if any roots are long enough. If not, reset the cutting and wait a few more days.

If it doesn't come right up, it is rooted and ready to transplant. To remove rooted cuttings from the medium, use a trowel or spoon to gently lift the roots intact. Plant at once.

Hardwood Cuttings. For hardwood cuttings, cut a longer piece with sharp pruners, but in the same way. Take more leaves off the bottom and sink the stick as far as 6 to 12 inches into medium. Use something deeper than a dishpan. Old picnic coolers work well. Or try the shaded sand bed for this. Hardwood cuttings take longer, up to several months to form roots, and I find them more difficult and less certain. But I have rooted some and met growers who prefer this method. With some types of plants, you have no choice. Check the plant-by-plant directory near the end of this book for each herb's preferred rooting method.

Tips on Growing from Cuttings.

It is not at all difficult to root softwood cuttings, but if your first ones do not root, do not be discouraged. Just try again. Last summer Grandma asked if I had any pink geraniums. Her friend would like some. "No problem. I'll root some cuttings for her," I said. Would you believe that two bunches rotted in the medium and none rooted until after the summer rains. I should have brought that dishpan inside. After September I could have rooted a thousand of them without a problem. Usually summer is an excellent time for rooting cuttings because of the rain and humidity, but not always. Plants with succulent stems may do better in the dry season or in a dryer summer. The point is, never give up. Just try again.

I was amazed the first time I tried softwood cuttings after we moved to Florida, and some coleus cuttings rooted in only a week.

I still haven't been able to root cuttings of silver dollar eucalyptus and one nurseryman said he couldn't either. Another pro has managed it in sand, so I may try again, though I think layering is our best bet for this plant.

Mound Layering.

This method of propagation works even for plants like lavender and rosemary that seem determined to produce a wide, branching plant from a single stem so you can't divide it. Scratch the skin on several of the the lowest branches on the undersides to expose the cambium layer that is just beneath. Then bend these branches to the ground (with eucalyptus a single stem will do), pinning them down with a bent pipe cleaner or wire if necessary. I set a limestone rock on rosemary stems. The lime that washes off also helps the plants. Then mound up good soil over the scratched point or points. Cover with mulch to help keep it moist.

Rooting this way can take from one to several months, depending on the plant and the season. Pull gently or dig down carefully to check, every month or so. When the roots beneath the scratched points seem to have anchored firmly, lift the entire new plant and have a look. If not enough roots have formed, re-cover the stems and wait longer. If roots seem sufficient, cut the rooted branches from the main plant. Cut or separate them into pieces if you buried multiple stems.

Be sure each has some roots attached. Then plant in pots or in the ground at once. Give them extra care for several weeks, even more care than transplants that were divided or separated.

DIVIDING CLUMPS OF HERBS

Many clump-forming herbs like comfrey, gingers, and lemongrass are easy to propagate by dividing established plants. Lift the plant carefully out of the ground with a spading fork or knock it gently out of the pot. If possible, break the clump into parts by hand. If not, use the prongs of two spading forks (or table forks for a

WATER-SAVING PRINCIPLES (XERISCAPING)

1. Design for conservation. Make the most of your site by taking advantage of wet and dry areas, windbreaks, sun and shade patterns, overhanging eaves, and other factors to situate plants in the conditions they prefer. Herb gardens need less work and water than lawn areas.

2. Select appropriate plants. For the backbone of your herb garden, use plants that thrive year-round in Florida, grouping those with similar water needs.

3. Improve the soil. Add as much organic matter as possible to help your herb garden soil retain more water and nutrients and sustain more beneficial microbes.

4. Mulch. Use mulch to soak up and hold in rainfall and irrigation. You'll reduce plant stress and encourage earthworms and enzymes to multiply.

5. Irrigate wisely. Water only when and as much as plants need. Keep equipment, from hoses to drip system to automatic sprinklers, working well. Use a rain sensor with automatic systems so you don't water while it is raining or too soon after.

6. Recycle water. Gather rainwater or use graywater from the washing machine when you can, especially on non-edible herbs. Some cities like St. Petersburg offer reclaimed water at lower cost and it is good for the garden.

small potful). If all else fails, use a butcher knife to get individual plants, each with some roots and a bud. Not only does this give you more plants, it helps stimulate their growth by eliminating crowded conditions.

New plants can often be cut from the side of a clump with a spade, knife, or trowel without digging up the main plant at all.

MAINTAINING YOUR HERB PLANTS

You don't have to work long and hard to keep your herbs in vigorous growth. But you do need to do the right chore at the right stage. If you do each job as needed, it takes very little effort or time. Ignore herbs, or any plants, when they are thirsty and they may forgive you, but not until after they have suffered dieback, sulked for a time, and finally recovered.

WATERING

If you move to Florida in the summer, as we did, or look up the rainfall statistics, you may not realize the importance of irrigation here. Florida is dry from September until May, and irrigation is needed for all but the most drought-resistant plants. Since fresh water is scarce in Florida, xeriscaping (water-saving landscaping techniques, see sidebar) will help your herbs grow better without contributing to the water scarcity problem.

Watering carefully means only when necessary, not because it is Tuesday or your house came with automatic sprinklers. Newly set plants, even the most drought-resistant, need constant watching and watering for a while. Even the most stringent water regulations give 30 days leeway for watering new plants any time. It probably won't be necessary but saving receipts is a good idea in case you need to prove that plants are new.

Try to group together herbs that need regular weekly watering, and do the same with those that need watering only when there is no rain for several weeks.

DAILY ROLL CALL
Constant observation is important. If you check every plant every day or at least every few days, you will notice which ones need water, mulch, or insect removal before it is too late. I must admit that I have remembered in the middle of the night that I hadn't seen the rue lately. And sure enough, when I checked the next day, it had disappeared completely. This is one disadvantage to having herbs all over. It happens less now that I have most of them together.

DAILY SHOWER
Plants benefit from a daily shower. This even works on roses and prevents the need for much spraying and dusting with strong chemicals.

This shower is, ironically, most important during the rainy season. A brisk midday spray with plain water from the hose nozzle, a spray strong enough to hit both sides of the foliage, will wash away most fungus spores before they settle in. It also dislodges most of the insects. And it relieves heat stress at the

DROUGHT TOLERANT HERBS		OASIS ZONE HERBS
Aloe vera	Hyssop	Basil
Anise	Lavender	Chervil
Borage	Parsley	Comfrey
Caraway	Rosemary	French Sorrel
Chamomile	Sage (all)	Leeks
Chicory	Shallots	lovage
Chives	Tansy	Mints
Cumin	Tarragon	Sweet Bay
Dill	Thyme (all)	Sweet Marjoram
Fennel	Winter Savory	Summer Savory
Feverfew	Wormword	Watercress
Garlic		Winter Cress

hottest part of the day. Of course, do not oversoak already damp soil.

I don't do this every day, but often enough to see the definite benefit. It's a good way to check on the herbs often, at the same time.

During the dry season, a shower once or twice a week is enough, and you can add more water for the thirstier plants, as needed. Certainly it is better to do the main watering in early morning or evening so less water is lost to evaporation. But I've saved more than a few plants from extinction with their noonday shower.

PEST AND DISEASE CONTROL

Although herbs are resistant to pests and diseases and we plant them to help with pest control in other states, in Florida they are definitely not immune. Here are practices that help reduce pest damage:

* Provide good soil drainage and aeration plus wide enough spacing between plants. Proper air circulation reduces diseases.

* Provide water and fertilizer as needed to keep stress to a minimum and therefore reduce the threat of pests.

* Grow several kinds of herbs together in the same bed or container rather than all one kind. They will do better. This works like any companion planting. One herb may repel the bug that comes to eat its neighbor. The bug that attacks comfrey may get discouraged and leave when its next bite is into a hot pepper or even a licorice scented Mexican tarragon.

* It can help to plant in more than one place. One plant may be chewed up while the same type in another location will be spared. See the example of grapefruit sage in chapter 1.

* In the rare case when a plant or part of a plant shows serious problems, discard it to the bottom of a HOT (fast-working) compost pile or in a sealed bag in the trash.

* Use the daily shower just mentioned as preventative or aid for sensitive or ailing plants.

FEEDING HERB PLANTS

Herbs in Florida's infertile soils will have to be fed, but you should never overfeed herbs. Overfeeding decreases the concentration of essential oils and therefore the fragrance and flavor. Too much nitrogen causes rapid, soft, lush growth of foliage but hardly any flowers or seeds.

Use any all purpose fertilizer after reading the label carefully. Then start with half of the recommended strength and see if that is sufficient. It is if the plant continues to grow and thrive with good color. If you have no instructions, scatter 1 to 2 pounds of 6-6-6 fertilizer over 100 square feet.

Most herbs will thrive with ordinary fertilizers. The humus you add to the soil, though it contains few nutrients, contains traces of many different needed elements. It helps make whatever nutrients are in the soil more available to plant roots. But now and then some plants may show signs of nutrient deficiency with lighter green or mottled leaves. In this case use a

The Native Americans buried a fish in every hill of corn. If you fish or know someone who will save fish scraps in the freezer until you can pick them up, use them. Leave them in the car or kitchen until you dig a hole or holes in the garden. Try not to disturb roots, but dig deep enough to cover the fish with at least 6 to 8 inches of soil. Put the fish into the hole without letting any of it touch the soil anywhere else and then cover with soil. This should prevent wildlife or neighborhood cats from digging.

fertilizer that includes not only the nitrogen, phosphorus, and potassium that plants need most but also the trace elements needed in small quantities. Read the labels carefully, for those that contain trace elements will say so.

If flowering plants seem to be all leaf and few blooms, decrease nitrogen and increase phosphorus.

WEEDING

Weeding is a pleasant chore in the herb garden because brushing against the foliage releases wonderful fragrances. Do it often to keep weeds from getting more than a few leaves and going to seed. Once a week is ideal. Use a hoe carefully and shallowly between plants. Weed close in by hand. Very soon plants will spread and shade out most weeds, especially if you mulch well.

PRUNING

Trim herbs as you use them or prune as needed with snips or shears. Even in hedges, keep plants far enough apart for good air circulation. Whenever you are pruning herbs, lay a piece of plastic, paper, or cloth beside and beneath the plant to catch the clippings, and use them all for cooking or potpourri. With formal

edges and hedges, keep the top narrower than the bottom so that the sun and air can get to the lowest branches.

Let plants grown for cut or dried flowers, like roses, purple coneflower, yarrow, sunflowers, feverfew, and nasturtiums, bloom freely and cut the bloom regularly or remove all dead blossoms. Shape and train the foliage before buds show and then not again until after bloom stops in most cases. If the nasturtiums are going too far across the sidewalk, just cut them back.

Cut rose blooms with stems long enough to snip just above a five-leaflet node (the ones closest to the bloom have only three leaflets) and you will get more bloom sooner.

Keep a calendar of blooming dates and you will soon know what to expect when.

Where fruits or seeds are wanted, in the case of anise, elderberries, nasturtium-seed 'capers,' coriander, and such, leave the flowers to fade naturally and cut the seedheads after they mature and dry somewhat, but before they open and scatter the seeds.

GROWING HERBS INDOORS

Just because you don't have to doesn't mean you can't grow some or all of your herbs inside. In N there are annuals like basil or perennials like lemon balm that you may want to save from winter freezes. In C and S there may be some like thyme and parsley that you want to save from summer sogginess. Others like rosemary, chives, fennel, and marjoram, you may just want to have handy so you don't have to run outside when you are cooking.

You can dig up whole plants if they are not too large and move them into containers. Or start them from cuttings or buy new plants. You may want to keep some plants in pots all year. When you move them, trim away any roots growing through the pot hole.

In Florida a great way to grow any houseplant is on the exchange plan. Have two of each. Move one indoors and use it as long as it looks good. I find that the air conditioning and lack of humidity indoors can eventually deplete houseplants as much as low light does. When this happens, move that pot to the place outdoors where it will do best and bring the other one into the house. By the time that one needs rest and restoration, the first should be in prime condition again. As long as I am moving the indoor pot to some

shade, I don't even do this gradually, but if it goes into full sun, it spends several days in partial shade first.

Herbs indoors should have at least five or six hours of sunlight daily in south or west-facing windows. With florescent lights, plants can brighten the darkest corner.

Be sure to keep the lights on only 12 to 16 hours a day. All plants need some darkness. You can use a grow-light or regular tubes: one cool and one warm work best. Incandescent bulbs can be used in combination with the fluorescent tubes, but alone they produce more heat than the kind of light plants need. Keep the tops of your plants within a few inches of the lights. Clean bulbs once a month and change them yearly whether they need it or not, for the rays weaken.

Indoor Care. Herbs don't need as much fertilizer in winter when they are growing more slowly. If you use houseplant food, cut amounts in half. When days lengthen in spring, feed them as often as every two weeks or as they seem to need it. Liquid fertilizers work best; dry powders are often too strong. But you can use slow release fertilizers. Work the little beads into the top half inch of soil and they will do their job for a good three or four months or more. Pest problems are unlikely and any mealybugs or aphids that do cause trouble can be washed away with soapy water.

HARVESTING HERBS

Of course, the schedule for harvesting herbs in Florida is going to vary from others places. In N and for frost sensitive herbs it will be

most nearly the same, harvest before frost. But even in N there is a much longer season with spurts of growth.

Most Floridians can use some herbs fresh all year. When growth is most abundant and the future most threatening, just before the heart of winter and summer, will be the best time to harvest for storage. You will soon learn which herbs to dry, freeze, or store fresh in the refrigerator and which ones are always available. Again you may prefer a bit of some in storage for hurried times.

The leaves of most culinary herbs reach peak flavor when the flower buds just begin to open. Gather leaves and flowers in the morning just after the dew has dried and before the sun dissipates the essential oils. If you want the whole plant, you can cut annuals back to 2 inches above the ground. Never take more than a third of perennials so as not to weaken the plant.

Otherwise, the best time for picking herbs is anytime you have clippers in hand and a use in mind. This can start from when you first transplant or thin them and continue all year. Pick mint or lemon balm for sun tea in the morning when you set it out for the best infusion or just before serving for garnish. When you gather vegetables or fruits for supper or canning, gather the herbs to put with them. When you are cooking dinner and find you need some rosemary, slip out and get it.

Cut a few chive leaves flush with the ground and leave the rest long so that plants will have green tips. Cut parsley, arugula, and many of the other leafy herbs to within 2 inches of the ground, leaving the

central growing point intact, or harvest by cutting as many leaves as needed from the side.

Pick fruit like elderberries when ripe but not too soft. Cut off full clusters and fork off the berries. Rose hips can get very dry and hard on the bush and will then keep indefinitely.

STORING HERBS

Wash culinary herbs well, then pat dry between paper or cloth towels. For fresh use that day, put them in a glass in the refrigerator. You can add a bit of water to the bottom and put the stems in this, but this isn't always necessary. Parsley is one herb that keeps well without it.

Dry herbs the same way as you would for crafts or potpourri (see page 20). Or dry them in the microwave oven. Spread dry herbs on clean white paper and remove any tough stems and leaves. Break the rest of the leaves into smaller pieces if you wish and pack into well labeled bags or spice jars. Dark colored ones are best but are not essential. For powdered herbs, put the dry leaves into a blender and whirl until the particles are small enough.

Freezing is easiest of all. Wash and dry the herbs and then put them in labeled packs or add them to the bag with the fruits or vegetables with which they will be used. I pick mint for my fruit shakes and add any extra to the bag of frozen strawberries. Most herbs will break apart when frozen, so this saves a lot of chopping.

Check the main chart on harvesting, storing, and using herbs, on page 38 to 41, for the best ways to handle dozens of home-grown herbs and spices.

REGIONAL DIFFERENCES

In Florida's main regions, northern, central, and southern, (N, C, and S), herbs have diffent needs and behaviors. There are herbs and spices that grow best in the different regions, too. In chapters 6, 7, and 8, expert growers in each region tell what they grow and how they do it, sharing insight on regional problems and possibilities.

Be aware that the borders of what we here call northern, central, and southern Florida are not straight lines across the state but wavy lines that tend to sink in the central counties and curve up along edges. The closer you are to the coasts, the warmer your garden will stay, so a garden in Melbourne may have much more in common with southern Florida than mine in Brandon, almost directly across the state and even a bit further south.

I am constantly amazed at the difference 100 miles, 50 miles, often even 10 miles can make. My son Tom is now going to school in Gainesville. "There is a line near Ocala," he says, "where I can feel the weather change every time I make the trip."

To take in as many of these varied climates and conditions as possible, I traveled both north and south and interviewed Florida growers as far flung as I could find. I urge readers who have or come upon additional tips, plants, or problems to share their experiences for future editions. Write to me at 1508 Burning Tree Lane, Brandon, Florida, or in care of B.B. MACKEY BOOKS, P.O. Box 475, Wayne, PA 19087.

Because the gardens I describe in these chapters were full of surprises and the growers had tips that can apply statewide, you may want to read about your section first, but read about the others as well. Good growing methods and especially hardy or desirable plants can often be adapted elsewhere.

5. Landscaping with Herbs

There are few aspects of gardening that are as much fun, not to mention interesting and useful, as growing herbs. It is natural for me to use herbs throughout my landscape, intermixing them with other plants as well as using them in beds and containers with others of their kind.

Whether you want a formal or informal look, a garden mostly for culinary herbs, for fragrance, for cut flowers, or for moonlight viewing of white and silver plants with wafting wonders of perfumes, you can work exclusively, largely, or partly with herbs. You'll find that they maximize your enjoyment and the effectiveness of your plantings as much as they multiply your uses of their leaves, flowers, fruit, and roots.

Before I tell you more about landscaping with herbs and give you the lists that will make choosing the right ones for the right places easier, I have to tell you about a man who makes his living landscaping with herbs.

BILLY DANIEL IS A SPECIALIST

Billy Daniel makes herb gardens happen, no matter what growing conditions he finds or where the gardens must be placed.

His Sweet William Herb Farm is on a rented property north of Tampa with definite limitations, but he makes great use of it. There he has a shade house and takes cuttings by the hundreds from purchased and homegrown plants. He starts his own from seed planted in pots or in the ground. He sows dill, the thicker the better, cilantro, chives, chamomile, yarrow, borage, marjoram, and several types of parsley, sorrel, basil, coneflower, sage, and thyme directly in rows at his nursery. He'd like more greenhouses when he gets his own land.

Waiting for better conditions for himself does not stop Daniel from developing ideal herb gardens for his clients.

A blues guitarist who first became interested in herbs when he saw them growing at Opryland in Nashville, Tennessee, Daniel brings a taste of rock 'n roll style to his plantings that mixes surprisingly well with the old-wives-tale folklore of herbal history. He also proves that there is a place for herbs in every landscape and every lifestyle.

A landscape designer who specializes in herb gardens, one of his finest achievements can be seen at Longboat Key Club. He furnished the plants for this impressive group of 32 herb beds of various shapes, all raised 12 to 18 inches above ground level. Each one is edged with large white limestone rocks, attractive yet functional. The rocks hold the special soil in place in its burlap lining, and every rain washes just enough lime into the beds to keep the soil pH at the right level.

The lavender he started for those beds in October was blooming with an abundance of two-foot long flower spikes by March. I had no idea that lavender could be that successful in Florida, but his photos and fragrant dried stems prove it. He sent me home to feed and speak kind words to my own summer-surviving plants.

Sous chefs visit that Longboat Key herb garden many times every day to clip sprigs of garlic chives, ferny fennel, tarragon, marjoram, oregano, rosemary, dill, bay, parsley, basil, mint, and thyme. Who could resist the cuisine in such a restaurant?

The Longboat herb garden was sponsored by Fetzer Vineyards of California. They have a five acre herb garden at their home office. The Florida facsimile was the showpiece for the Florida Winefest and Auction held there recently.

Daniel planted another Fetzer herb garden at Innisbrook, near Tarpon Springs. There the 3-foot wide rows are bordered with a combination of lemon grass and pineapple sage, both of which thrive year round throughout Florida. The sage is one of several which bloom abundantly.

He favors herbs that flower, like the false tarragons, sage, sunflower, nasturtium, and yarrow. He also makes good use of foliage color and texture. One of his best beds combines bronze and green fennel in a cloud of subtle color. "I add zinnias and sunflowers to all my plantings for a bit of zing," he says.

Raised beds can be shaped freeform or as circles, rectangles, hearts, stars, crescents, or whatever suits the mood of the garden.

The building material selected also defines and shapes the mood of the garden. Raised beds can be built of old brick, landscape timber, large rocks, or various other materials, each of which adds its own unique look and feel to the garden design. Using the same material throughout the garden contributes to its harmony.

In landscaping private homes, Daniel plans, constructs, and plants more modest mazes of raised or in-ground beds. He also blends herbal trees, shrubs, or herbaceous plants into the other plantings. Herbs come in all shapes and sizes.

He is a firm believer in plant selection and grouping according to water needs, both to save water and for more successful growing.

"Basil, mint, dill, fennel, chamomile, cilantro, tansy, and chives like moist soil and need to be watered often," he says. "The same conditions could kill the dry herbs like rosemary, thyme, sage, lavender, bay, marjoram, and oregano.

PLANNING YOUR HERB GARDEN

Billy Daniel advises people who are starting with herbs or expanding to new beds, "Spend some time and take some care. Don't get frustrated and never give up."

My own advice is to play as you plan. Plunge in. You are more likely to enjoy the results of a few dollars spent on herb plants than on lottery tickets. We all lose some plants in the learning, but at the same time some succeed and spread. Study this book. Study other gardens you see and like. Then make your own plans and change the details to suit yourself and your family.

Design your plantings with color, texture, fragrance, height, time of bloom, time of blahs, your own personal prejudices, and your own time and energy allocation in mind. The garden is one of the few places where you can turn your wishes into reality.

Also plan with careful consideration for the views from your windows, the places you see often like your entranceways, and your rest and relaxation areas. There is nothing more pleasant than brushing against the lantana or plucking a leaf of scented geranium as you walk into the house, or looking out in the morning from your breakfast table to see mounds of colored and textured foliage and flowers, washed with dew.

You may not want to have your herbs in a separate garden, especially if these plants are new to you. Plant herbs among your garden and landscape plants and get used to how easy and rewarding they can be, and start building up your stock of plants. Later on, designing a separate herb garden will seem more natural.

Because herbs go so well with food, whatever fruits or vegetables you are growing will influence both what and where you plant herbs. Herbs are high on the list of plants that attract birds, bees, and butterflies, so plant them where you can watch the lively company they draw from indoors and out.

Herbal foliage and the flowers of herbs give an extra dimension to cut flower arrangements. If you keep a cutting garden, be sure to include herbs such as salvias, sunflowers, and yarrow. If you need a tree, a shrub, or a bit of color in your landscape, your choice can just as well be a herb.

You will soon learn which herbs are most reliable from reading about and growing them. Make them the backbone of your plantings. Put the ones that are fussy in a place where a summer slump won't ruin the scene. Because of the nature of year-round growing in Florida, and because new herb plants spread and mature so quickly, your herbal landscape may change and develop faster than other kinds of plantings. That's all right. Just be flexible and enjoy it.

HERB SELECTION LISTS

There is a herb for nearly every place and every purpose. The lists in this chapter will help you classify, know, choose, and use them. Look for further information on each herb in the plant-by-plant directory at the end of this book.

These lists will help you work herbs into your landscaping plans. Herbs don't need to be in a separate garden unless you want them in one. And even there, you'll want to know which ones are annuals that will need replanting every fall or early spring and which are perennials that live for years.

There are herbs like loquat that will serve you as shade trees and some like citrus are great small specimen trees. The shrub herbs can be used for framing or screening your home from the outside and improving the views from the windows from inside.

Several herbs make very good ground covers, neat and dependable. Others such as nasturtiums and pennyroyal will serve as ground covers for most of the year but die out in summer. If they are growing in mulch, the empty spot can blend right into your landscape plan.

Whatever special conditions you have in your yard, you'll want to check which herbs will do well with those conditions: salt spray, extra dry or extra moist soil. Most herbs that need full sun elsewhere will be grateful for some shade in Florida, especially in late spring and summer in the late afternoons. Very few will grow in deep shade, but almost all will grow with light to partial shade.

Add to these lists as your own experience in your own garden dictates. Remember that they are specifically for Florida and will therefore help you adjust information from lists in other herb books. I find such lists in any book to be my most useful resources, so I made these as extensive as I could. You will want to refer also to the plant lists in chapters 6 (N), 7(C), or 8(S) to check which plants do best in your section of Florida.

A SAMPLING OF COLORFUL HERBS

While all herbs are interesting, some are also colorful. Silvery artemisia, purple basil, forest green parsley, chartreuse sorrel, orange butterfly weed, variegated ginger, and firecracker red peppers add a zestful dash of color to the garden. Yet herbs have mainly low-key colors that seldom clash, especially with all those shades of green surrounding them. So blend colors for harmony or for contrast, and give each section of the garden some color and accent.

I am color conscious in my garden, so I put all the yellows and oranges on one side and all the pinks and purples on the other. Blues and whites go anyplace. Reds can be orangey-red or purplish-red, and I place them accordingly.

You are your own best judge of color in the landscape, for you need only suit yourself. Colorplay is stricltly for enjoyment, and your herbs are easy to move if you later find a better combination.

Be most careful in placing large plants like angel trumpet and hydrangea or trees like redbud and loquat. Also consider carefully before placing spreaders like lantana, goldenrod, and passion flower.

COMMON NAME	BOTANICAL NAME	COLORS
Aloe	*Aloe*	flowers red or orange
Alyssum	*Lobularia*	flowers white, pink, or purple
Angel trumpet	*Datura*	flowers white, peach, or lavender
Anise hyssop	*Agastache*	flowers purple, red, pink, or white
Basils	*Ocinum*	foliage green or purple
Bergamont, Beebalm	*Monarda*	flowers red, lavender, white, or pink
Borage	*Borago*	flowers blue, pink
Bugleweed	*Ajuga*	foliage green, purple, or silver
Butterfly weed	*Asclepias*	flowers orange or red
Calendula	*Calendula*	flowers yellow, orange, cream,or red
California poppy	*Eschscholzia*	flowers orange, gold, red, or pink
Chamomile	*Chamaemelum*	flowers white
Chicory	*Chicorium*	flowers blue, white, or pink
Chives	*Allium*	flowers pink, lavender, white
Elderberry	*Sambucus*	flowers white, berries ripen purple
Goldenrod	*Solidago*	flowers yellow
Hydrangea	*Hydrangea*	flowers blue, white, pink, or tan
Lantana	*Lantana*	flowers in any color or multicolored
Lavender	*Lavandula*	flowers white or purple, leaves silver
Loquat	*Eriobotrya*	foliage blue or silver, yellow fruit
Marigold, French	*Tagetes*	flowers yellow, orange, mahogany
Mondo grass	*Ophiopogon*	leaves green, lavender or purple fls.
Mustard	*Brassica*	flowers yellow
Nasturtium	*Tropaeolum*	flowers yellow, orange, cream, or red

(–continued)

A Sampling Of Colorful Herbs (continued)

COMMON NAME	BOTANICAL NAME	COLORS
Passion flower	*Passiflora*	flowers white, lavender, or bright red
Pepper	*Capsicum*	fruits red, yellow, white, purple
Perilla	*Perilla*	foliage purple, flowers white or blue
Periwinkle	*Catharanthus*	flowers white, red, pink, or lavender
Pinecone ginger	*Zingiber*	cones red, leaves green or variegated
Pokeweed	*Phytolacca*	berries purple
Poppy	*Papaver*	flowers red, pink, white, salmon
Portulaca	*Portulaca*	flowers all colors but blue
Prickly poppy	*Argemone*	flowers yellow
Purple coneflower	*Echinacea*	flowers lavender or greenish white
Redbud	*Cercis*	flowers purple
Rose	*Rosa*	flowers all shades but true blue
Sage	*Salvia*	flowers all shades, varied by species
Society Garlic	*Tulbaghia*	flowers lavender
Sunflower	*Helianthus*	flowers yellow, orange, cream, red
Tarragon, Mexican	*Tagetes*	flowers yellow
Thyme	*Thymus*	flowers pink, white, purple
Ti Plant	*Cordyline*	leaves pink to deep red
Violets, pansies	*Viola*	flowers in all shades

PINK, VIOLET, AND SILVER HERB BORDER
18 ft. long by 4 ft. wide. 1 block equals 1 sq. ft.
The top of grid is the back of the border, featuring taller plants.

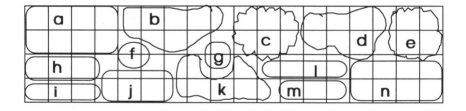

a. purple coneflower (4)
b. hydrangea, pink (3)
c. eucalyptus (1)
d. ti plant (3)
e. lantana, lavender (1)
f. fennel, bronze (1 clump)
g. angel trumpet (1)

h. basil, purple (6)
i. alyssum (6) Society garlic (3)
j. lamb's ear (8)
k. periwinkle 'Tropicana Pink' (6)
l. perilla (6)
m. lavender (3)
n. portulaca, 'Peppermint' (12)

HERBS WITH SILVER FOLIAGE

A patch of silver artemisia beside white violas will show up in the moonlight, and beside a carpet of white purslane, it will shine in the sun. All leaf colors come mainly from the pigmentation in the cells: much of that is the chlorophyll that makes leaves green. Another factor is how much the chlorophyll blocks or does not block the other pigments. Beyond this, leaf colors can get an additional silver plating from the "bloom" or silver dusting in plants like silver dollar eucalyptus. Some plants like lamb's ears are more shimmering because of a flocking of fine hairs by which nature protects them from intense sun and heat, dry soil, or wind.

Some herbs like lamb's ears and artemisias are almost entirely silver or shades of gray of varying darkness. Others like thyme, tansy, and chives may have one or two silver varieties among their many greener ones.

Some foliage that is basically green, like silver thyme, takes on a silver sheen from simple variegation, be it edging, stripes, dappling, or spots.

Herbs with silver foliage look elegant anywhere and help other colors blend better. For the ultimate effect, plant them near blue or purple flowers or herbs with red foliage. For formal or knot gardens you may want a complete ribbon of silver-leaved plants, but most often they are used as pleasant accents.

COMMON NAME	BOTANICAL NAME	REGION
Artemesias	*Artemisia* species	NC
Bugleweed, variegated	*Ajuga reptans*	NCS
Catnip	*Nepeta* species	NCS
Chive, silver or corkscrew	*Allium senescens glaucum*	NCS
Clove pink	*Dianthus caryophyllus*	NCS
Comfrey, variegated	*Symphytum officinalis*	NCS
Curry plant	*Helichrysum*	NCS
Eucalytpus	*Eucalyptus* species	NCS
Germander, silver	*Teucrium fruticans*	NCS
Horehound	*Marrubium* species	NCS
Lamb's ears	*Stachys* species	NCS
Lavender	*Lavandula* species	NCS
Mint, pineapple	*Mentha suaveolens variegata*	NCS
Sage, some	*Salvia* species	NCS
Santolina	*Santolina* species	NCS
Sea holly	*Eryngium* species	NCS
Tansy, silver-leaved	*Tanacetum vulgare*	NCS
Thyme, silver leaved	*Thymus vulgaris argentaeus*	NCS
Wormwood	*Artemisia* species	NC

HERBS THAT CAN BE GROUND COVERS

Ground covers are elegant additions to any section where it is difficult to mow grass, as on slopes, in small sections or strips, or where using the lawnmower is impractical because of tree roots, rocks, or other obstacles. Or use ground covers simply to cut down on the work of mowing, Once established, they are much easier to maintain than a lawn.

Ground covers are also more interesting. Without other necessity, use them where you want a different color or texture. Where more than one ground cover is involved, plant a harmony of colors and textures as you would for a flower garden, but make the drifts of each kind considerably larger. This will give the scene undulating shapes with a feeling of motion.

The herbs listed below will vary in height depending on both variety and climate. Some nasturtium types will climb any support to the roof line of a one story house, while others stay low.

These are also mostly very spreading plants, so give them ample room. Most will spread slowly enough, but Aztec sweet shrub has taken over a whole section of the herb garden in a year. Some people still have mint that threatens to take over, but I find that summer checks its invasiveness in my yard. I am delighted with the spread in any case, but knowing beforehand helps you plan more effectively.

HERBS FOR GROUND COVER

COMMON NAME	BOTANICAL NAME	REGION	HEIGHT (inches)
Aztec sweet shrub	*Lippia dulcis*	NCS	6-12
Bugleweed	*Ajuga reptans*	NCS	6-10
Chamomile	*Chamaemelum nobile*	NC	1-8
Gotu kola	*Centella asiatica*	NCS	6-8
Lamb's ears	*Stachys* species	NC	6-24
Mints	*Mentha* species	NCS	2-24
Nasturtium	*Tropaeolum majus*	NCS	8-12
Oregano, creeping	*Origanum* species	NCS	6-12
Rosemary, prostrate	*Rosmarinus officinalis*	NCS	12-18
Santolina	*Santolina chamaecyparisus*	NCS	8-18
Violets	*Viola* species	NCS	4-8
Yarrow	*Achillea millefolium*	NC	2-18

ANNUAL HERBS

An annual is a plant that sprouts, grows vegetatively, blooms, and goes to seed in a single season and does not come back from the same roots. Most are so special and profuse in their bloom, seed production, or culinary uses that they are well worth planting again and again. Most of the annuals on this list should be replanted every fall and will last until the next spring or summer. Marigolds and dianthus will grow anytime but have more limited lifespans and will bloom themselves to death in a few months. Some annual salvias will last longer than marigolds, but you should still plan to replace them when they look straggly.

Annuals grow anywhere, but not any time. There are annuals for all seasons in Florida, and different ones prefer different seasons. Winter doesn't automatically come to end their growing season. Sometimes we wonder why something is dying and the only cause is the end of their life cycle. Annuals will need to be replanted from seeds or cuttings to keep a continual supply, and some of them can only be grown in certain seasons, usually from September to May.

TRUE ANNUAL HERBS

COMMON NAME	BOTANICAL NAME	REGION
Anise	*Pimpinella anisum*	NCS
Arugula	*Eruca vesicaria (E. sativa)*	CS
Basil	*Ocimum* species	NCS
Borage	*Borago officinalis*	NC
Calendula	*Calendula officinalis*	NC
Chamomile	*Matricaria* species	NC
Chervil	*Anthriscus cerefolium*	NCS
Clove pink	*Dianthus caryophyllus*	NC
Coriander	*Coriandrum sativum*	NCS
Cumin	*Cumin cyminum*	NCS
Curry plant	*Helichrysum angustifolium*	NCS
Dill	*Anethum graveolens*	NCS
Marigold	*Tagetes patula*	NCS
Marjoram, sweet	*Origanum majorana*	NCS
Savory, summer	*Satureia hortensis*	NCS
Sunflower	*Helianthus annuus*	NCS
Shoofly plant	*Nicandra physalodes*	NCS
Portulaca	*Portulaca oleracea*	NCS

HERBS OFTEN TREATED AS ANNUALS IN FLORIDA:

Some of these are perennial in other places and climates, but here the heat and humidity of summer does them in and we must restart them again in the fall.   And some of these like sage and lavender you may eventually learn to save over the summer and can then treat like perennials.

COMMON NAME	BOTANICAL NAME	REGION
Beebalm, lemon mint	*Monarda citriodora*	NC
Caraway	*Carum carvi*	NCS
Chamomile, Roman	*Melissa officinalis*	NC
Lavender	*Chamaemelum nobile*	NCS
Lemon balm	*Lavandula* species, some	NCS
Marjoram	*Origanum majorana*	NCS
Nasturtium	*Tropaeolum* species	NCS
Rue	*Ruta graveolens*	NCS
Sage	*Salvia* species, some	NCS
Savory, winter	*Satureia montana*	NCS
Tarragon	*Artemesia dracunculus*	NC
Thyme	*Thymus* species, most	NCS
Yarrow	*Achillea* species	NC

a. bark mulch
b. arugula
c. 'Ruffles' basil
d. perilla
e. marigold 'Jaguar'
f. lemon tree,
     pruned high

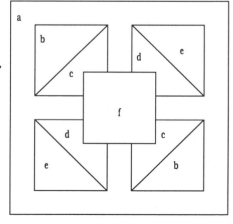

HERBS THAT ARE PERENNIAL IN FLORIDA

Most perennial herbs are relatively carefree and permanent. They fit into flower gardens as well as herb gardens, and can make the backbone of your garden plan. Be sure to divide them when they are too crowded. A few, like ferverfew, chicory, and anise hyssop may last a few years and then disappear. So replant them as needed or take cuttings for new plants every few years.

Ajuga, bugleweed	*Ajuga reptans*	NCS
Aloe	*Aloe* species	CS
Angel trumpet	*Datura* species	NCS
Anise hyssop	*Agastache foeniculum*	NCS
Bay laurel	*Laurus nobilis*	NCS
Butterfly weed	*Asclepias* species	NCS
Cardamon	*Elettaria cardamomum*	NCS
Caraway	*Varum carvi*	NC
Castor bean	*Ricinus communis*	NCS
Chicory	*Chicorium intybus*	NCS
Chives	*Allium schoenoprasum*	NC
Comfrey	*Symphytum officinale*	NCS
Costmary	*Chrysanthemum balsamita*	NC
Feverfew	*Chrysanthemum parthenium*	NCS
Fennel	*Foeniculus vulgare*	NCS
Garlic chives	*Allium tuberosum*	NCS
Geraniums, scented	*Pelargonium odoratissimum*	NCS
Gingers	*Zingiber officinale*	NCS
Goldenrod	*Solidago* species	NCS
Gotu kola	*Centella asiatica*	NCS
Horehound	*Marrubium vulgare*	NCS
Horseradish	*Armoracia rusticana*	NCS
Lavender	*Lavandula* species, some	NCS
Lemon balm	*Melissa officinalis*	NCS
Lemon grass	*Cymbopogon citratus*	CS
Lemon verbena	*Aloysia triphylla*	NCS
Mints	*Mentha* species	NCS
Oregano	*Origanum* species, some	NCS
Parsley	*Petroselinum crispum*	NCS
Passion flower	*Passiflora* species	NCS
Peppers	*Capsicum* species	NCS
Perilla	*Perilla frutescens*	NCS
Rosemary	*Rosemarinus officinalis*	NCS
Sage	*Salvia* species, most	NCS
Sorrel	*Rumex scutatus*	NCS
Southernwood	*Artemisia* species	NC
Tansy	*Tanacetum vulgare*	NCS
Tarragon, Mexican	*Tagetes lucida*	NCS
Tumeric	*Curcuma domestica*	S
Vick's salve plant	*Plectranthus* species	NCS
Watercress	*Nasturtium officinale*	NCS
Wormwood	*Artemisia* species	NC
Yarrow	*Achillea millefolium*	NCS

HERBS YOU'LL SEE GROWING WILD IN FLORIDA

Some of these you'll want to grow in your yard. For others it will be enough just to know that the roadsides are yellow with mustard in early spring or that you can gather the chickweed or dandelion greens to add to your salad. Some on this list are edible and some are poisonous, so check further, as in the plant-by-plant section, before you gather any to eat. Many of these are native plants.

COMMON NAME	BOTANICAL NAME	REGION
Angel trumpet	*Datura species*	NC
Bayberry, wax myrtle	*Myrica species*	NCS
Bay, red, laurel	*Persea borbonia*	NCS
Bixa	*Bixa orellana*	S
Butterfly weed, milkweed	*Asclepias species*	NCS
Castor bean	*Ricinus communis*	NCS
Chickweed	*Stellaria media*	NC
Dandelion	*Taraxacum officinale*	NCS
Deadly nightshade	*Atropa belladonna*	NCS
Dill	*Anethum graveolens*	NCS
Elderberry	*Sambucus canadensis*	NCS
Goldenrod	*Solidago species*	NCS
Goosefoot, fat hen	*Chenopodium species*	NCS
Holly	*Ilex species*	NCS
Juniper, red cedar	*Juniperus virginiana*	N
Lantana	*Lantana species*	NCS
Mint	*Mentha species*	NC
Mistletoe	*Phoradendron serotinum*	NCS
Mustard, black	*Brassica species*	NCS
Nightshade	*Solanum, Atropha species*	NCS
Passion flower	*Passiflora species*	NCS
Periwinkle, Madagascar	*Catharanthus roseus*	NCS
Plantain, goosetongue	*Plantage major*	NC
Portulaca, purslane	*Portulaca species*	NCS
Prickly poppy	*Argemone mexicana*	NC
St. John'swort	*Hypericum species*	NCS
Salvias, some	*Salvia species*	NCS
Star anise	*Illicium floridanum*	N
Sweet bay	*Magnolia virginiana*	NCS
Vanilla orchid	*Vanilla planifolia*	S
Violet	*Viola species*	NCS
Watercress	*Nasturtium officinale*	NCS

HERBAL SHRUBS AND LARGE GRASSES

You can work herbal shrubs into your landscape as part of foundation plantings, shrub borders, or the understory of a woodland. Most of these are reliable and easy to grow. Some can be pruned to grow as small trees if you want. Some like boxwood or roses can be trained as standards growing on tall stalks above your other herbs. Others, like ginger, grow in a clump. For easiest maintenance, let these grow naturally and put them where pruning will not be a constant problem.

Ginger, because of its size, looks and acts like a shrub in the landscape, though it is a grass and not woody. Other herbs which are grasses behave similarly, for instance cardamon, lemon grass, khus-khus, and vetiver.

Frost tender plants die to the ground after a freeze and usually come back from the roots. The farther into S you live, the less frost you will have, and the surer you can be that these plants will make it back after they are set back. They will be shrubs again within a few months and perhaps for a few years until another hard frost hits. Some that are shrubs in N because of being trimmed back by annual frosts may be fine small trees in S. Prune and train accordingly. If you want bay or star anise to be trees instead of bushy shrubs, remove all but one main branch from the young plant and let that become the trunk with all branches coming from it.

COMMON NAME	BOTANICAL NAME	REGION	HARDINESS
African mint bush	*Ibosa riparia*	CS	frost tender
Angel trumpet	*Datura* species	NCS	frost tender
Bay	*Laurus nobilis*	NCS	frost tender
Bixa or Bixia	*Bixa orellana*	NCS	frost tender
Boxwood	*Buxus sempervirens*	NC	hardy
Castor bean	*Ricinus communis*	NCS	frost tender
Curry tree	*Murraya* species	CS	frost tender
Elderberry	*Sambucus canadensis*	NCS	hardy
Eucalyptus	*Eucalyptus* species	NCS	hardy
Gingers	*Zingiber* species	NCS	go dormant
Hibiscus	*Hibiscus* species	NCS	frost tender
Holly	*Ilex species*	NCS	hardy
Hydrangea	*Hydrangea* species	NCS	hardy
Jamican mint bush	*Micromeria viminea*	NCS	frost tender
Juniper	*Juniperus* species	NCS	hardy
Rice paper plant	*Tetrapanax papyriferus*	NCS	frost tender
Rose	*Rosa* species	NCS	hardy
Star anise	*Illicium verum*	NCS	fairly hardy
St. John's wort	*Hypericum* species	NC	hardy
Ti plant	*Cordyline terminalis*	NCS	frost tender

HERBS THAT ARE TREES

These herbs may be used as trees in the landscape. Smaller trees like allspice and cinnamon in S, bayberry and ginkgo in N and C, are great for accent or shade in or near your herb garden. Any that are also on the shrub list can be kept small. Try one in the very center of the herb garden or in the center of each section. Or let them make a border behind the herbs.

Larger trees like loquat, sweet bay, walnut, and willow can get quite large and serve as shade trees and framing for your house. Keep these far enough from your herb garden to allow at least 6 to 8 hours of sunlight on the ground-level herbs, preferably morning sun. Loquat and citrus produce abundant and delicious fruit, and are beautiful trees that just happen to have many herbal uses.

COMMON NAME	BOTANICAL NAME	REGION
Allspice	*Pimenta* species	S
Angel trumpet	*Datura, Brugmansia* species	NCS
Bayberry	*Myrica* species	NCS
Camphor tree	*Cinnamomum camphora*	NCS
Cinnamon	*Zeylanicum* species	S
Citrus	*Citrus* species	NCS
Curry leaf	*Murraya* species	S
Eucalyptus	*Eucalyptus* species	NCS
Ginkgo	*Ginkgo biloba*	NC
Juniper	*Juniperus* species	NCS
Loquat	*Eryobotrya japonica*	NCS
Neem	*Azdirachta indica*	CS
Pine	*Pinus* species	NCS
Red bay, laurel	*Persea borbonia*	NCS
Redbud	*Cercis canadensis*	NC
Sweet bay	*Magnolia virginiana*	NCS
Walnut	*Juglans* species	NC
Wax myrtle	*Myrica cerifera*	NCS
Willow	*Salix* species	NCS

HERBS FOR SEASIDE GARDENS

Only these few herbs, mainly natives, will live on the salt side of the dunes or coastal beaches. Even these may sometimes suffer wind damage that is quite similar to that of salt. Remember that the salt spray itself comes farther inland during storms and hurricanes.

For the most part, try to separate your main and culinary herbs from the ocean or gulf by at least a building or an expanse of salt-tolerant trees and shrubs (see page 98).

COMMON NAME	BOTANICAL NAME	REGION
Aloe	*Aloe vera*	CS
Bay	*Laurus nobilis*	NCS
Germander	*Teucrium fruticans*	NC
Lambs quarters	*Chenopodium* species	NCS
Lantana	*Lantana* species	NCS
Lemon balm	*Melissa officinalis*	NCS
Juniper	*Juniperus* species	NCS
Mondo grass	*Ophiopogon* species	NCS
Portulaca	*Portulaca oleracea*	NCS
Rose	*Rosa rugosa*	NCS
Rosemary	*Rosemarinus officinale*	NCS
Sage	*Salvia* species	NCS
Santolina	*Santolina chamaecyparisus*	NC
Wax myrtle, bayberry	*Myrica cerifera*	NCS
Yaupon holly	*Ilex vomitoria*	NCS

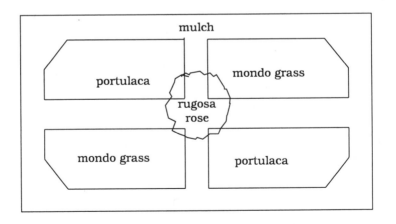

DROUGHT TOLERANT HERBS

With Florida's long dry winters and hot dry May and June, you need to read over the following lists carefully and group your plants together according to water needs. Remember that even drought tolerant plants need frequent watering until they become established. After that they need it only occasionally, which may be every four to six weeks during the winter or every four to six days in May and June. Let common sense and your own knowledge of your soil and shade patterns, and in extreme cases wilting leaves, be your guide. It also helps to dig down in the soil and feel for moisture or push in a trowel or an asparagus cutter/weeder to see how far down that last rain really went.

COMMON NAME	BOTANICAL NAME	REGION
Aloe	*Aloe vera*	NCS
Bayberry	*Myrica* species	NCS
Borage	*Borago officinalis*	NCS
Burnet	*Sanquisorba minor*	NCS
Caraway	*Carum carvi*	NC
Chicory	*Cichorum intybus*	NCS
Cumin	*Cuminum cynimum*	NCS
Feverfew	*Tanacetum parthenium*	NCS
Garlic	*Allium sativum*	NC
Lamb's quarters	*Chenopodium* species	NCS
Lantana	*Lantana camara*	NCS
Lavender	*Lavandula* species	NCS
Parsley	*Petroselinum crispum*	NCS
Rosemary	*Rosmarinus officinalis*	NCS
Sage	*Salvia* species	NCS
Santolina	*Santolina chamaecyparisus*	NCS
Thyme	*Thymus* species	NCS
Wormwood	*Artemisia* species	NCS
Yarrow	*Achillea* species	NCS

HERBS FOR MOIST CONDITIONS

These herbs should be grouped together nearest the hose or wherever you will water most often. If you haven't done this yet, at least be aware that these don't like to grow in dry soil. Mulch them well and and stand over these longer when you are running around with the hose.

COMMON NAME	BOTANICAL NAME	REGION
Basil	*Ocimum* species	NCS
Chervil	*Anthriscus cerefolium*	NCS
Chive	*Allium* species	NCS
Cilantro	*Coriandrum sativum*	NCS
Comfrey	*Symphytum officinale*	NCS
Dill	*Anethum graveolens*	NCS
Fennel	*Foeniculum vulgare*	NCS
Leek	*Allium porrum*	NC
Marjoram	*Origanum marjorana*	NCS
Mint	*Mentha* species	NCS
Sorrel	*Rumex scutatus*	NCS
Sweet bay	*Magnolia virginiana*	NCS
Tansy	*Tanacetum vulgare*	NCS
Watercress	*Nasturtium offinale*	NC
Viola	*Viola* species	NCS

HERBS THAT DO WELL INDOORS

The more air conditioning you have in your home, the harder it will be on plants. Most of them love humidity, so you may want to put them out on the porch or patio IN THE SHADE for an occasional treat. Or have duplicate containers that you can alternate from indoors to out as needed. But always remember to make the transition gradually, a few more hours in the new place every day for a week until the plants become adjusted. Here are some of the herbs you can grow indoors. Experiment, for success with these and other herbs depends on your indoor conditions.

Aloe	*Aloe* species
Basil	*Ocimum* species
Bay	*Laurus nobilis*
Chervil	*Anthriscus cerefolium*
Chives	*Allium schoenoprasum*
Lemon balm	*Melissa officinalis*
Lemon verbena	*Aloysia triphylla*
Mint	*Mentha* species
Myrtle	*Myrtus communis microphylla*
Parsley	*Petroselinum crispum*
Rosemary	*Rosmarinus officinalis*
Scented geranium	*Pelargonium* species

HERBS THAT ATTRACT
BUTTERFLIES AND HUMMINGBIRDS

These herbs, especially when in bloom, will draw flying, fluttering color to your garden and give you the most pleasure if they are within view of your windows so you can watch. Many of the same plants also attract bees. A few, like butterfly weed and fennel will be food sources for the caterpillars and therefore sometimes be eaten. I find that the insects go on to their next stage before they do any permanent damage. Do not use any insecticide, not even soap, on these for the most butterflies. Fortunately these same herbs help attract beneficial insects to your garden.

COMMON NAME	BOTANICAL NAME	REGION
Anise hyssop	*Agastache foeniculum*	NCS
Bergamot	*Monarda* species	NCS
Butterfly weed	*Asclepias* species	NCS
Catnip	*Nepeta cataria*	NCS
Fennel	*Foeniculum vulgare*	NCS
Foxglove	*Digitalis purpurea*	NC
Goldenrod	*Solidago* species	NCS
Passion flower	*Passiflora* species	NCS
Pineapple sage	*Salvia elegans*	NCS
Purple coneflower	*Echinacea purpurea*	NC
Roses, single	*Rosa* species	NCS
Sages (other)	*Salvia* species	NCS
Scented geranium	*Pelargonium* species	NCS
Sunflowers	*Helianthus annuus*	NCS
Wax myrtle	*Myrica cerifera*	NCS

BUTTERFLY AND HUMMINGBIRD BORDER
1 block equals 1 square foot, 16 ft. x 4 ft.

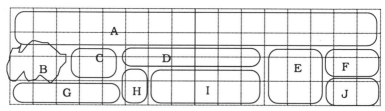

A. mixed sunflowers (12)
B. shrub rose (1)
C. bergamot (1)
D. purple-leaved fennel (6)
E. pineapple sage (red) (4)

F. goldenrod (1)
G. white sweet alyssum (12)
H. purple-leaved sage (1)
I. anise hyssop, purple (10)
J. Salvia farinacea 'Victoria' (4)

6. Growing Herbs and Spices In Northern Florida

Northern Floridians come closest to being able to grow herbs the way it is done in northern states and described in most books. They can grow most of the same plants, plus several hot-climate spices like the gingers. And they can grow and use some herbs and spices very nearly year round with only a little winter protection.

The farther north and west into the panhandle you live, the more like the rest of the country your growing conditions will be. But, even close to the Georgia border, there are differences. Summers are hotter and more humid and this is increasingly true the farther south you live. Winters are mild but temperatures can vary widely from day to day or year to year. Soil can vary from red or yellow clay near Georgia through red and yellow sands in the western counties to the gray and black sandy soils that predominate in much of Florida.

Some plants still go dormant, but many become evergreen, and a freeze can catch them with their sap still high and vulnerable to frost. Protect your plants outdoors or keep cuttings indoors for starting over after a freeze.

In Northern Florida, expect winters to be dry, so irrigation is important. Days are shorter and growth is slower, so patience is needed. Overwatering or overfeeding herbs in winter can be fatal.

To the surprise of Floridians farther south, northern growers sometimes have long spells of cloudy days in winter when overwatering leads to fungus. So does the high humidity of summer. For growers all over Florida, the great advantages of year round growing are balanced by the fact that some plants will have times when they look pretty peaked.

In researching this chapter, I visited several herb gardens located in Northern Florida in order to find out what grows best here. Expert gardeners shared tips and techniques for growing an extensive list of herbs and spices, making the most of a growing season that is about twice as long as that in most northern states.

Their experiences should help Northern Florida herb growers understand the plusses and minuses of this climate, and nurture a healthier and more diverse personal herb collection.

JAMES STEELE'S HERB GARDEN

James Steele makes his living growing about 160 different herbs and spices in large gardens and greenhouses, but his delightful business, *The Herb Garden*, located less than an hour's drive east of Gainesville, is anything but cold and commercial.

Steele tends a well landscaped acre and a quarter. Beds of stock plants thrive below and around trees and shrubs in beds along the road with a wildflower garden around a vine-covered gazebo just beyond. Toward the back his home is tucked neatly behind an office as picturesque as the photos in the herb books. Three greenhouses blend into the scene, also a potting shed, a shade structure, and rows of blooming, thriving herbs in pots.

From the front fence to the back border, The Herb Garden is an attractive demonstration site where public television has done shows on herbs three times.

The Start

In 1969, James Steele was looking for landscaping plants for his new house in Miami. Instead he brought home herb plants and has been growing them ever since. He has a degree in horticulture and managed a nursery in Gainesville for eight years. Five years ago he almost started his business on three acres in North Carolina, but he is glad now that he didn't, for in northern Florida he can work outdoors most of the year and in the 12,000 square feet of greenhouse the rest of the time.

His sales are mostly wholesale to markets within 50 miles: Jacksonville, Gainesville, and Ocala. They take all he can grow and cry for more. He is also open for retail trade. Right now his biggest day of retail sales is at the Spring Plant Festival at Kanapaha Botanical Gardens in March.

To increase retail trade and educate the public, he finds time in a busy schedule to teach classes in the local adult education program and at The Herb Garden. Subjects include medicinal preparations, growing and using herbs, herbal cosmetics and teas, cooking with herbs, container growing, and wreath making.

Classes at the garden are free except for supplies and are usually held on Saturday morning from 10 a.m. until noon every other week in the spring and fall.

Janette Hughes, Sales Manager, Jan Malmborg, Production Assistant, and Steele make up the workforce. There is a down-to-earth, natural feeling here, a place where enthusiasm and common sense priorities result in high quality herb plant production.

Climate

Summers are hard on many herbs here, as in other areas of Florida, especially when we get as much rain as usual.

"One of the reasons I keep plants in the greenhouse in summer is to keep the rain off them," said Steele. Gardeners without greenhouses can set plants on porches or other covered areas for a similar benefit.

He uses very little heat in winter, keeping only one greenhouse at about 45 degrees at night for the basil. The other greenhouses are kept just above freezing.

"Our plants are toughened to natural conditions," said Steele. "The biggest problem in winter is that this area sometimes gets rainy or cloudy weather for 10 days straight."

Steele pays close attention to the weather reports and waters accordingly. "Better to let critical plants get too dry than too wet," he said. "Herbs are tough. They bounce back from being too dry but they die from being too wet."

He also tells customers and classes that fall is like spring, for it is the beginning of the Florida growing season. They need to know that some plants are going to look a bit ragged for a time in either winter or more likely summer, but will come back and look great again. Too many people give up and pull them out. The best thing to do in summer is to wait until after the rains, then cut back about half of the green growth. What is cut off is used as the herb harvest or to propagate new plants.

With summer-blooming plants like *Rudbeckia* and *Echinacea* that go dormant in winter, he does not prune too early or this might encourage new, too-tender growth. He waits for a frost, which usually arrives in December, then cuts the tops off at pot rim level late enough to send plants into dormancy.

He uses Osmocote (TM) fertilizer on small plants in the greenhouses, but in the ground he relies mostly on cottonseed meal and bone meal and uses these fertilizers according to label directions. Both are slow releasing and he only applies them once a year as a rule. If a plant seems to need something more, he uses blood meal and compost. His soil is sandy, but constant application of compost has greatly improved most of it.

The Herb Garden is listed in the Herbal Green Pages (published annually by Maureen Rogers, P.O. Box 345, Silver Springs, PA 17575). Steele also uses that book to visit other herb growers if he travels anywhere.

"I'd like to do more teaching and get the public more involved with herbs. I'd like this to be a place people would stop for a workshop and to see the demonstration gardens when they are traveling." He is already more than halfway to that goal. For more information on workshops, a price list, and a brochure, contact him at The Herb Garden, 693 SR 26, Melrose, Florida, 32666.

A Walk Around the Steele Herb Garden

In mid November after a very rainy late summer and fall, James Steele gave me a tour of his gardens. I was delighted to see wormwood thriving in the first bed.

"It comes through the summer for you?" I asked.

Replied Steele, "Most everything comes through the summer for us. The problem herbs are mostly the lavenders, sages, and thymes, the dry Mediterranean herbs. They look bad, but most of them come right back and fill out in the fall."

He has found that the lavenders tend to get a fungus disease from the damp ground that can be controlled with a thick mulch of oak leaves or white sand that keeps the foliage from coming into contact with the soil. One clump did well for four years and then died back when the sand mulch had dissipated and the soil fungus got through.

English lavender blooms from May through July. French lavender, the one with deeply cut leaves that has done best for me, blooms earlier for him and extends the season.

"Lavenders do very well in clay pots that have been in place long enough for the roots to run down into the ground beneath. Rains just flush right out. They should be a bit potbound so the soil doesn't hold too much water."

James Steele's valerian had died back in the rain but was reviving well in the next bed. "It gets real tall,' he said. "I make a lot of tinctures from this."

Costmary does well beside it, but has not bloomed. Vervain does well and blooms. So does lobelia.

THE HERB GARDEN
List of Plants Grown for Northern Florida Gardens

Agapanthus
Ajuga, Bronze
Ajuga, Burgundy
    Glow
Aloe
Alyssum
Anise
Artemisia, Silver King
Artemisia, Silver
    Mound
Artemisia, Sweet
    Annie
Aztec Sweet Herb
Balm of Gilead
Basil, Holy
Basil, Lemon
Basil, Purple Ruffle
Basil, Spicy Globe
Basil, Sweet
Basil, Thai
Basil, Tree
Bay, Sweet
Borage
Burnet, Salad
Calendula
Caraway
Cardamon
Catmint
Catnip
Chamomile, German
Chamomile, Roman
Chaste Tree
Chervil
Chicory
Chives

Chives, Garlic
Coltsfoot
Comfrey
Coneflower, Purple
Coreopsis
Coriander,
    Vietnamese
Coriander/Cilantro
Costmary
Culantro
Curry
Dill
Epazote
Equisetum
    (horsetail)
Eucalyptus
Fennel, Bronze
Fennel, Florence
Fenugreek
Feverfew
Garlic
Geranium, Apple
Geranium, Scented
Germander
Ginger
Gotu Kola
Horehound
Hosta
Hyssop
Hyssop, Anise
Lady's Bedstraw
Lady's Mantle
Lamb's Ear
Lantana
Lavender, English

Lavender, French
Lemon Balm
Lemon Grass
Lemon Verbena
Licorice
Lime Balm
Lobelia
Lovage
Luffa
Marjoram, Sweet
Marjoram, Creeping
Marshmallow
Mint, Apple
Mint, Blue Balsam
Mint, Candy
Mint, Chocolate
Mint, Corsican
Mint, Eau de
    Cologne
Mint, English
Mint, Jerusalem
Mint, Lavender
Mint, Lebanese
Mint, Lemon
Mint, Lime
Mint, Mountain
Mint, Peppermint
Mint, Pineapple
Mint, Spearmint
Monarda (Beebalm)
Motherwort
Mugwort (*Artemisia*)
Mullein
Myrtle
Nasturtium

THE HERB GARDEN
List of Plants Grown for Northern Florida Gardens

Nettle
Onion, Welsh
   Bunching
Oregano, Dittany of
   Crete
Oregano, Greek
Oregano, Mexican
Oregano, Variegated
   Cuban
Oreganum x
   ma joram
Parsley, Curled
Parsley, Italian Plain
Patchouli
Pennyroyal
Perilla
Phlox, Perennial
Primrose, Evening
Prunella
Purslane
Pyrethrum
Roquette
Rosemary, Pine-
   Scented
Rosemary, Prostrate
Rosemary, Upright
Rudbeckia
Rue

Sage, Autumn
Sage, Cleveland
Sage, Garden
Sage, Golden
Sage, Grapefruit
Sage, Indigo Spires
Sage, Mealy Cup
Sage, Mexican Bush
Sage, Pineapple
Sage, Purple
Sage, Purple Majesty
Sage, Russian
Sage, Scarlet
   (*S.Coccinea*)
Sage, Tricolor
Saint John's Wort
Salvia, Sky Blue
Santolina, Gray
Santolina, Green
Savory, Summer
Savory, Winter
Skullcap
Soapwort
Sorrel
Southernwood
Stevia
Stokesia
Sweet Grass

Tansy
Tarragon, French
Tarragon, Mexican
Thyme, Caraway
Thyme, Coconut
Thyme, Creeping
Thyme, Garden
Thyme, Golden
   Lemon
Thyme, Lemon
Thyme, Longwood
Thyme, Mother of
Thyme, Orange-
   Balsam
Thyme, Silver
Thyme, Wooly
Tilo
Trumpet Creeper
Valerian
Vervain
Violets, Wild
Watercress
Woodruff, Sweet
Wormwood
Wormwood, Fringed
Yarrow

"Mullein grows as a biennial. It grows wild farther north in Florida and blooms along the roadways." Pyrethrum and St. John's wort were thriving. Both bloom well. The latter gets about 12 inches tall here, almost like a ground cover, reseeds very easily, and blooms in late spring. Greater chamomile blooms in midsummer. Comfrey has not bloomed for him (it has, sparsely, for me). Marshmallow goes dormant in the winter. He had lady's mantle but lost it in the rains. Mugwort has pink flowers in late fall and grows to about 3 feet here.

Gotu kola was spreading and thriving as it had all summer. Catnip blooms in late summer.

Small sassafras trees provide summer shade and let in winter sun for the wildflower garden. Limbs were almost bare in mid November. He had planted the trees as foot-tall plants four years before and they were 12 feet high already. "Ocala is about the southern limit for them" he said.

Violets, which are rare and tender in my yard, were spreading like a ground cover here. "I started with just a few flats and they've spread all over," he said. Many coneflowers grew above and among the violets and some were still blooming.

Said Steele, "They bloomed mostly in September and are going dormant now. The perennial herbs that go dormant are often the stronger medicinal herbs. Most of the nutrients settle down into the roots and that makes them more powerful."

Many of the ornamental sages were still blooming. A big patch of lady's bedstraw, which is in the woodruff family, goes dormant for winter here.

A Wide Selection of Culinary Herbs

Prostrate rosemary blooms mostly in early fall, sometimes also in early summer. Creeping thyme can look ragged in midwinter but a 2-year-old patch was lush in November, has pink flowers in June, and attracts bees.

James Steele had a fine specimen of *Lippia graveolens* (Mexican oregano) near the front gate, a small bush about 3 feet tall. It has white flowers in summer and a very strong flavor for authentic southwestern cooking. It was still fully leaved in mid November but Steele said it goes dormant and dies to the ground every winter. Its relatives such as the Aztec sweet shrub and a licorice-scented Lippia grow much the same way.

"We're in the borderline area for bay laurel. We'll get branch dieback [when temperatures are] in the low 20s. Any further north and I'd recommend bringing them in for the winter."

Some of his bay trees were too large for easy transport.

Fennel grows all year long here. Rose hips do well but *Rosa rugosa* can take over if you let it.

He explained that his marjoram, a cross between marjoram and oregano, blooms very heavily in late August. In early September and October it has a short dormancy, then it starts filling right out. The *Oregano* x *marjoram* is quite hardy. A non-stop plot of this cross does well with just a few pine needles for shade. They fall from far above.

"The regular marjoram up here really struggles with the rains we have," he said. "It likes the fall and winter but not the wet summer."

Mexican tarragon was fading out. Culantro (not the same as cilantro) does well as a perennial that reseeds very easily and looks like a thistle. Cut off the blooms if you don't want the seed, but this is one of those plants that goes rapidly from vegetative to reproductive growth, and not much can stop the cycle. Culantro is growing in popularity here.

Vietnamese coriander (*Polygonum odoratum*) was a healthy looking mat. A new plant last spring, it had not yet bloomed, but usually does in the summer. This and culantro are perennial and have the same strong flavor, while cilantro is annual and milder in taste. True coriander or cilantro goes to seed all summer long but is great in winter and does not go dormant. It gets only a little leaf burn until plants fade out in late spring.

He gave me a taste of *Stevia rebaudiana*, which struggled for him in the rain and wet soil. It is native to Texas, Arizona, and South America. The leaves are as sweet as sticky buns with a delightful aftertaste. It has small leaves and tiny white daisy flowers and the one I brought home has stayed about the same since.

"Let it go dry," said Steele. "I expect it to be a perennial."

Lovage is a nice winter herb here. Parsley does very well. Sometimes it even blooms but it does not die down, just keeps on growing like a perennial.

Lemon grass grows with chickasaw plums and dogwood in the front bed. His cardamon grows only about 2 1/2 to 3 feet tall and he has never seen it bloom, but it makes a lovely ground cover under a tree.

"In the winter it will get ugly but will keep trying to grow. It will grow even farther north, but may go dormant. The leaves are very aromatic."

A licorice plant grew well for him, about 3 feet starting at the end of February, then died in the late summer rains. It was in a clay pot but sitting where there was too much clay underneath. Steele thinks it should work with better drainage.

Steele starts garlic bulbs in pots. If he plants them out in November, they make bulbs that he can braid by February. He grows pennyroyal and uses it as a tea rinse to keep fleas off of his dog. He has watercress, which resembles the pennyroyal, but the watercress leaves are larger and they taste different.

"I find that watercress grows better in a pot of soil than in water that isn't moving. It dies in standing water," he said, ending my lifelong search for a way to grow it.

Tansy thrives here in a roadside bed and sometimes blooms. It tends to get knocked back in the winter but revives in the spring. Some of his patches had trouble in the rain, but others did not mind, another reason to plant the same variety in several different places.

"Vitex or chaste tree grows very well and quickly here and has tons of fragrant lilac blossoms in July. The black berries can be used as a pepper substitute," says Steele.

Santolina does well here.

Germander is evergreen all year. In the fall it will have a little change of color and start growing more slowly. In winter it thins out and keeps the top leaves. In spring he'll cut off half of these and the whole plant will fill out. It blooms in late spring or early summer.

Silver mound artemisia does well here in the winter, but looks terrible in the summer.

He said, "Two months ago it really looked raggy. I'm trying a drier soil mix for plants like this."

His grapefruit sage, *Salvia dorisiana*, gets about 3 feet tall and has creamy yellow flowers in early summer. Mine has bright pink ones. Snails can be a problem.

Artemisia and Cleveland sage are hard to keep here in summer. The Cleveland survives but does not proliferate. True edible ginger does well. It goes dormant in the winter, also. Galangal (*Alpinia galanga*), with gingerlike leaves, grows even taller and has yellow buds and red flowers, a very pretty a pretty combination.

Evening primrose grows very well and blooms in late summer. Agastache goes dormant but comes back in spring.

He has a ginkgo tree but they are not common except up in the panhandle as an understory tree. They need shade when young. Rue does very well and blooms in midsummer. Eucalyptus is iffy. There are some large trees in Gainesville, but this is about the northern border for uncovered eucalyptus.

"False balm of Gilead is good for potpourris. It is not edible. It goes dormant but comes back," he said.

Purple sage is one of his biggest sellers. One pot had a thick carpet of Corsican mint at the base. "The mint will cascade over the sides by spring." The one I brought home spread amazingly.

In the greenhouse various lavenders were trying to resist a soil

fungus that causes rot. "It took me four years to find that resistant strain," he said as I added that plant to my collection.

Basils grow in the greenhouse in winter. The sensitive herbs huddle here out of the drenching rains in the summer. Seeds are started here, transplants conditioned, and orders segregated.

James Steele's *Herb Garden* and the people who work there give visitors a living demonstration of the many possibilities for use and enjoyment that herb plants can provide. They send people home with new information, thriving herb plants, and that wonderful I-can-grow-anything feeling.

O'TOOLE'S HERB FARM

Betty and Jim O'Toole own O'Toole's Herb Farm (P.O. Box 268, phone 904-973-3629) in Madison, Florida, about 20 miles from the Georgia border and just a bit farther north and east of Tallahassee. They sell largely wholesale to nurseries and grow culinary herbs for markets and restaurants. They have a small retail store, offer tours of their garden, and do several workshops each spring and fall.

"Summers are the most trying of times." writes Betty.

"We've found that several things like thyme do much better in raised beds. Our winters are relatively mild. We usually have a hard frost by early November, then temperatures will drop into the 20's, even the teens, but rapidly warm back up. This is hard on any plant, but still not as hard as August and September. We cannot grow basil after frost, even in greenhouses, due to lack of light, I guess. It just will barely stay alive. We cannot use grow lights because we are Certified Organic Growers.

"We plant most of the perennials in the fall, also lots of annuals that do well here in winter: dill, parsley, chervil, cilantro, marjoram..."

Lemon balm has bloomed for them in spring, also marjoram and many thymes, of which they recommend lemon thyme and creeping thyme. Rue has lovely foliage and blossoms and is a great butterfly attractor.

Wormwood 'Powis Castle' blooms in the fall. Elephant garlic does very well for them. They dig bulbs in June and July after bloom. Lovage does well in cool weather, but barely survives August. Costmary is a good evergreen that does especially well in winter. Patchouli does beautifully in warm weather but they take it into the greenhouses for winter. Santolina is lovely in winter, blooms nicely in spring, but hates August.

Other herbs on their list are Balm of Gilead, borage, caraway, germander, horehound, hyssop, lambs ears, salad burnet, French sorrel, southernwood, tansy, and three kinds of yarrow: 'The Pearl,' 'Parker's Gold,' and 'Summer Pastels.'

KANAPAHA BOTANICAL GARDENS: THE BIGGEST HERB GARDEN IN FLORIDA

The time to see the most in the herb garden at Kanapaha Botanical Gardens, in Gainesville, would be April or May. But the best time to come is whenever you can, as often as you can. It is one of the finest anywhere.

"Dr. Jordan Goodman, the wife of director Don Goodman, designed the herb garden, selected the plants, and did a great deal of work there," said my guide, Barbara Bennett, chief horticulturist. "She also researched the plant histories and compiled the labels and the booklet." A series of grants in the early '80s helped.

KANAPAHA'S HERB BOOKLET

The office and gift shop are cozy and warm with a potbellied stove in the center and the smell of wood smoke. The one thing you may want to buy there or at least look at before you go out to the gardens is a small booklet, *The Herb Garden of Kanapaha Botanical Gardens,* which lists all the plants that you will find there and the information that is contained on the labels.

In fact, this little 28 page booklet is so informative, especially about which plants are herbs and how they were used medicinally, that herb growers may want to write for a copy to use until they can make a visit: $4 will cover cost, tax, postage, and handling. Write to Kanapaha Botanical Gardens, 4625 SW 63rd Blvd., Gainesville, FL 32608, 904/372-4981.

The labels throughout the garden are excellent, easy to find and read, with several lines of information in addition to the plant name. They are perhaps the best I have seen in any garden.

"Over the years we have grown some 463 different herbs here," said Bennett. "The booklet tells about 280 of them. But lately we are settling for fewer but more dependable plants. We could grow almost any herb here at some time of the year if we had the time and help. We do the best we can."

"Mugwort, which gets much higher in the north, gets only about 12 inches tall here. This patch has already bloomed.

"That group of nasturtiums astonished me by living through the summer," she said. It was already blooming again in mid November.

The herb garden has three main features. The largest is the medicinal garden with its intricate design of small in-ground beds and old brick walks. A small mimosa tree (this species is used by the Chinese as a tonic and treatment for wounds, boils, and swellings) stands in the small circle in the center, bare by November, but with purslane still colorful at its feet. Around the outside edges of the design are shrub and tree herbs including:

-root beer plant, *Piper auritum*, which was used to treat stomach disorders as well as to flavor meat and tamales.

-Japanese raisin tree, *Hovenia dulcis*, whose fruits were used as a cooling diuretic, especially for treating drunkenness.

-Jerusalem cherry, *Solanum pseudocapsicum*, whose leaves and fruit were once used medicinally. However this plant can be toxic. I have one of these and find it great for watching birds that come to eat the orange berries, but did not realize it was a herb.

-Spanish bayonet, *Yucca aloifolia*, which has edible flowers. The roots were used by Native Americans for treating skin disorders. The leaves contain salicylic acid (as in aspirin) and were used for fever, pain relief, headache, and arthritis.

-Ti plant, *Cordyline terminalis*, whose sacred leaves were soaked in cold water and tied around the head to cure headaches.

-Loquat, *Eriobotrya japonica*, the tree with the delicious fruit and large leathery leaves. The latter were used for coughs, stomachache, nausea, ulcers, and nosebleed.

-Common camellia, *Camellia japonica*, was used medicinally in China. The seeds are the source of a non-drying hair oil. *Camellia*

sinensis, also growing in Kanapaha, is a commercial source of tea. I was amazed at the difference that traveling 130 miles north could make in the plants one could grow successfully. Some plants I had not seen in Florida before: witch hazel, mullein, devil's walking stick or *Aralia*, Solomon's seal, wall-flower, agrimony, soapwort, cardoon, sweet woodruff, licorice, linden tree or *Tilia*, burdock or *Arctium*, caraway, goutweed or *Aegopodium*, hawthorn, English daisy, wild indigo or *Baptisia*, winged sumac, and Jack-in-the-pulpit.

There were other plants I had seen often but did not know had herbal qualities: saw palmetto, Swedish ivy, kalanchoe, crape myrtle, figs, tapioca plant, Virginia creeper, winged elm, coontie, arborvitae or *Thuja*, asparagus, beauty-berry, beggar's tick (our weed *Bidens*), black-eyed Susan or *Rudbeckia*, coral and Japanese honeysuckle, bachelor buttons, cotton, daylily, candle plant or *Cassia alata*, English ivy, evening primrose, four-o'clocks, nandina, lily-of-the-nile or *Agapanthus*, luffa, oak leaf hydrangea, *Ophiopogon* or mondo grass, photinia, red clover, red maple, red mulberry, redbud, rose balsam, roselle, and sweetgum or *Liquidambar*.

Kanapaha grows true Queen Anne's lace; Barbara brings seed from North Carolina wildflowers every summer to start it over. It blooms in the spring, and by keeping some plants in the shaded nursery longer before setting them out, the staff prolongs its blooming season.

Many of the medicinal plants that were once used have not been researched in modern days. The booklet emphasizes: "This garden is not intended for prescribing medications, curing afflictions or replacing the services of a physician, but rather to provide evidence of the importance of these plants throughout history." The same can be said of this book.

Many of the plants are poisonous, as the chemicals which have pharmacological activity are also in many cases extremely toxic, making the plants dangerous for personal use.

Nevertheless, according to the Kanapaha herb book, in these modern times "the World Health Organization estimates that 75 to 90 percent of the world's rural population relies on herbalists for most of their medical care. Plants are the source of about 25% of all prescription drugs..."

The Knot Garden

The second section of the herb garden is an excellent example of a knot garden. The outside is a clipped hedge of dwarf holly about two feet high, not strictly a herb, but very effective in this situation. Inside, boxwood is used for making the loops of a bow and is clipped to a neat square ribbon about a foot high.

Berried nandina filled in some of the center with color. "We've tried marjoram and lavender and they were not reliable enough. We may try Texas sage next," said Bennett.

The Scented Garden

This smaller garden is made mainly of beds raised not just a little but waist high so you can smell without stooping. Many of the culinary herbs are included here: mints, sages, chervil, fennel, marjoram, coriander, anise, dill, thyme, lemon balm, perilla, basils, garlic chives, bay laurel and rosemarys. It also features wormwoods, southernwood, false Balm of Gilead, and curry leaf.

"We have trouble with hyssop, the savories, sages, marjoram, and thymes coming through the summer," said Bennett, making me feel better about my failures.

Other Features

During my two hour visit, I saw part of the butterfly garden at the entrance and the vinery and bamboo garden, but I had to forego seeing the water lily pond, cycad garden, palm hammock, carnivorous plant garden, fern cobble, rock garden, hummingbird garden, spring flower garden, sunken garden, and wildflower walk. There is a sales area and also picnic tables where school tours have lunch.

Information can be gotten and special group tours can be arranged by calling or writing to:

Kanapaha Botanical Gardens
4625 SW 63rd Blvd.
Gainesville, FL 32608

904-372-4981

Garden Tips from Kanapaha

*You don't have to tear out all of an invasive plant if it has qualities you like. They have controlled Black-eyed susan vine, bamboo, and false roselle, among others, with great effect.

*Just because a job is impossible doesn't mean it can't be done. What Kanapaha has done with only two full time people, a marvelous

core of volunteers, and community service help is quite astounding. Maybe we overwhelmed gardeners should recruit volunteers among our apartment-bound friends.

*Plant those vegetables which are herbs, like onions, garlic, peppers, mustard, and radishes, in the herb bed where they can be decorative for their leaves, textures, flowers, and seeds, and still harvested when ready.

*Mix herbs into other plantings to find more growing space.

*For beebalm that blooms, grow wild bergamot (*Monarda fistulosa*) and horsemint (*M. punctata*), instead of *M. didyma*, which has not bloomed here. They haven't had luck getting lemon mint started.

*Try *Plectranthus madagascariensis*, variegated. It is a low ground cover in Kanapaha. It has smaller leaves and a different scent from my Vick's salve plant, a similar *Plectranthus* which has not done well there.

*Use *Ophiopogon japonicum*, mondo grass, as an edging in the herb garden and as a ground cover under the trees. At Kanapaha it has made a vast, dark green carpet only a few inches tall.

7. Growing Herbs and Spices in Central Florida

Growers here, of whom I am one, deal with a climate that is betwixt and between. Sometimes it is too warm and humid, sometimes too cold. But, like my fruit growing friend Al Hendry, look on the bright side. He says, "Some years it stays warm and some things do better and other don't. Other years it gets cold and we lose a few tropical plants, but the cold lovers thrive. Either way, we always have something."

You can get around half of this problem, cold, by planting only the hardier herbs. There are plenty. But most of us like the challenge of trying the tropicals and spices like Cuban oregano, allspice, and even cinnamon, and we either protect them with covers or bring them inside in containers when frost comes.

You can get around the summer slump also by planting only the tough summer survivors, but most of us nurture a few of the more difficult herbs, such as the lavenders and thymes, finding ways to keep them going. Or else we just start them over again when it cools down in the fall, and still enjoy a good eight to nine months of lush growth from them.

The soil is easy to work with here but usually needs additional organic matter. Most of us have either gray or black sand, or, near water, a richer muck soil.

LORETTA CLEMENTS' HERB GARDEN PROVES THE POSSIBILITIES

Herb growers of Central Florida, raise your expectations! In summer, thyme can not only survive but can thrive and bloom. So can lavender and yarrow. Sorrel and sage can come through. Basil can bloom and spread. Once summer is past, there is a nine-month growing season that can make a herb garden here at least as lovely and doubly as productive as most throughout the country.

Loretta Clements of Brandon (near Tampa) readily admits that growing herbs can be a challenge here, but she has an ambitious new herb garden that proves the possibilities and is only just beginning. A pretty, perky, ladylike person, she has a suprisingly adventurous approach to designing and creating a herb garden.

After raising herbs in her regular gardens for years, in January of 1993 she built herself a formal herb garden that extends across most of the back of her yard, approximately 20 ft. x 60 ft. It is in full sun, summer and winter. Herbs surround the bird bath in the center and fill the central beds completely. Vegetables sneak in at one end and flowers at the other, with shrubs and trees in the background and a low white fence at the front.

"I had a man with a small tractor come in here and take off the sod before I started," she explains. "It wasn't easy for him to get to the area and I thought some of my shrubs were ruined by the tracks he had to make. Finally he tied all the shrubs tightly together to get by them." But the shrubs survived and the job got done.

Could Anyone Build Beds Like Loretta's? Perhaps anyone (even I) could lay out the beds the way Loretta has done hers. She simply laid landscape timbers, available at any builder's supply store, around the beds. She cut the ends to shape with an electric saw. They meet only at the inner edge of some rounded ends, but they look fine and do their job. She put "staubs," little stakes, 2 by 8 inches, on alternate sides to keep the timbers in place. The staubs hardly show. You can buy them when and where you get the timbers.

"Instead of timbers, a person could use bricks, stones, edging, or anything that will elevate the beds at least four inches," Loretta Clements says.

She spread five yards of peat moss, delivered by truck to the front driveway and hauled by wheelbarrow with her daughter's help. Then she dug this about 8 inches deep into her sandy soil. The paths are mulched with wood chips. We walked around the garden within half an hour after a heavy storm and hardly noticed the dampness, so good is the drainage.

"Most herbs will survive in very poor soil but they will not give you the nice healthy growth you want if they are struggling," she says. She suggests that people clear their soil, spread at least an inch or more of peat and/or compost, and dig this in. Drainage is essential. But if soil does not drain, raised beds usually solve the problem. It is best not to use creosoted wood.

"The space you select does not have to be large," she said. "A 4 by 8 foot spot will provide you with room for 16 to 20 plants. A container garden is very rewarding if you live in an apartment. Strawberry jars, half whisky barrels, large clay pots or their plastic lookalikes, wooden soft drink carriers, and other sizeable containers are good choices for container gardening."

She recommends planning on paper with height, color combinations, and a framework of perennials in mind. Then fill in with annuals and biennials. "By replacing the annuals as they complete their life cycle, you keep your garden looking well groomed and can try new plants all year long, as well as have a constant supply of fresh herbs."

CAREFUL SOIL PREPARATION AND SEEDING
"Leave the bed alone for a few weeks for all the microorganisms to

work away before planting. I also highly recommend having the County Extension Office test a sample of soil taken from several places in the garden. Most of Brandon's soil is slightly alkaline. I have mine tested at least once a year and follow instructions for amending," she says.

Loretta keeps her seeds in a cool dry place in the air conditioned house, and some packets stay viable for several years. Other growers keep seeds in packets or coffee cans in the freezer.

Loretta's herb garden is a year-round project, but she gets a new start in late September or early October, depending upon when the heat and rain let up.

She sows seeds directly in the soil for calendula and alyssum and they germinate quickly for an almost instant garden. She also sows basil, dill, marjoram, oregano, sage, savory, and borage directly. Sometimes she manages to transplant borage, but she finds it does better if sown in place. Planted in fall, it will bloom until late spring.

When she plants in the ground, she just barely covers seeds. "They don't want a blanket, they only need a sheet in Florida," she says. "I just sprinkle a little soil over them and pat the soil down to firm out the air spaces." She waters with a watering can so she doesn't wash them away, and always labels them.

SOME HERBS ARE BEST STARTED IN POTS

She buys parsley or grows it in pots. She finds anise, caraway, and fennel easy to grow from seed.

She plants many seeds in pots, transplants them to larger pots, and puts them into the garden when they are about 4 or 5 inches high after hardening off.

"I'm not a carpenter by any means, but I built myself a potting shed last year." It has lath sides, a corrugated vinyl roof to let in some sunlight, hooks and shelves in one corner for pots and tools, and benches to hold pots with young plants and trays of vermiculite with rooting cuttings. It is quite decorative from outside and wonderfully functional and no carpenter could have done a better job. I, who had never considered such building a personal possibility, was awestruck even at the attempt, but even more so at the results.

When transplanting, Loretta thoroughly waters the potted plants an hour before moving them. When she turns a plant out of the pot, she breaks off or tears apart outside roots if they are matted. This exposes more area to take in nutrients and grow out from the planting hole. She digs her hole two to three inches larger than the plant root system.

"Pat the bottom of the hole firm so your plant won't slip down further below the planting line or this could cause root rot," she advises. Then she fills the hole with water to which she has added fertilizer at one fourth the recommended strength and lets it drain down, then sets in the plant, fills in the soil, and does not water any more at that time. New plants usually need watering every day unless it rains.

LORETTA CLEMENTS' HERB COMPANIONS

BENEFICIAL PARTNERS
Coriander: plant with anise but not with dill
Rosemary: plant with sage
Basil: plant with tomatoes but not with rue
Marjoram and oregano: good with most herbs,
    plant throughout the garden
Sage: plant with rosemary or carrots but not
    near cucumbers

HERBS THAT HELP WITH INSECT CONTROL
For aphids: chives, coriander, anise, lavender
    pennyroyal, spearmint
For ants: pennyroyal, peppermint, spearmint, tansy
For bean beetles: rosemary
For black flea beetles wormwood
For flies: basil, tansy, nicandra
For tomato worm: borage
For plant lice: pennyroyal
For mosquitoes: pennyroyal

"Watch the weather," she says, "and water deeply enough so the water gets down to the roots."

Sometimes she cuts a clump of plants like chives in half, one for her garden and one to give away. But she prefers to grow her plants in the ground rather than in pots after their infant stage. She finds that they do better for her that way, even thymes over the summer. Watering is less critical in the ground.

In dry times all her plants get watered as needed, from every other day to twice a week, but only after she digs down and checks how the soil feels. She has soaker hoses in some of her beds, but she hasn't yet decided whether she likes hand watering or soaker hoses the best.

"Don't get plants too close together," she warns, "or they won't develop as well. They need good air circulation to avoid dis-ease. This also lets you enjoy the beauty of each individual plant."

**PEST PROTECTION
IS CRUCIAL**

Loretta encourages natural predators to move into her garden and patrol for pests. She keeps the birdbath clean and filled with fresh water. The birds won't let mosquitoes breed there. She has at least two toad houses made from overturned, broken pots that are as decorative as they are useful.

She often puts four toothpicks around a single-stemmed herb to foil the cutworms.

"Bat houses are good in herb gardens," she says. "Bats will eat more than their weight in bugs every night."

She sprays the plants after planting with soapy water. After that, whenever she notices any sign of insects or their damage, or otherwise at intervals of about two weeks, she again sprays plants in both garden and potting shed. In order to to cover the life cycle of as many harmful insects as possible and get a more complete kill, she sprays once a day for three days straight.

She had been using two tablespoons of dishwashing soap to a gallon of water, but when another grower told her that she used four tablespoons, Loretta decided to double the strength of her attacks.

Bt *(Bacillis thuringiensis)* or any product containing this natural insecticide will kill any insects in the worm stage safely. If something stronger is needed, she uses Sevin dust.

Loretta banks sensitive herbs through the frost-warning weeks with white sand to a depth of 4 ot 6 inches. This way, if the tops die down, the plant will come back again in the spring. She does not use cypress mulch.

EVERY HERB GARDEN IS UNIQUE

Loretta planted her favorite herb plants just last January in this garden. Every herb garden will be different according to what the grower wants: herbs for cooking, for crafts and bouquets, dyes, or potpourris. Just about anything that you can grow in the spring, you can grow in the fall also in this area. Herbs make tremendous growth before summer sets some of them back.

Yes, a few die over summer even for her, but very few. She is leaving the dried stems of one Lady Lavender in place in hopes that it will send up new growth from the roots when spring gives the signal.

"Every spring I treat myself to two plants of true tarragon that I order from Sandy Mush Herb Farm.

I guess it's because I like to suffer. By midsummer they are long gone. They can't take the high heat and humidity but yet they need the sun. Just buy them and let them tease you and then let them die," she said.

This year in late October there is some new growth coming back from the base of one of those tarragons.

"Spring is when I get the creative juices going and like to try new things," says Loretta. "I keep planting through February. I will cut back some of the fall planted herbs in late February or early March." She especially likes sage for stuffing the Thanksgiving turkey and a chocolate mint that she cuts up to use in her chocolate chip Christmas cookies.

She recommends that everyone have a container of the plants they want to use a lot either on the kitchen window sill or porch or by the back door, where they are easy to reach.

Weeding is very important. It takes seven years to get out all the weeds that will germinate if you let one go to seed.

Loretta stresses that using the herbs often is an important factor in herb gardening. "Select recipes that use herbs, make potpourris, put together flower arrangements, or simply dry herbs to replenish your supply," she says. "The more you use them the more they will grow."

SOME OF THE HERBS GROWN BY LORETTA CLEMENTS

Artemisia, southernwood,
   wormwood, silver kind,
   for potpourri
Basil, she uses purples
   to make vinegar pink
Calendula
Catnip
Chives
Cilantro
Clary sage
Coneflowers
Culantro
Digitalis, one species has
   grown and bloomed for
   her for years
Dill
Garlic and elephant garlic
   have made bulbs
   but had no blossoms.
Lavenders, several kinds
Lemon verbena, protect from
   wind, which can
   defoliate plants
Lovage
Marjoram, grows as an annual
   and blooms
Mints
Monarda, lemon mint
Myrtles
Nasturtiums
Orris root, grew well
   through the summer
Parsley, curled and Italian
Patchouli
Rosemarys
Salvias
Santolina
Savory
Sorrel
Sweet cicely
Thymes, several bloomed
   through summer
Tansy
Tarragon, French or true
Tarragon, false (*Tagetes
lucida*), a southern
perennial she uses in
vinegars and on chicken
Violas, pansies, johnny-
   jump-ups
Yarrow, several kinds and
   colors

HERB GARDENS AT THE UNIVERSITY OF SOUTHERN FLORIDA

Tampa is a busy place. The University of Southern Florida (USF) is one of its busiest hubs. But except for the days of special sales, the USF Botanical Gardens are a place of serenity, peace, and all-but seclusion. If you meet others, you are free to pass silently, though the pull of kindred spirits often leads to easy conversation or comment on some plant's amazing behavior. Visitors can drive right into the greenhouse area and park among a few other cars, as a rule.

There is a mailbox to the left of the greenhouse clearly marked with trail maps inside. And one of the first features beyond it, not a stone's throw from the parking area, is the fine, new herb garden completed in 1994.

It started small but is well designed with four five-sided beds of neat and thriving herbs at each corner and paths of hexagonal bricks. The center bed is raised enough to sit on its edges and has a sundial for a focal point. Scented geraniums of four different kinds and prostrate rosemary surround the base of the sundial and emit wonderful fragrances when brushed or rubbed.

THE TAMPA UNIT OF THE HERB SOCIETY OF AMERICA

"This is a culinary garden," says Peggy Davis, president of the Tampa Unit of the Herb Society of America, whose members are responsible for the new addition to the USF herb garden. "We hope in the future, with the help of the university, to do additional gardens. We're planning on a fragrance garden, an antique rose garden, and a dye garden. It's an ongoing project.

The Tampa group is the only Florida unit of the Herb Society of America and its members are dedicated. They meet, often at the garden, every second Saturday of the month except July from 10 am until noon. There are at least two meetings a year open to the public and members can bring guests to any meeting.

To join, one must commit to 30 hours of volunteer service to the community a year, attend at least 8 of the 11 meetings, and be willing to hold office. It is not a group for the faint of heart, though Loretta Clements says the hours are easily and happily spent with normal contributions to meetings and workshops. She manages fine in spite of her full time job and work in her own garden.

Herb growers can benefit from the group's work even if they cannot presently make the commitment required for membership.

Besides this new demonstration garden, the Tampa Herb Society sponsored an excellent all day workshop last October that promises to be an annual event. Most of the 80 people who attended plan to go back, because workshops came in groups of three and it was wrenching to go to only one. Peggy Davis gave an entertaining talk on the folklore of herbs.

She told how rosemary was used for both weddings and funerals, how juniper was planted at the door because a witch would have to count every needle on the tree before she could enter, how royal herb strewers in England spread bushels of petals and herbs and were only stopped in the reign of the present Queen Elizabeth II. Other folklore she related: lavender is said to kill tuberculosis germs in 12 hours and was burned in French hospitals during the war. If you put a sprig of mugwort in your shoe, you are supposed to be able to walk 40 miles before noon and not be tired.

Some of the herbal tales, of course, are farfetched. Others contain enough truth for drug companies to be

very interested in herbs and use them in many prescription medicines.

The Tampa unit of the herb society is dedicated to research and education about herbs, and achieves their goals admirably at USF. The plants in the garden are well labeled with common and botanical names, whether they are perennial, biennial, or annual, and their uses, origins, and plant family. You can touch and see the herbs and spices, learning to recognize them as they develop, grow, bloom, or fade as the seasons progress.

By visiting often, you can watch how cold, hot, dry, and wet periods affect some herbs drastically and others hardly at all. I saw that the sweet marjoram label marked a missing plant and felt better about some of mine that disappear. But the Italian oregano, *Origanum* x *marjoram*, was growing lushly. Cinnamon basil was thriving and blooming in mid-December. I want to watch how the cold affects that variety that seems so much hardier than most.

There is a bench beside the herb garden, handy for dropping a purse or bag so both hands will be free to touch the herbs gently and write down names to remember. It is a pleasant place to stop and rest peacefully for a moment in a beautiful setting.

USF gardens, in Tampa, are open from 8 to 5 on Mondays through Fridays, from 8 to 1 on Saturday. Admission is free. Guided tours are available for clubs and groups that call ahead. The entrance to the garden is marked and most easily reached from Bruce B. Downs Boulevard just north of Fowler Avenue, where you turn east

or right on Pine Avenue. The entrance is on the corner of Pine and Alumni Drive.

The plant sales in spring, fall, and December are crowded events and great fun. Various plant societies bring in a great array of plants, most not available in ordinary nurseries. Volunteers in golf carts will help you bring your purchases to the parking area. Some people come with garden carts and wheelbarrows strapped to the top of their vans. There is a smaller but still very choice and unusual selection at the greenhouse every Saturday morning, without the crowd. If you are looking for some unusual plant, they may be able to find it for you even if they don't have it at the time.

Call 813-974-2329 for exact and additional hours, to arrange tours, or for further information.

8. Growing Herbs and Spices in Southern Florida

In southern Florida (S), it rarely freezes. Sunshine tends to be constant and intense, a bonus during all but summer months, when shade is welcome for some herbs and spices, although unnecessary for others. Summers are steamy with frequent heavy rain and high humidity.

Soils here vary dramatically. Most are sandy, gray and black flatwoods soil over lime materials. Some are so thin over rock so hard that an auger is needed to dig holes for planting trees and shrubs. Muck and peat pockets are found mostly inland in a few narrow bands in the eastern counties. Then consider the swamps of the everglades and the dry sand of the keys, and you see why your garden may have unique needs that differ from other gardens not far away.

Wind protection can be very important, especially near the coasts. Irrigation is necessary through the dry months of fall, "winter," and spring while some plants may survive the summer only if they can be protected from the heavy rains.

Growers in this area have serious summer problems, especially with lavender, thyme, and other herbs from the dry Mediterranean area. They have more herbs to add to the list of those that are difficult in Florida, and must wait longer for their herbs to recover lush growth in the fall, because cooler weather comes so late in the year.

Summer problems can be partly alleviated by planting herbs under light shade. Fortunately there are temporary shade plants such as pigeon peas which are allowed to grow through the summer and then are pruned down or pulled out for winter. You can also move container-grown plants around to grow in or provide shade beneath, as needed. Don't forget to put the herbs back into more sun gradually in the fall.

Frost-tender, heat-loving spices that must be coddled as shrubs in C will grow to be trees here, and a wider variety of them can be grown. When that occasional frost or freeze comes along, these tender plants are more likely to die back only to their roots and then recover, instead of dying out entirely.

MOUNTS BOTANICAL GARDEN

A great demonstration garden for South Florida herbs can be found at Mounts Botanical Garden in Palm Beach. It is easy for travelers to find at number 531 on the east side of Military Trail. This main north/south road runs about three miles from both I-95 and the Florida Turnpike. Get off the Interstate at Exit 53 or the Turnpike at Exit 99 and go south on Military Trail.

Mounts is right across the road from the Palm Beach International Airport with planes almost in the treetops adding to the interest.

The garden is open Monday through Saturday from 8:30 a.m. to 5 p.m (closed holidays) and Sunday from 1 to 5. There is no admission charge. At present, guided tours start every Saturday at 11 a.m. and Sunday at 2:30 p.m. (Call ahead to check.) Call 407-233-1749 for information or to arrange special tours for groups of ten or more.

There are over 14 acres here, always changing, large enough to spend a day if you want, but small enough to see a great deal in a quick walk. It's a nice place for a lunch stop, even if you have come with a non-gardening group.

There is a wide paved path leading near enough to all the plantings for wheelchair or stroller traffic (bring your own wheels). Parking lots are ample in front, back, or along the side.

Mounts Garden was developed and continues under a program of the Palm Beach County Cooperative Extension service to foster plant appreciation and provide a center for teaching, display, conservation, and research. It was started in 1954 by Marvin "Red" Mounts, then the county agricultural extension agent.

Now Gene Joyner holds that title and the garden is widely known as Gene Joyner's place, but is not to be confused with Joyner's private collections at his home nearby. He somehow found time to give a private tour of Mounts to my friend Betty Mackey and me as we searched for great herbs for South Florida in January.

THE HERB GARDEN AT MOUNTS

Roses and fruit, shady paths, and flowering trees greet you at the gate. But not far along the main trail is the herb garden where you'll want to stop, study the labels, rub the leaves, and sniff. This large garden was designed and is maintained by two very active groups from the area, the Morning and the Evening Herb society.

The raised beds are made of molded concrete with sides high enough to sit on. The four beds in the center are labelled according to

the uses for the herbs within: tea, culinary, folklore, and potpourri. Behind the potpourri garden, around the outer edges, are dye plants. Behind the folk healing garden are insect repelling herbs.

A great thing about such a public garden is that you can visit at various times of the year and study the herbs that thrive in the area in their different stages of growth. If you are visiting from elsewhere, Mounts is well worth the stop. Many of the plants are the familiar ones we raise statewide, but they tend to look and act somewhat differently in each setting. The spices grow larger or taller than they do farther north, and more of them will thrive, either with or without protection.

star anise

A hedge of star anise protects the garden on the west and east sides from winter winds and summer sun This plant adds a licorice taste to recipes. Leaves and fruits are good in potpourris. It can eventually grow to 20 feet in this zone (compared to about 3 feet tall after several years in C), but they keep it cut down to about 6 feet. This will take some but not an unmanageable amount of pruning in the future.

The beds are watered with drip irrigation, which means that an emitter must be cleaned now and again. But for the most part, the plants get the amount of water they need with only periodic readjustment of the timer. They use no bug spray, for this is a garden to touch, taste, and smell.

Here, as in all of Florida, lavender and the herbs that like it dry suffer in the humid summer. In S, rosemary and scented geraniums have to be added to the list of herbs with this problem. The solution at Mounts is to grow them in a light soil mix containing plenty of perlite.

Mounts used to have 27 different scented geraniums, but fungus presented a major headache. Of course, in the winter, when I saw it, even the lavender looked great and one plant was two feet tall. And James Steele's protective mulch might well make a difference even here (See chapter 6, page 103)

In spite of summer problems, several herb growers in the West Palm herbal societies report using rosemary as an ornamental hedge, and one has a rosemary "tree" that is as tall as she is.

Among the rare plants to be seen here is a Jamaican mint bush, *Micromeria viminea*. This also grows at Kanapaha Gardens in the N., similar to but not quite the same in leaf or in size as the Costa Rican mint, 4 foot tall and wide, nearby. Labels here contain only common names so far.

Tilo (*Justicia pectoralis*, related, though no one would guess, to the shrimp and flamingo plants) was clinging to the ground, but sending up shoots of tiny purple flowers as if it could not help itself. It looked much like Vietnamese coriander to us until we found that label nearby and saw the differences.

We had already seen Brazilian lettuce in Marian Van Atta's garden in central Florida. It is thriving here.

The allspice (*Pimenta officinalis*), a small evergreen with glossy, leathery, aromatic foliage, was placed in the center of the garden and makes a fine focal point. It is surrounded with colorful nasturtiums in the spring and purslane in the summer.

Several other spice trees grew nearby: big and littleleaf curry (*Murraya* species), cinnamon (*Cinnamomum zeylanicum*), with its unique banded pattern of veins, and bay rum (*Pimenta acris*), used for perfume in the Caribbean, surround the herb garden.

When asked about his own favorite herbs, Gene Joyner replied, "I like the basils because there are so many of them. I've grown 12 to 15 different kinds with odd flavors, lemon, anise, licorice and different shapes and colors."

He also described the various teas with a chuckle. "So many herbs are said to be good for tea, but no one mentions that only a few people might want to drink the tea." Apparently they've had gatherings where the other extension agents sampled herbal teas and found rosemary, for instance, quite "yukky" but other teas like lemon mint were excellent. However, those who want the properties of the less pleasant tasting herbs soon learn to mix them with lemon, honey, or other herb or fruit flavors.

HERBS GROWING AT MOUNTS IN WINTER

POTPOURRI OR CRAFT GARDEN
Patchouli, blooming
Lavender-scented
    geraniums
Lemon mint
Lemon basil,
    blooming
Pennyroyal
Rose geranium
Jamaican mint bush
Pineapple sage,
    blooming
Orange mint
Fennel
Thyme
Tansy
Tagetes 'tarragon,'
    blooming
Oregano
Lemon balm
Garlic chives

CULINARY GARDEN
Dianthus, blooming
Spicy globe basil
Bronze fennel
Parsley
Calendula, blooming
Cuban oregano
Sage
Thyme
Nasturtium, blooming
Chives
Purple basil
Ruffled basil
Tagetes 'tarragon'
Arugula
Vietnamese coriander
Sorrel

FOLKLORE GARDEN
Lavender
Sorrel
Calendula,
    blooming
Anise hyssop
Sweet basil
Chamomile
Aloe
Rosemary

TEA GARDEN
Many of the culinary
    herbs, plus
Catnip
Spearmint
Tilo, blooming

ADDITIONAL HERBS IN EDGING BEDS
Peppers
Porter bush, blue and
    pink
Comfrey
Pandanus
Dill
Horseradish
Fennel
Iboza, bush about to
    bloom
Star anise
African blue basil
Rose, blooming
Borage
Henna
Cinnamon basil
Citronella grass
Lemon grass
Salad burnet

INSECT REPELLENT HERB GARDEN
Artemisia
Bay
Eucalyptus
Feverfew
Garlic
Ibosa riparia, African
    Moth Plant
Lavender
Lemon balm
Pennyroyal
Sage
Southernwood
Tansy
Thyme
Wormwood

DYE-MAKING HERB GARDEN
Barberry
Betony
Chamomile
Comfrey
Dandelion
Elderberry
Fennel
Feverfew
Goldenrod
Henna
Marigold
Marjoram
Onion
Pokeweed
Rosemary
Tansy

The Mounts herb garden is in almost full sun. Plans are afoot to extend it across the path with an area of equal size that will include overhead latticework for shade and many hanging baskets.

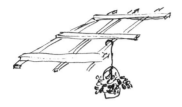

OTHER FEATURES

Near the herb garden, Mounts has a display garden featuring 40 kinds of poisonous plants, some that give people rashes to touch and some that can kill if people eat them. It included one of my favorite plants, *Datura*, known as angel's trumpet or jimsonweed. It has large, fuzzy, some-what coarse gray green leaves and prickly egg-sized seed capsules, but exquisite long-throated lilylike fragrant flowers.

The plants in this garden, at varying degrees of toxicity and in great variety, give people a more realistic outlook on the idea of poisonous plants (many of which are important herbs). I have always found that most children over a few years old can be shown toxic plants and given common sense warnings, and will be impressed enough to leave them alone.

The walk crosses over a bridge to an island of flowering trees that were not then in flower. They included the jacaranda and the floss silk trees that bloom in spring and fall. Only a white shaving brush (*Bombax ellipticum*) was blooming in January, with a pink one to follow soon. Tabebuias will

be blooming by April and the red royal poinciana will bloom in June. While Joyner named them, I was hoping to come back again and again to see the blooms reflected in little Lake Orth.

Tropical vegetables. To this former farmer who used to think of gardens, before I moved to Florida, as rows of vegetables to feed a big family of hearty eaters, the tropical vegetable plot at Mounts was fascinating. Most of the plants were vines growing up arbors, but they can be adapted to long expanses of privacy fence with proper support to get them started on their climb. I am ready to try, or try again with jicama, luffa, winged beans, tropical yams, and red lima beans. There was a thriving patch of malanga and a fruiting narangilla that can be used for a drink, and water chestnuts thriving in the muck of sunken wading pools.

Ornamentals. Another garden of flowers is an official All America Display and Research Garden. This will vary greatly at different times of the year. January is probably its least colorful time, but we found new salvias, a Philippine violet, and a Jamaican croton to add to our wish lists. Local nurserymen are encouraged to grow plants that do well in these trials. Different Florida lawn grasses in 18 separate trial plots grow close enough for comparison.

All plants in Mounts are well labeled with color coding so you can tell at a glance if a tree is mainly for fruit, shade, or flower, or if a herbaceous plant is for ornamental or edible purposes.

For a list of events and speakers here or more information, write or call:

> Mounts Botanical Garden
> 531 North Military Trail
> West Palm beach, Fl 33415
> 407-233-1749.

HERBS IN JUPITER FARMS

In nearby Jupiter Farms, Janice DiPaola grows over 100 varieties of herbs at her nursery, *Full Moon Over Florida*, and specializes in topiary.

She and other professional herb growers have a wealth of experience with a wider variety of herbs than most home growers will ever try. You can be sure that those they grow commercially are reliable for the climate.

Here is the list of herbs she grows and sells. I find lists like this a great resource for checking on what grows where. If a plant is missing, it probably means that it is not a good risk in this region. If it is included, success is not only possible but probable, because nurseries cannot afford to bother with borderline plants.

Herbs Grown at
Full Moon Over Florida

anise hyssop
arugula
Australian violet
Aztec sweet shrub (*Lippia dulcis*)
balm of Gilead
basil, many forms
bedstraw
betony
borage
burdock
burnet
calendula
caraway
catnip
camomile
chives
cilantro
comfrey
coneflower (*Echinacea purpurea*)
coriander
cumin
dill
epazote
eucalyptus, silver dollar
fennel
feverfew
germander
gotu kola
henna
hyssop
lavender
lemon balm
lemon grass
lemon verbena
marjoram, sweet
mint, American, Corsican,
orange,and lemon
mojean tea
mugwort
nasturtium
parsley
patchouli
pennyroyal
peppers, chile, several types
primrose, evening
Queen Anne's lace

rosemary
sage, many types
sesame
soapwort
sorrel
stevia
tansy
thyme, several types
valerian
vervain
vetiver
vidalia onion
yarrow

She recommends:
caraway
cardamon, part shade, slow grower
chamomile, easy in full sun
costmary
dittany of Crete, nice in a hanging
    basket
gotu kola, grows in pots, shade,
    prone to spider mites
lemon balm, easy from seed, likes
    shade
marjoram, easy in full sun
mojean tea herb, native of Jamacia,
    full sun, perennial, stir tea
    with a stem for vanilla flavor
patchouli, grows like a weed in
    shade, keep moist
rue, blooms here, beware of skin
    problems
santolina, lives 2 to 3 years, keep
    head dry, grow in full sun
sesame, lovely, blooms November
stevia, similar to sweet Aztec herb,
    fast growing, ground cover or
    hanging basket, leaves are
    very sweet
sweet woodruff, grow in shade,
    lives 1 to 2 years
thyme, from cuttings, full sun, run
    dry, blooms spring

Some that failed for her after
several tries are foxglove, lovage,
orris root, and sweet cicely.

ECHO

Across the state in Fort Myers
is ECHO, the small farm where
Educational Concerns For Hunger
Organization develops its food growing methods and trains missionaries
and others who work with people in
Third World countries. Don't miss a
tour of this facility if you are anywhere nearby (see Places to Visit at
the end of this book)

They also have a nursery with
the following herbs for sale as well
as a seed list.

Herbs available at ECHO
butterfly pea
caraway
chervil
cotton
curry plant
ginger
Mexican tarragon (Mexican mint)
oregano substitutes
papyrus
quail grass
roselle
scented geraniums
society garlic
thyralis
vanilla orchid
vicks salve plant
Vietnamese balm
Vietnamese coriander

"THE MOST EXPENSIVE HERB GARDEN IN THE WORLD"

"Aren't you tired yet?" asked one of the volunteer workers at Mounts Botanical Garden. He was older than we were and going strong, but he figured a few hours of trailing Gene Joyner should have done us in long ago.

Betty and I went back over much of the gardens, read more labels, wrote more notes, and took more pictures. Then we brought our fruit from the car, bananas from my yard, grapefruit Marian Van Atta had given us. We shared the bananas with a group of school children who had never tasted anything like our small but extra sweet homegrown bananas, who took the grapefruit seeds home to plant, and who thanked us with hugs. And then, suddenly, we were tired.

"Should we go to the Grand Hotel?" we asked each other. Joyner had recommended it. "Or should we just head for home." We ignored the vote of old bones and decided it would be a shame to miss the Grand Hotel, "since we've come all this way."

We drove east on Southern Boulevard as far as we could go and then turned south. In the early afternoon, even in January, the traffic was not heavy. We drove among the beautiful homes and yards and took in the plantings with the appreciation of gardeners.

Before we knew it, we were pulling into the driveway of the Four Seasons Ocean Grand Hotel. Well, actually we drove by it at first, but we turned around at the next light and came back. Betty was still ready to leave when she saw the valet parking, but I drove left to the lot where the staff must park. I'd already had a glimpse of

the garden. Suddenly we weren't tired anymore.

The Chef's Herb and Citrus Garden is just inside the gate to the left and well labeled, so you don't need a guide to enjoy it. It seems small at first, but has an impact that is irresistible. Neither of us had ever seen a more colorful herb garden. The focal feature is a series of three raised, tiered beds. The first had pansies blooming at the base in many colors with coreopsis at the top along with a cascading carpet of purple alyssum. The middle tier featured a densely growing herb with uniform spires of lavender-purple, above a sign saying *Chef's Herb and Citrus Garden*, edged in almost matching lavender.

We got out cameras and notebooks and went to work.

"Look, this alyssum is mixed with Australian violet," I was thrilled to recognize one of my newest discoveries, *Viola hedera*, a violet that blooms all year in Florida with round, dark green leaves that spread by runners and delicate white violets stripped with purple. The alyssum dominated colorwise, but both seemed to be thriving.

We'd been told of this garden by several herb growers in the area and given location instructions by Gene Joyner. "Everything is well marked," we'd been assured. "You can enjoy it even if Chef Hubert is not available." And we did.

First we rushed from plant to tree to flower. Most of the garden is heavily mulched with wood chips, but under and around the trees were herbs as groundcovers: mints, oregano, culantro, nasturtiums. Fruit trees and shrubs were mostly labeled. I saw my first mamey sapote with both fruit and flowers. The garden was in excellent condition, but some work must have been in progress, for many labels were gathered on the ground instead of on the plants.

We recognized most of the herbs and trees, but there were a few that stumped us still. We studied every plant and every planting situation attentively.

"I have a tripod in the trunk," I remembered. "Get it," Betty said, "This is surely a garden worth the extra effort."

Finally we decided that there were at least two healthy clumps of herbs we couldn't name and had to know, so I gave Betty the tripod and hurried into the hotel to ask if Chef Hubert or the sous chef might have a minute to talk to us. The concierge put in a call, and I relaxed in the sumptuous lobby while I waited. Then a young man in a chef's hat came out and walked with me back to the garden. It had been sunny when I went inside, but it started to rain just as we came out. Chef Hubert didn't seem to mind, so neither did I.

Chef Hubert Des Marais apologized for the garden, which we considered about perfect except for the missing labels. Herb gardens in Florida are hardly ever totally in peak form, since year round growing has such a variety of challenges, especially in southern Florida.

"The garden has its ups and downs," he said. "But the food is always 100 percent. I use all these herbs either for flavoring or for garnish. That one? It's beebalm or *Monarda*."

We didn't know it would grow in Florida, let alone South Florida, and we still don't know if it will bloom, because he has been keeping it cut off for the three months or more it has been thriving there. The other mystery herb was a Japanese parsley with variegated, ivy-size leaves.

He had a pandanus which he uses with poultry. It is of the same genus as the screwpine and will eventually grow into a tree, but it grows very slowly. I've seen three of them now in herb gardens, and none was taller than 4 feet, although the screw pines at the Marie Selby Botanical Gardens in Sarasota are 12-foot trees.

Chef Hubert showed us his purple-leaved sweet potato, which was growing as a groundcover. He uses the leaves as a garnish or like spinach, and also cooks the fleshy root when it matures.

"This is probably the most expensive herb garden in the world," he said. "We've moved the trees around a few times. And those timbers in the raised beds came from Home Depot, but they are the best kind."

The hotel spares no expense on the material or the work. Chef Hubert planned the garden and oversees it, but there is a gardener who keeps it up. It runs about 100 feet long by 40 or 50 feet wide from the front gate to the tennis courts.

"We're far enough from the ocean [it is on the other side of the hotel] not to have salt problems but close enough to enjoy the frost protection." There was some wind protection, as well, which is important, for winds tend to be severe on the beaches but were calm in the garden.

"One of the best things here is the drip irrigation system," he said. "We can regulate it to supply all the water needs of the plants without stress."

The garden is about five years old. The rain and sun played tag while he proudly showed us every plant and answered all our questions. We almost forgot to ask about the purple spires: they were anise hyssop in full bloom, pruned to perfection. They (and Chef Hubert) are pictured on the cover of this book.

Chef Hubert is also a member of the Rare Fruit Council International. He has even more herbs and fruit as well as orchids in his home garden.

It was easy to see he loved his work. Months later we learned that

he had been named one of the country's ten best chefs (Food and Wine Magazine).

"We're breaking in a new menu tonight and I have to get back inside," he finally said. The hotel has a main dining room that is open only in the evening. But there is a Bistro open all day. It didn't take us long to decide we needed some dessert.

The chef took us in through the kitchen and showed us some of the working area. Then he sent us into the elegant Bistro overlooking pool and ocean.

On the chef's recommendation, we ordered the triple chocolate cake and the passionfruit cheesecake with macadamia nut crust. After a basket of herb bread and butter, we were brought the extraordinarily elegant desserts. The cake accompanied by colorful fruit sauces striped with chocolate made the plate look liked a stained glass window, and fruit and mint garnishes were beautiful as well as edible. We shared tastes and then strolled on the beach, agreeing that this was a perfect way to end a day of studying herbs growing on the Gold Coast of Southern Florida.

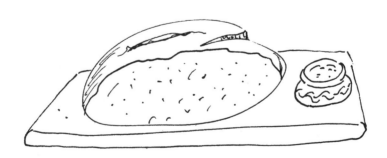

9. Plant by Plant Directory of Florida Herbs and Spices

This directory features folklore, description, cultivation, and uses of herbs and spices you can grow in Florida. It reflects my own experience plus that of the many gardeners I interviewed and writers whose work I studied. The information presented here is not intended to be used to treat any ailment or condition which requires medical attention, Sample unfamiliar herbs cautiously until you are sure that no one involved is sensitive or allergic to them.

This section summarizes a great deal of information, and the best way to keep it from running together is to read about just one or two herbs every day. Start with the ones you grow. Bring in a sprig and take in the look and scent as you read. Then move on to the ones you want to acquire next or that you see in the wild. Getting to know them will be an adventure.

If you discover something important or interesting that I haven't mentioned, or if you prove me wrong, please write (see page 84) and let me know so we can continue to build and share herbal knowledge for this region.

AFRICAN MOTH PLANT
Ibosa riparia
(I-BO-za)
Mint family
Native to South Africa
Uses: insect repellent
Grows best in S

Leaves are nettlelike. Plants can get 4 feet tall. They repel insects and moths with pungent, camphor-scented leaves. Flowers are plumes of white fluff. Plants cannot take freezing.

Florida Culture: Grow in pots in N and C, for it dislikes temperatures below 45 degrees (F). Propagate with seeds or cuttings. Pinch back to make plants bushier. Keep soil evenly moist through summer and until bloom stops, then let soil dry between waterings.

ALLSPICE, CAROLINA
Calycanthus species
(ka-lee-KAN-thus)
Calycanthus family
Native to China and
   temperate N. America
Uses: culinary, medicinal, ornamental
Grows in N, C, and S

This relative of the sweet shrub is a deciduous shrub that grows 3 to 10 feet tall from Virginia to Florida. Leaves are five inches long. Dark reddish brown, 2-inch flowers are many petaled and fragrant. This plant has been used as an aromatic stimulant and

---

* Throughout this section, N refers to Northern Florida, C to Central Florida, and S to Southern Florida (see climate zone map on p. 8).

flavoring in tonic. The bark makes a cinnamon substitute.

ALLSPICE, TRUE
Wild Clove
Pimenta officinalis, P. acris
(pi-MEN-ta)
Myrtle family
Native to tropical America
Uses: culinary, oil, perfume, potpourri, medicine
Grows in C or S, in containers in N or C

The leathery leaves of this attractive shrub are very fragrant when crushed. The dried, unripe fruit of the allspice is a spice or condiment used in curries, rice, pudding, pickling, and wine. Sprinkle powdered seed over potpourri. Use the ground powder, which combines the flavors of nutmeg, clove, and cinnamon, in cakes, apple and pumpkin pie, gingerbread, soups, stews, pot roast, hard sauce, marinades, and Swedish meatballs.

Wild clove (*P. acris*) produces the oil used so much in hair tonics as Bay Rum.

Both trees are evergreen with large, lance-shaped, aromatic leaves on long stalks, dotted with black underneath.

Florida Culture: Allspice and wild clove both become small trees in S but make good pot plants in C or N, though they seldom flower. They need a frost-free climate and do best with a minimum temperature of 55 degrees.

Propagate by taking cuttings of well ripened shoots in late summer, or layer. Prune in March. Plant in full sun to partial shade. Enrich the soil with compost and after plants are established, allow it to dry out between waterings.

ALOE
Burn Plant, Bitter Aloe
Aloe vera or
  Aloe barbadensis
(AL-oh or AL-oh-ee)
Lily family
Native to Africa and the
  Mediterranean
Uses: first aid, cosmetic, ornamental
Grows best in C and S

The history of aloe goes back at least 2000 years. Alexander the Great is said to have conquered Madagascar to acquire a good supply of it, either to treat the wounds of war or perhaps for the source of the beautiful violet dye yielded by species there.

It has dozens of uses around any house and I suggest you keep a plant in a pot on the doorstoop

or patio where you can easily reach it at night or in the rain. Breaking off a piece and rubbing the gel on the skin will take the itch out of rashes and bites, the soreness out of minor wounds, and the pain out of burns. Used leaves heal over with a brown crust you can rub off, so try to use an inconspicuous leaf repeatedly to preserve the beauty of the plant. Aloe is a fine border or accent plant and is especially good with modern or Spanish architecture.

The 350 species and even more varieties vary in size, color, and texture, but all have a basal rosette of thick, straplike green or gray-green leaves. Some have spiny edges. Both leaves and flowers are often dappled with gray or white. Most types stay low in Florida and send up flower spikes periodically, usually in summer, to 3 feet in height. These branch at the top and bear a showy raceme of tubular red, purple, orange, or yellow flowers, which are striking in flower arrangements.

Florida Culture: Grow this foolproof succulent plant as a perennial in a container in colder regions, in the ground from Tampa south. It will take full sun to partial shade and the only way to kill it is to switch from shade to sun too abruptly, in which case it seems to stew in its own juice. It is supposed to perish at 41 degrees, but mine has been through several light frosts with no problem. It needs only a little feeding and will survive on very little water but tolerates summer rain and humidity. Propagate easily by dividing offshoots.

ANISE
> Aniseed
> *Pimpinella anisum*
> (pim-pi-NEL-a)
> Carrot family
> Native to Asia Minor, Egypt
> Uses: baked goods, sachets, medicines
> Grows well in N, C, and S

The Romans so valued anise that it was one of the herbs used for paying taxes. Pliny, the Roman naturalist, wrote in the first century about chewing anise seed to freshen the mouth in the morning and it is now used in toothpaste, mouthwash, perfume, and soap. Crushed seeds add fragrance to sachets.

Mostly it is grown for its flowers and seeds, but the leaves can be used fresh in salads, as a garnish, or dried in a tea that aids digestion and may increase mother's milk. Add seeds to cookies, eggs, cooked fruits, spinach, carrots, and meats.

The plant is lovely in the garden where it blooms with dainty white flowers. It resembles Queen Anne's lace or the more delicate Bishop's weed, *Ammi*, but is less showy and vigorous than either one. Leaves are rounded or heart-shaped at the base and toothed, with leaflets becoming more feathery as plants mature. The fruits (seeds) are flattened ovals, 1/8 inch long with a lengthwise rib and licorice taste. Anise gets 2 feet tall with spindly growth that needs wind protection or staking.

Florida Culture: Anise likes warm weather for seed germination and a long season of growth, so it is a good annual for Florida. Start seeds in a sunny place in the fall in C and S, in spring in N, and sow thickly enough so that plants help support one another. Hilling up earth around the plants after they are growing well helps, too.

Anise makes an attractive border with its many white flowers. It takes many plants to get a significant amount of seed. If the days get hot too soon, the plants may bolt into bloom while still too spindly for much seed production. Transplanting also delays flowering and reduces yield. Use leaves fresh. Harvest seed when it turns brown.

ANISE, STAR OR CHINESE ANISE, FLORIDA
> *Illicium verum, I. floridanum*
> (il-LI-si-um)
> Magnolia family
> Native to Asia
> Uses: culinary
> Grow in N, C, and S

Star anise produces anise-scented leaves and seed that is used as a condiment in the Orient. An attractive evergreen shrub, it has leaves similar to magnolia, but smaller. Flowers are whitish, yellow, or purple with many narrow petals followed by star-shaped gray-brown fruits. These grow in most of Florida in zones 8 to 10.

The Florida anise, with reddish purple flowers and fruit, grows wild in N and can be cultivated elsewhere. As a tea, both are used to promote digestion and appetite, to relieve gas, as a cough medicine, and for antibacterial properties.

Florida Culture: This is easy to grow, almost carefree in full sun to partial shade. Propagate by layering, sowing seeds, or taking cuttings. Prune back as desired. Anise has low salt tolerance, medium drought tolerance, and can be subject to scale, although mine has never been bothered by anything.

ANISE HYSSOP
> Giant Blue Hyssop, Fragrant Giant Hyssop
> *Agastache foeniculum*
> (a-GAS-ta-she)
> Mint family
> Native to midwestern US
> Uses: ornamental, cut flower, tea, garnish
> Grows in N, C, and S

This beautifully flowering perennial herb is neither an anise nor a hyssop, but it tastes more like anise. The Chippewa used it for lung formulas and the Cree carried it in their medicine bags. It is a fine bee plant that produces nectar all day and is grown commercially for delicious honey. It also attracts hummingbirds. The plant resembles mint or salvia. I grew some from seed said to produce different colored flowers: yellow, red, pink and white, on differently scented plants: peppermint, spearmint, anise, or licorice. All of mine had dark blue spires on plants 3 to 5 feet tall with a licorice fragrance. I like them well enough, but will try again for more variation.

Florida Culture: Start seeds indoors or in peat pellets or start from cuttings. Germination takes 1 to 2 weeks. Plant 12 to 18 inches apart in enriched soil in full winter sun or partial summer shade. You can take cuttings to change locations for the seasons. Grow it as a tall back-of-the-border plant, or trim it way back for more uniform growth (see cover photo). This grows wild and is even a nuisance plant some places, but not in Florida. Mine did fairly but not outstandingly well. Feed and water as needed. It may self seed.

ARTEMESIA
> Mugwort, Southernwood,
> Wormwood
> *Artemisia vulgaris, A. arbrotanum, A. absinthium*
> (ar-te-MIZ-i-ah)
> Daisy family
> Native to E. Europe
> Uses: ornamental, culinary,
> medicinal, crafts
> Grows best in N and C

This genus of 200 aromatic plants is named for the botanist wife of the Persian King Mausolus. After his death in 353 B.C., she had a wondrous tomb built, from which comes the word mausoleum. Artemisias have been used through the centuries as insect repellents, to treat drowsiness and infections, as a poison antidote, as an antiseptic, and to expel worms.

Most artemisias are difficult in Florida. I have lost many of these plants in my Tampa area garden though they grew almost wild in my Iowa garden. I enjoyed every month that they survived. Now I have three reliable kinds and am seeing more plantings, especially of southernwood, that do well year round.

Most of the artemisias are perennials with silvery, finely-cut,  many branched lacy foliage that varies with each species and cultivar. They tend to stay shorter here than the same kinds would in northern states. Some have small yellow-white flowers. Others seldom bloom or set seed.

All the foliage dries well and is good for making wreaths, crafts, and dried bouquets. I have one with tall, finely cut, beautifully silver foliage that wilted almost at once in bouquets, until I learned to condition it by submerging it entirely in a sink of shallow water with something to hold it under. Now it stays perky, then eventually dries in the vase.

The leaves are good as strewing herbs, can be burned to improve kitchen odors, and are soothing in a bath. A decoction of southernwood and barley is a good wash for acne. Wormwood contains several toxic substances and should not be taken internally.

Other artemisias include:

-**true tarragon,** *A. dracunculus*, so good in French cooking and with poultry, but limited here by summer heat. As a rule, plant it each fall for use until late spring. Use *Tagetes lucida* as a heat-tolerant substitute (page 221).

-**Roman wormwood,** *A. pontica*, which is used to flavor vermouth and other wines and also said to be good for digestion.

-**Silver King artemisia,** *A. ludoviciana* and 'Silver Mound' or *A. schmidtiana* are both used mostly in ornamental plantings.

-**Sweet Annie or sweet mugwort,** *A. annua* is an annual whose foliage is extremely fragrant and dries to a lovely yellow-green.

-**Beach wormwood or old woman or dusty miller** (there are other dusty millers in other genera), *A. stellerana* thrives in sandy soil and full sun and is not so temperamental.

-**Young Lad's Love and Old Man's Beard,** *A. arbrotanum* var. *Tangerine*, whose ashes were once used to stimulated beard growth.

Florida Culture: All artemisias start easily from seeds or cuttings, some of which root slowly, root divisions, and layering. All except white mugwort, which likes moist soil and some shade, do best in full or partial sun and light, dry soil. Mulch them, especially in the summer, and set them in light shade then if possible. Be careful where you plant wormwood, for it could inhibit fennel, sage, caraway, anise, and possibly other herbs nearby.

ARUGULA

Roquette, Garden Rocket
Eruca vesicaria sativa
(e-RU-ca)
Cabbage family
Native to Europe and Asia
Uses: gourmet salads,
   seasoning, garnish
Grows well in N, C, and S

Although this was once used as a cough syrup and the ancient Romans liked the flavor, it is now used only for eating or garnish. The fact that arugula means deceit in flower language doesn't mar the flavor at all. This has lately been quite the "in" vegetable and with good reason. A few leaves will spice up a tossed salad delightfully. A salad of arugula leaves, papaya or citrus, nuts, and celery seed dressing is delicious and one of my favorites. The flowers can also be added to salads. Young leaves are milder, but old leaves are not too bitter, unlike lettuce.

This looks just like cabbage when the seedling sprouts, often within two days of planting. It soon has dark green, deeply cut leaves growing in a basal rosette. Crush them for the aroma or taste for the flavor. When the weather gets warm or after a few months in winter the plants send up 2 foot stems that branch with many small, creamy white flowers. It is attractive enough to grow in the flower garden or among the shrubbery, or in containers on porch or patio mixed with flowers. Use fresh. Arugula does not dry or freeze well.

Florida Culture: Grow arugula as an annual starting with seed in August or September. It is easier here than lettuce and lasts longer. Plant in improved soil in full sun for Florida winters and give at least occasional watering for best results. As soon as the leaves are large enough to use, cut them to within an inch of the ground and they will grow back again. Resow at least once or twice through the winter for a continuous supply.

Except for the centers, which are protected by outer leaves, arugula freezes out at 25 degrees. My plants died in summer until I put one in a container outside under an overhanging roof. There it gets morning sun, afternoon shade,and protection from excessive rain.

Cut back and use often to prevent bolting. Someone gave me plants once, but my seeds sown at the same time matured first.

AZTEC SWEET SHRUB
Sweet Herb of Paraguay,
   Mexican Lippia
Lippia dulcis
(LIP-pi-a)
Verbena family
Native to South America
Uses: culinary, ornamental,
   ground cover
Grows in N,C, and S

The leaves of this herb have a sweet flavor when chewed or added to foods. Its use as a sugar substitute is under study. One four-inch

plant spread to cover a 10-square foot space in my garden and it has grown merrily on through two summers and one winter so far, though it may prove frost tender in N. Take cuttings the first winter to be sure. The leaves are about one and a half inches long, rough to the touch, opposite, and a lighter green underneath. Two little cloverlike white flowers come out at each node. Seed capsules are green. *Stevia rebaudiana*, which has an even sweeter taste and better aftertaste, is not nearly as easy to grow.

Florida Culture: This grows easily from cuttings or divisions and spreads abundantly in full sun to light shade. Give it plenty of room.

BASIL
Ocimum species
(OS-i-mum)
Mint family
Native to India
Uses: culinary, ornamental,
   cosmetic
Grows well in N, C, and S

A French expression, seeding the basil, refers to ranting and raving because this herb is traditionally sown with much shouting and stomping. This is not neces-

sary in Florida. Another tradition held that if a man gave a woman a sprig of basil, she would fall in love with him and never leave him. In some cultures basil was considered sacred and laid on the breasts of the dead to protect them in the next life.

Basil is widely used in Italian and Thai cooking and is the predominant ingredient in pesto. Basil is great with any tomato recipe, and also for vinegars, salads, or for flavoring meats, pastas, or eggs. It repels flies and mosquitoes, so plants are used on tables in outdoor cafes. A tea from the leaves is said to help sufferers of colds and fevers. Use it also as a hair rinse.

Basil is a tender, tropical plant and one of the most important of the culinary herbs. There are many forms which vary in leaf size and color, but the opposite, oval leaves are usually 2 to 3 inches long. The enduring fragrance varies from lemon to cinnamon to licorice. Colors vary from bright green to deep red-purple and textures and form can be glossy or velvety, ruffled or smooth-edged. Basil makes an excellent container plant, and *Ocimum minimum,* the tiny-leaved basil preferred for pesto, is especially fine for this purpose. Leaves of lettuce leaf basil make exciting sandwiches combined with meat, tomatoes, or cheese.

Leaves and stem are dotted with tiny oil glands that release fragrance if touched or even moved by a breeze. Blooms are tiny and white or purplish, borne in whorls of six around mint-like spikes. Plants grow from 1 to 3 feet tall.

Florida Culture: Basil is an annual that sometimes lasts so long in Florida that we are surprised when it dies out. It can be started from seed planted thickly in fall in C and S, early spring in N. Thin so that plants are at least 3 inches apart. It is also easy to start from cuttings, which will root in a glass of water or in moist soil or vermiculite.

Basil plants like enriched soil and mulch. Frequent use will keep them trimmed and bushy. Use just as the flower buds appear for best fragrance and taste. Purple basil is more resistant to pests but the green bears wind better. I find the variety 'African Blue' by far the easiest and most reliable.

BAY

Sweet Laurel, Bay Laurel
Laurus nobilis
  (LAR-us)
Laurel family.
Native to the Mediterranean area
Uses: culinary, herbal arts, ornamental garden, dye
Grows in N, C, and S.

This evergreen tree yields the bay leaves you buy in the herb section of the grocery and that I've always added, one leaf per pot, to every batch of tomato juice I've ever canned. Breaking the leaf releases the aroma.

These are the laurel leaves that were worn by the Greeks and Romans as a symbol of reward and glory. *Laures* means to praise and *nobilis* means the famous. Baccalaureate and bachelor are modern words derived from

this ancient custom. A convalescent home in Russia urges patients to smell bay leaves to sharpen the memory. The ancient Greeks and Romans used it thus, also for headaches. Nero once fled during a plague to a place where bay trees purified the air. This is the bay that is part of *bouquet garni*, a favorite seasoning of French chefs. A paste of ground bay leaves and honey is said to help remove skin blemishes.
The bay tree can grow 60 feet tall and 30 to 40 feet wide. It stays small in containers and grows very slowly. The shiny gray bark and alternate, glossy, leathery, dark green leaves, gray green underneath, are up to 3 1/2 inches long and 1 1/2 inch wide. Flowers are small and yellow in small umbel clusters, so not very showy, and are followed by dark purple to black berries. There is also a variety 'Aurea' or golden bay with bright yellow leaf ends and an 'Angustifolia' or willow leaf bay with narrow leaves.

Florida Culture: Bay laurel will grow from seeds but they take 3 to 6 months to germinate. Most of us start from plants, and even they grow slowly at first. Put them in a place sheltered from wind. They like full sun to partial shade and sandy soil. Plants will tolerate a wide range of soil pH. They do fine in summer heat, are hardy from zone 8 to 10, will bear temperatures down to 28 degrees, but will die in an extended freeze. They are difficult to root from cuttings of green wood, often taking six to nine months, so don't hesitate to buy plants when you see them. Pinch terminal buds to force lateral branching and keep pot plants full and shapely. Shift to larger size pots as needed. Watch for scale.

Other bay trees. Bay laurel, *Laurus nobilis*, is the bay referred to in literature and cookbooks. However, there are other bays that can be used as culinary substitutes. The California bay or laurel, *Umbellularia californica*, does not, as far as I can find out, grow in Florida. The following two bays, however, are native to our area and thrive in Florida.

Red bay
Laurel, Isabella Wood
Persea borbonia
(PER-se-a)
Laurel family
Native to southeastern U.S.
Uses: ornamental, shade,
    food, lumber, flavoring
Grows in N, C, and S
    through zone 10

The red bay grows wild in Florida's zones 8 and 9, in swamps, hammocks, and along coastal shorelines as an evergreen tree often reaching 30 to 50 feet. It is in the same genus as the avocado, and also related to camphor, sassafras, and swamp bay. Leaves are 2 to 5 inches long, narrow, leathery, and glossy with pale undersides. Yellowish-green flowers bloom in the spring. The bark is dark red and deeply grooved. The rose-colored wood was used for fine furniture and finishing before the influence of mahogany.
Red bay leaves can be dried and used like *Laurus* leaves for flavoring foods. They are best harvested in spring, but can be picked

anytime and will keep, dried, in a glass jar for up to two years. The dark blue, one-seeded berries that ripen in late summer and fall are sometimes eaten raw or made into jams and jellies, or used in wine.

Florida culture: Red bays may be hard to find in nurseries, but the wave of interest in native plants should increase their availability. They grow best in full sun to partial shade in moist, acid, well drained soil. They grow very well in wet places but also thrive in dry ones. Salt tolerant, they are often found along the coast. Their main problem is galls. There is a somewhat dwarf variety, *P. humilis.*

Sweetbay
Magnolia virginiana
Magnolia family
Native to southeastern U.S.
Uses: ornamental, culinary
Grows in N, C, and S
to zone 10

The sweetbay grows wild in many parts of Florida. Marjorie Kinnan Rawlings writes about it in *Cross Creek.* There are several in a nature preserve I see from our yard, and they are full of bloom all summer, much more so than the southern magnolia, which is more formal with much larger leaves and blooms. There is even a tree at the side of our yard, so I can gather leaves and use them and will always happily associate the sweetbay with Florida summer.

BAYBERRY
Saw Myrtle, Sweetgale
Myrica species
(my-RI-ca)
Bay family
Native to southeastern U.S.

Uses: candles, fragrance, soap
Grows in N, C, and S
to zone 10

It is from the wax of the northern bayberry, *Myrica pensylvanica*, iffy even in Georgia, that the traditional bayberry candles are made. My Aunt Joan always burned them on New Year's Eve and as a child I thought they stunk, but love the fragrance now.
Bayberries were reported at Williamsburg in 1699. Thoreau used bay to remove pine pitch from his hands. It is good for soaps and ointments. A bayberry tea was used for sore throats and nasal congestion, and poultices from the roots were considered good for healing ulcers, cuts, bruises, and insect bites. An infusion of the bark is astringent and recommended for lotions or baths. The berries dry well and are decorative in dried bouquets or wreaths.

There are some 50 bayberry species, mostly evergreen shrubs or small trees found in moist woodlands or on the sandy rims of ponds and swamps. Saw myrtle (*Myrica cerifera*) grows wild in Florida.

Bayberries are characterized by grayish bark, waxy branchlets, and small alternate, narrow, delicately toothed, dark green leaves that are dotted with resin glands. Leaves give off a distinctive fragrance when crushed, especially in the spring. Flowers are inconspicuous yellowish catkins with separate male and female blossoms, usually on separate plants, so two or more plants are needed for production of the small, gray, fleshy or nutlike berries covered with an aromatic resin.

Florida Culture: Buy bayberry plants or start fresh seeds in moist, peaty soil with a pH of 5.0 to 6.0. Cut seedlings back to half their height when transplanting. Old, leggy shrubs can be renewed by cutting them back to the ground. Shrubs will grow in infertile soil, but respond so well to good watering and nutrition that they grow very quickly to 15 to 25 feet. They have high salt tolerance and grow along the coast, and high drought tolerance in spite of their liking wet places. They do best in fairly sunny to partly shady places. They put out root suckers profusely and can be weedy or invasive. Berries can stain masonry.

BEEBALM
>Bergamot, Oswego Tea,
>*Monarda* species
>   (moh-NAR-dah)
>Mint family
>Native to eastern U.S.
>Uses: ornamental, tea,
>   potpourri
>Grows in N and C, also in
>   S as an annual

Herbalist Kaye Cude and I both tried to grow the bee balm with dark red flowers that I had loved in the north. It is supposed to grow in Florida as a herbaceous perennial and bloom with its two tiers of asymmetrical, tubular blossoms in whorls around a button of bracts. It lived but did not bloom for us.

Then Kay discovered the lemon beebalm, *M. citriodora,* and I put one into a container without a great deal of hope. But it thrived all winter with long, narrow leaves of light green. It did not resemble the one I'd known but was delightfully fragrant with a lemony scent.

By spring it was a sprawling plant that bloomed profusely, in fact it turned into a cloud of dozens of lavender flowers, somewhat like beebalm (*M. didyma)* in shape, but continuing to open with more whorls along the stem ends until the flowering part was about 5 inches long. It looked like lavender wild bergamont. It died in summer, but I'll start over with the seeds I saved.

Beebalm was a gift from our native Americans and made a popular tea to replace the black china tea that the English taxed and the Colonists dumped into Boston Harbor. The Shakers used it also for medicine.

Horse mint, *M. punctata,* common on the coastal plains of N and C, is a wild cousin that has whitish green spotted blossoms with purple and pink bracts. Wild bergamot, *M. fistulosa,* with upright lavender bracts, and horsemint both grow at Kanapaha Gardens (see chapter 6).

All monarda flowers attract butterflies and hummingbirds.

Add the leaves to salads for an orange-lemon flavor. Use the flowers for garnishes and salads or add them to jelly or fruit punch. Use the leaves in potpourris, lotions, and baths, in herb wreaths, or in dried or fresh arrangements. A sprig tucked under a garden hat or into the hair is said to keep away mosquitoes and gnats.

Florida Culture: So far, I've found that the monardas are best grown as annuals in most of Florida, but be prepared for surprises. In the north it is perennial, spreading by underground runners like its mint cousins. It needs ample water. My lemon beebalm bloomed in Florida in full sun, but in Iowa I kept the other kinds in shade, so try both. Set plants two feet apart and mulch.

Some sources say that the lemon beebalm also has varieties with yellow flowers and that seedheads are attractive when dried.

BIXA

Bixia, Annato, Achiote, Uruca,
Lipstick Tree
Bixa orellana
(BI-ha)
Bixa family
Native to tropical America
Uses: ornamental, food coloring, flavoring, fiber
Grows in pots in N and C, in ground or in pots in S

Bixa grows to be a small evergreen tree with many five-petaled rose, pink, or white flowers with yellow stamens. The heart-shaped spiny seedpods grow in a striking cluster. Each one is maroon to vivid scarlet and 2 inches long.

For thousands of years the natives of the Amazon region used the red dye from the seedcoat as face and body paint. Bixa is used for food coloring and dye for soap, cheese, cloth, paint, lipstick, and margarine. Watch out: it stains tablecloths and napkins, too.

Bixa, the "poor man's saffron" lends rice and meat dishes a distinctive, mildly pungent flavor and colors them from gold to bright red.

In the Middle Ages, merchants caught mixing saffron with less expensive dyes and spices such as bixa could be burned at the stake, but today this commonsense substitute is widely used in dishes like Spanish paella and English red cheese. You can buy bixa or achiote seeds in Latin specialty stores or get a powder called *bijol* in small plastic packets or cans. Add a teaspoon to the water when cooking rice, soup, or chicken for a rich golden color and a mild flavor. Tie seeds in cheesecloth and heat them in cooking oil for red food color.

Florida Culture: This is a good hedge or bee plant in southern Florida. Plant seeds 1/8 inch deep, barely covered. Germination can be irregular and take anywhere from 20 to 180 days to sprout, according to some sources. Be watchful when you read such predictions. One of my seeds came up in about 10 days and was three inches tall before the next one sprouted. Rooted cuttings will fruit and flower earlier than seedlings.

Grow bixa in containers in N and C, for the plants are sensitive to frost.

BLACK PEPPER
Piper nigrum
(PI-per)
Piper family
Native to tropical America,
Ceylon, Peru, Malaysia
Uses: culinary, medicinal

This tender perennial vine grows mainly in the tropics and I have not yet seen a plant in Florida. Most of the black pepper we buy is grown in India or Malaysia from this tender, vining perennial. Both black and white pepper come from *P. nigrum*; black pepper from the unripe fruits and white pepper from the ripe fruits with the rind removed.

Beside adding flavor to food, black pepper helps kill bacteria and acts as a food preservative. Medicinally it has been used as a diuretic, stimulant, and digestive aid.

The pepper vine grows in shade and reaches up to 20 feet on strong, woody stems that twine around supports. Leaves are broadly oval, glossy dark green, with prominent veins. Flowers appear in summer in white clusters, with the aromatic, globular, wrinkled red fruit following.

There are several ornamental kinds that make good houseplants, especially the Japanese pepper, *Piper futokadsura*. Related species that grow in Florida include *P. auritum*, acoyo or root beer plant, which grows as a weedy small tree. Leaves smell like root beer, but it was used to treat various stomach disorders as well as to relieve pain. It is a flavoring for meat and tamales.

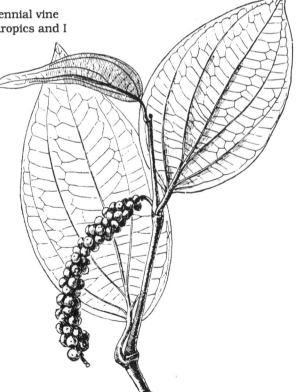

BORAGE

Talewort, Cool-Tankard
Borago officinalis
(bo-RAY-go)
Borage family
Native to Syria but
widely naturalized
Uses: ornamental, bee
plant, salads, drinks,
edible flowers
Grows in N, C, and S

Borage has been known down through the ages as an antidepressant, a herb of gladness and a comfort for sorrow. Just the thought of it does all of the above for me. I planted it once in Iowa and had it ever after and its dainty pink and blue flowers seemed appropriate for a home in which there was almost always a baby.

The loveliest borage I ever saw was in a hanging basket where the flowers made full impact on the eye, but I've never quite matched that perfection of plant growth and presentation.

Ancient soldiers drank borage wine to calm their fears, give them courage, and lift their spirits. If I plant as soon as the summer is over, perhaps I can have enough to flavor the plum wine next spring.

Borage is a cousin to comfrey and the leaves are similar in their slightly hairy texture. They also grow from a rosette, with stems reaching about two feet tall, sometimes more. The soft gray-green leaves can be used, like comfrey, as poultices that are cooling to skin irritations and swellings.

The one-inch flowers are star shaped and delicate, borne in profusion in lovely nodding clusters. The plant is somewhat showy in the border, attracts bees, and is a good companion for strawberries.

Older leaves are on the coarse side. The hollow stems and young leaves lend a crisp cucumber taste to salad, but use borage in moderation for it contains the same alkaloids as comfrey. It can be sauteed or steamed with or like spinach or other greens or added to cheese, poultry, vegetables, drinks, pickles, or salad dressings. The flowers are a pretty garnish and are good in salads, on sliced tomatoes, candied, or frozen in ice cubes. Pop off the prickly backs for company. Charles Dickens was especially fond of borage punch. Combined with any lemon flavored herb, borage makes a nice tea. Store borage leaves in vinegar or freeze them. Borage blends well with dill, mint, and garlic.

Florida Culture: Borage is an annual that grows easily from fat, black seed. Plant it 1/4 inch deep in late summer or fall in peat pellets or where they are to grow. Germination takes 7 to 10 days. Thin plants to stand 9 to 15 inches apart. Give borage full sun in winter, increasing shade in the spring. It prefers a slightly alkaline soil so it grows well near the foundation of a house. It is drought resistant, but will need occasional watering in the dry heat of April and May.

It grows with a taproot that makes transplanting difficult.

Stems snap off easily. Shade it for summer, but don't feel bad if it succumbs to the heat.

BOXWOOD
Box, Boxtree
Buxus sempervirens
(BUX-us)
Box family
Native to the Mediterranean
Uses: herb garden edging, woodworking, crafts
Grows in N and C

Boxwood is one of the best edgings for formal herb gardens and will take shearing for knot gardens or to form special topiary shapes. It does well as far south as the Tampa area.

Most of us think of boxwood as a purely ornamental plant with a formal feeling, but it was once considered a medicinal plant and used to treat epilepsy and toothaches. It is considered of little use by modern pharmacologists. Be warned that the leaves are poisonous and have caused animal deaths.

Boxwood plants are dense, slow-growing evergreen shrubs with small, dark green, elliptical to round leaves up to an inch long. Mature plants bear inconspicuous yellow green flowers followed by green capsules of shiny black seeds.

The densely grained wood is highly prized for fine inlay work, chess pieces, decorative boxes, and musical instruments.

Florida Culture: Boxwood is usually started from nursery plants or hardwood cuttings that need some coddling until they become established. You can take cuttings at any time of year. Box will grow in acid or alkaline soil but needs good drainage and constant moisture. The root system is shallow, so mulch is important and cultivation should be done with care.

Protect young plants from intense sun the first summer, and from drying winds. A spraying with one of the anti-transpirant coatings will help in the latter case. Once settled in, boxwood bushes take minimal care. Be sure to prune the top more narrowly than the bottom so the lower branches will not be shaded out.

BUGLEWEED
Carpenter's Herb, Middle Comfrey
Ajuga reptans
(a-JOO-ga)
Mint family
Native to Europe
Uses: ornamental, medicinal, dye
Grows in N, C, and S in Zones 8 to10

Many of us have grown bugleweed as a groundcover for years without realizing that it is a herb. It has been used to cure coughs, ulcers, rheumatism, and hangovers. Probably the most authentic medicinal claim was as an aid to healing cuts, for it contains tannin and plants with tannin are known to slow bleeding, thus the name carpenter's herb.

For most of the year this neat, popular plant consists of rosettes of spoon-shaped, wavy-edged, green, bronze, or variegated leaves. The latter can be in shades of lavender, cream, and green as in 'Burgundy Glow' or bronze, orange, cream, and green as in 'Multicolor Rainbow.' There are many named varieties, including 'Artic Fox' with striking silver and green wrinkled leaves. I find the variegated ones just a little less easy to grow.

Ajuga's candles of white, pink, purple, but usually dark blue flowers bloom briefly in spring. Leaf rosettes stay under 6 inches tall and flowers seldom get as tall as 12 inches. Trim off the stems after the blooms fade.

Florida Culture: Ajuga is an excellent, easy-to-grow perennial ground cover for sun or shade, dry or moist soil. It spreads quickly and is good for edging walks, but if you use it in a rock garden, it may elbow out its neighbors. The one potful I bought quickly spread over 10 feet square until some asparagus fern moved in and overtook some of it while I was busy elsewhere. In other spots, plants originally from the same pot have been doing well with very little care for seven years.

This plant needs occasional watering. It is not salt tolerant and can succumb to nematode damage. It will do better in partial shade than in full sun. Dividing the clump and transplanting plants a foot or so apart will help them spread faster.

BURNET
> Salad Burnet, Pimpernelle
> *Sanguisorba minor* or
> > *Poterium sanguisorba*
> > (san-qwi-SOR-ba)
> Rose family
> Native to eastern North
> > America
> Uses: cooking, landscaping,
> > tea
> Grows in N, C, and S

The 16th century British herbalist, Gerard, calls the flavor of burnet leaves a combination of melon and cucumber, mostly cucumber. Thomas Jefferson used it to graze animals and once sent two boys to pick 6 to 8 bushels of burnet seed, a job that could take forever, even plucking the seedhead whole.

The plant does not thrive in our humidity but I have managed to grow it through the winter as an annual and others have kept it for years as a perennial. It is a neat, low-growing plant with gracefully arching stems of small, toothed, opposite leaves. Even in Iowa I never saw it bloom, but if it does, the flower stems shoot above the foliage and have small, pink to purple tufts of bloom. The lower flowers are male only, those in the middle are both, and the upper rings of flowers are female, just like bananas.

Use the tender young leaves for cucumber flavor in salads, vinegars, and marinades, in herb butters, in beverages, or as a unique garnish. Chop leaves into coleslaw or chop with beets, dill, and yogurt for a relish. The flavor dies in drying but the leaves can be frozen. Chewing the leaves is said to aid digestion and it has been used for treating wounds.

Florida Culture: Burnet does well in containers as long as it has 5 or more hours of sunlight a day. It is attractive in flower or herb gardens. Plant seed or root divisions in fall in enriched, well-drained soil. Seed germinates in 8 to 10 days. Plants will not spread far here. Thin seedlings to 8 to 12 inches apart. Trim and use the foliage often enough to encourage tender new growth. Plants tolerate cold weather very well.

BUTTERFLY WEED
Asclepias species
(as-KLEE-pee-as)
Milkweed family
Native mostly to N. America
Uses: Garden, bouquets, to
attract butterflies
Grows in N, C, and S

Native Americans and early
settlers used this for a wide range
of ailments. The powdered root
made a paste for sores and a tea
from the root treated respiratory
problems. They cooked shoots like
asparagus, ate the pods, and made
sugar from the flowers. But don't
try these, because now we know the
plant can be poisonous in large
doses.

Several species grow wild in
Florida in N, C, and S. Mine is *A.
curassavica*. This perennial gets 3
feet tall and blooms all year round
in mild areas with bright clusters, 3
to 5 inches across, of dark red buds
and opening flowers of yellow and
orange. Lance-shaped leaves of
dark green are paler underneath
and usually opposite. It has a
milky juice that can stain clothes
and is best cauterized with a flame
for longer lasting cut flowers. Butterflies love the blooms and larvae

will eat the leaves, but seem to
pupate before they harm the plant.

Florida Culture: Fresh seed
is best. Keep it moist at about 75
degrees F until it germinates. Outdoors I find self-sown seedlings
coming up all over in sunny spots.
It is drought resistant, not too invasive, and easy to grow. Cut
back when necessary or it will
get leggy.

CALENDULA
Pot Marigold
Calendula officinalis
(kah-LEN-deu-lah)
Daisy family
Native to southern Europe
Uses: ornamental, cut
flower, culinary, dye
Grows in N, C, and S

We first grew this bright orange
daisy in our greenhouse in Ohio,
took it to the wholesale house in a
squat diaper pail, and sold many
because they were striking in bouquets, inexpensive as florist
flowers go, and we were the only
ones in the area growing it. Since
then I have grown it as an annual
every place I've lived.

The name came from the Romans noticing that the flowers of
calendula bloomed on the first day
of every month. It won't do that in
Florida. Strong calendula tea
brings gentle relief from skin rashes. During the Civil War and World
War I it was used to slow bleeding
and speed healing of wounds.

It is highly decorative, indeed it
is one of the biggest and brightest
of the herb flowers with large, flat,
daisylike blooms, 2 to 4 inches
across, with several rows of ray petals in brilliant shades of yellow

and orange, some with dark centers. There is also a dwarf variety for edging, but the types with longer stems are preferred for bouquets. Leaves are long and narrow, light green, growing from a basal rosette until the stems elongate. Plant calendulas in beds, borders, or containers. They dry well for winter bouquets or herbal wreaths. This is not the marigold that helps control nematodes. Flower petals are edible and add color and mild flavor to salads, teas, butters, soups, and rice. Dry the petals for use the rest of the year as a saffron substitute. Calendula rinse brings highlights to blond and brunette hair and makes a stimulating herbal bath.

Florida Culture: Calendulas are easy to grow in full sun and sometimes self sow. Plant in earliest spring in N. In C and S, for the longest period of enjoyment, either start seed in late summer and provide plenty of water and fertilizer for quick growth, or buy bedding plants in the fall. As long as you pick the flowers or deadhead, they keep on blooming. They respond well to soil enrichment, feeding, and watering, but can suffer from rot if overwatered. They are also susceptible to nematodes, so treat accordingly (see page 17).

CAMPHOR TREE
Cinnamomum camphora
(sin-a-MO-mum)
Laurel family
Native to Japan and China
Uses: potpourri, moth
    repellent, oils
Grows in N, C, and S

Camphor tree is a broad-leaved evergreen, up to 45 feet tall and wide, round headed in youth with wide, spreading branches at maturity. The new leaves are red-bronze turning to glossy dark green, alternate, oval, 3 to 6 inches long, in a palmate pattern. Flowers are fragrant, greenish-white, tiny, in 2 to 3 inch panicles in spring followed by 1/3 inch black berries that can be a nuisance over a driveway or patio but are not showy.

The camphor tree is often seen in Florida and is a handsome shade tree with leaves that are fragrant when bruised and useful in certain potpourris. You can also strew them among blankets and sweaters or use in sachets in the closet to keep clothes or blankets smelling fresh.

This is a tree to know and appreciate but not to plant in Florida because it is on the Category I list (the worst) of Florida's most invasive plants. The roots grow at the surface and are very competitive, the stumps resprout, and the fruits can be messy. The tree is also an irritant to some people.

Florida Culture: Camphor grows quickly, likes acidic soil, either sandy or high in clay, and full sun to partial shade. It has low salt tolerance but medium drought tolerance once established. Scale and root rot can be problems.

The tree will live as far north as coastal Georgia but dies back at 20 degrees. The leaves turn yellow green in wind or cold. They are usually pushed off by new ones in late winter or early spring.

CARAWAY
Carum carvi
(Kay-rum)
Carrot family
Native to Europe
Uses: culinary, medicinal
Grows in N, C, and S

For years I considered this difficult, mostly because my seeds did not germinate, but suddenly they did and it is growing well. Indeed it thrived all summer in a clay pot with the carport protecting it from rain. Besides the seeds that are so popular in cabbage dishes, cheeses, liqueurs, breads, and Hungarian goulash, caraway has been used since ancient times for treating stomachache, colic, gas, and menstrual cramps. Seeds serve as an aid to digestion, perhaps as a love potion, taste good, and are pleasantly chewy. Plants grow much like carrots but the glossy green foliage is even more delicate.

Florida Culture: Sow seeds in individual containers or in place. They take 1 to 2 weeks to germinate. They are supposedly hard to transplant, but mine had no trouble. Plant or thin them to 8 to 12 inches apart. Harvest when ripe and dry in the sun or in bags in a warm, airy place.

CARDAMON
Cardamom Ginger
Elettaria cardamomum
(el-et-TAR-i-a)
Ginger family
Native to India
Uses: ornamental, culinary
Grows in N, C, and S

I knew this would thrive in Florida the minute I saw it. It looks like the edible and ornamental gingers with its long, silky, palmlike leaves. It is more a spice than a herb, a tropical perennial that grows 6 to 12 feet tall in the jungles of India and Guatemala where the rainfall is as much as 150 inches a year. The contents of each ribbed seedpod, up to 18 seeds, make only 1/8 teaspoon of spice when ground. So it is no wonder that cardamon is one of the most costly of the spices, second only to saffron. Every seedpod must be snipped by hand.

Most cardamon grown in Florida is from Malabar cultivars that flower on long stems that sprawl along the ground. Plants grow less tall the farther north you live in the state. Bloom depends on both weather and pollinating insects, varying from year to year. Bloom is both possible and likely even farther north than Florida. When seeds form, harvest them slightly unripe so you won't lose any if the pods split.

Commercial crops come mostly from Mysore cultivars with upright flower stalks that have a definite bend near the base but otherwise look much like shell ginger when in bloom. The leaves grow in a clump from thick rhizomes.

> I saw cardamon growing six feet tall in George Riegler's garden just north of Tampa with numerous flowerstalks and one seedpod drying on each. The start George gave me has bloomed but is not yet as large as his.

You can use cardamon seeds or ground powder in homemade curry powder (recipe page 43), fruit punches and marinades, orange marmalade, and fruit salad dressings. Chew on the seeds to relieve indigestion or gas and to sweeten breath. Use the leaves between linens and blankets or add leaves or seeds to the bath for an invigorating soak. Add seeds to potpourri.

An essential oil from the seeds is a stimulant, like ginger. The seeds taste a bit like a gentle ginger with a touch of pine and can be used whole after shelling, or ground when green or after roasting. Seeds keep their flavor best if stored in their pods until you are ready to use them.

Florida Culture:　Grow this in N in containers, where it will stay small and you can bring it indoors in winter. Or let it die back to the ground every winter and come back from the rhizome. In C and S give it plenty of room outdoors with medium light. It has moderate drought resistance but will grow faster with more water. It thrives in hot summers. Propagate by seed or dividing the clump.

CASTOR BEAN,
　　Castor-Oil Plant, Palma
　　　Christi
　　Ricinus communis
　　　(RISS-i-nus)
　　Spurge family
　　Native to tropical Africa
　　Uses: ornamental, oil,
　　　possible pesticide
　　Grow in N,C, and S

This poisonous plant thrives in Florida, grows as tall as a small tree, and under good conditions spreads until it makes a grove.

Dark velvety red, palmate leaves and seed clusters are striking in appearance.

Warning: The seeds are so poisonous that one seed can kill a child, so do not grow these until after your youngsters pass the stage of putting things in their mouths. Also be sure to warn visitors with small children. Other parts are irritating only to people who are sensitive to ricin, a protein found in castor bean plants. I've grown many poisonous plants and my children ignored them all, but this one scares me.

It is, however, considered an important enough ornamental to have several cultivars: the more compact 'Gibsonii,' 'Red Spire' with red stems and bronze-green foliage, 'Sanguineus' with blood-red stems and leaves, and 'Zanzibarensis' with bright green, white veined leaves.

This source of castor oil has been used medicinally for years. Seeds were found in Egyptian tombs from 4,000 years ago. Castor oil is used in soap making and for lubrication of jet engine parts. The stems are used in papermaking, and natives in Ecuador string the seeds together and burn them as candles. Some say the presence of castor bean will deter rabbits, moles, and mosquitoes from the garden.

Florida Culture: Castor beans are easy to grow in Florida and will thrive in full sun. They quickly make an exotic screen or background, or bold accent. Some varieties can be invasive. This herbaceous perennial comes back from the roots after frost.

Before sowing, soak seeds overnight in water. They will sprout in 18 days in warm soil. Space plants 4 feet apart. For safety you can cut off the flowers before the toxic seed forms.

CATNIP
Catmint
Nepeta cataria
(NEP-e-ta)
Mint family
Native to Europe
Uses: tea, cat toys, dye, ornamental
Grows in N, C, and S

This plant that grew as a weed in the Midwest takes a bit of care in Florida. Catnip was valued enough for the colonists to bring it along, and it soon escaped into the countryside.

Catmint usually refers to the closely related *Nepeta mussini*, an ornamental catnip that does not attract cats, which is grown for its gray green foliage and attractive blue flowers.

Catnip was once used as a culinary herb, but its rather rank odor relegated it to being used more as medicine. A tea made from the leaves is said to reduce fever and the symptoms of some childhood diseases and it has also been used as a relaxant.

With its grayish green, heart-shaped, scallop-edged leaves, catnip is especially attractive when planted with blue flowers such as torenia and sage. The inconspicuous flower spikes can be dried and used in wreaths. The whole plant makes a yellow to gold dye.

Most catmint is grown for cat's delight. Some cats ignore it, but most will play for hours with simple toys made of cloth filled with the dried herb. It seems cats chew on the leaves to release the aroma, for it is the smell they are after. The same smell is said to repels rats and insects.

There is an old adage that says: "If you set it, cats will get it. If you sow it, cats won't know it." I can bear witness to that. Our cats ignored it when it was a plentiful self-sown weed but my present pets go crazy when I try to transplant a cutting or new plant. Perhaps cats smell when a plant is stressed, as when a plant is transplanted. And that is when they attack. Or maybe they become immune to its charms when it is plentiful.

Some of my catnip plants did well enough for a while. Then they disappeared. I brought one back from Iowa this spring and planted it under a milk jug beside which I often saw the mother cat sitting in contemplation. Soon after I took the jug away, figuring the plant was settled in, the catnip went away, too. It is better to cover plants with chicken wire cages until they are large enough to resist rolling felines.

I have outsmarted the cats by hiding plants in various places. One is doing okay in a container that also contains Vick's salve plant, which effectively covers the catnip scent. The one over by the horseradish in the far garden is safe, too. The third is in a container at the base of the black sapote along with a lemon balm that is sulking through the summer. But the safest one of all is in a hanging basket.

Florida Culture: Catnip is a perennial that does not thrive through Florida summer, but most of my plants are surviving both summer and cats so far. Catmint is drought resistant but more lush with regular watering. Aroma is strongest in full sun but leaves are larger and more tender in partial shade. Sow seed in fall or spring. It takes 7 to 10 days to germinate. When larger, thin plants to stand 14 to 18 inches apart. Catnip roots easily from cuttings, and clumps can be divided. It is slow to flower here, but mature plants will bloom in the spring.

CHAMOMILE

    Roman Chamomile, English
       Chamomile
    Chamaemelum nobile, true
       chamomile
    Matricaria chamomilla,
       sweet false or German
       chamomile
    Daisy family
    Native to Europe
    Uses: tea
    Grows in N and C

The Greeks named this the ground apple for its applelike fragrance, and the ancient Egyptians dedicated it to their sun god. But chamomile is best known as the tea given to Peter Rabbit by his mother, to calm him down after his adventures in Mr. McGregor's garden. The true chamomile is considered best for tea.

Both chamomiles have fernlike, gray-green to bright green foliage that stays low until bloom. Flowers are single white daisies with fresh apple scent. True chamomile gets only 1 foot tall while false can grow to 2 or 3 feet. German (false) chamomile is milder, with a sweeter fragrance. There is a depression in the yellow center of the flowers.

Florida Culture: Chamomile grows here as a tender annual that we can enjoy only from September to May. It grows easily from seed sown shallowly in pots in late summer. Germination takes 10 to 12 days. When several inches tall, plants should be set out 6 to 12 inches apart. Provide full sun in cooler months, shade it in hot weather, and discard it when it gets too leggy.

CHERVIL

    French Parsley
    Anthriscus cerefolium
       (an-THRIS-kus)
    Carrot family
    Native to Russia and
       western Asia
    Uses: culinary garnish, wine
    Grows in N, C, and S

Chervil came to Europe ahead of the Christians. The Romans called it the leaf of joy. Its uses are mostly culinary, though poultices of the leaves can be put on boils, bruises, and other skin irritations. The plants resemble finely cut parsley and have a delicate anise flavor and fragrance.

Chervil grows as an annual and forms low mounds with long, lacy leaves, curly or plain, from the center. Stalks of small white flowers are best cut off to keep the leaves growing. Some plants will produce thickened, edible roots.

Chervil makes a lovely garnish and adds flavor to salads, soups, sauces, stews, and marinades. Use it in bearnaise sauce, in *fines herbes*, to flavor cheese and egg dishes, and in vinegars. Add it at the last minute when cooking or the delicate flavor will vanish.

Florida Culture: Sow fresh seeds in late summer or fall in C and S, in fall or early spring in N, either in place in the garden or in pots for transplanting when small. Germination takes 7 to 14 days. Thin or set 12 inches apart. Chervil likes some shade. Start cutting and using it 6 to 8 weeks after sowing and you can use it all winter. Plants will sprout again after most freezes and also do well in containers or indoors. They will bolt to seed when it gets too hot, and the leaves may turn purple from heat stress. Let some go to seed then and it may self seed.

CHICKWEED

Stitchwort, Starweed
Stellaria media
(ste-LA-ree-a)
Pink family
Native to Florida
Uses: culinary, medicinal, wild herb
Grows in N and C

Chickweed, a useful weed, sprawls happily in Florida yards from Orlando and Tampa north, pops up in flower pots, and might as well be put to use. It is a creeping annual with small, succulent, opposite, ovate light green leaves that are hairy underneath. Edges are smooth. Small, starlike flowers bloom year round with green centers and five white petals so deeply cleft they appear as ten. Straggly stems are branched and brittle and the leaves fold up at night.

The seeds and buds are favorite food of many birds, especially caged birds. Leaves are rich in Vitamin C and phosphorus and are tasty raw in salads, chopped into omelettes, added to biscuits, or boiled with or as greens. Leaves also make a soothing poultice for skin irritations.

Florida Culture: This is easy to grow or find, for it self sows readily. It prefers moist soil and full to partial sun but tolerates a wide range of conditions, including frost.

CHICORY

Blue Sailors, Coffeeweed
Succory, Witloof
Cichorium intybus
(si-KOH-ri-um)
Daisy family
Native to Europe
Uses: ornamental, culinary,
coffee
Grows in N, C, and S
through zone 10

The chicory that lines the highways of the Midwest has long been my favorite weed. There is something about the color of those ragged blue daisies reflecting the morning sky that lifts my heart, especially when they grow on the rocky edges of clumps of Queen Anne's lace. Chicory closes near noon, but makes summer morning trips a delight and roadside spraying abhorrent to me.

I never managed to grow the weeds "in captivity," but chicory seeds purchased from a catalog grew plants with much wider shiny, lighter green leaves starting in a rosette and growing up a tall column that got 3 to 4 foot tall and needed staking. But it did produce the same blue flowers. I didn't like it as well as the weed, but it was a suitable substitute, especially in Florida where I've never seen the other. The flowers can be candied for cake decorations.

The ancient Greeks and Romans used chicory as a vegetable. A close relative of endive, it is popular in Europe where they eat the roots and forced leaves as Belgian or witloof endive. Up to 20 cultivars are known and you might be surprised to learn that trendy greens like radicchio and treviso are actually forced leaves of special varieties of chicory.

Chicory is famous as a substitute for coffee. Research shows it safe. It is less of a strain on the heart and nerves since it has no caffeine. Use the leaves in salads or cook them like or with spinach and other greens. Leaves are not good dried or frozen, but roots can be dried and ground for use as a coffee substitute or additive.

Florida Culture: Enrich soil with compost. Cultivated chicory does not prefer poor soil as the weed does. Sow seed or set plants or roots in full sun in fall. Germination takes 7 to 14 days. Set 10 to 12 inches apart. Weed and water as needed. Pinch back or stake to keep the stalk from falling over. Treat as an annual and gather seed or place some where irrigation will bring up new plants when summer is past. It's possible to force roots for Belgian endive. Cut off thick pieces of root and place them upright in a bucket of damp sand. Put them into a cupboard or other cool, dark place until the blanched shoots are ready to harvest.

CHIVES

Allium schoenoprasum
(AL-i-um)
Lily family
Native to Siberia
Uses: culinary, garnish
Grows in N and C

This onion relative is a hardy perennial and grew as a beloved weed for me in Ohio and Iowa. In the Orient, chives were used as a cold, flu, and lung remedy.

In Florida, I confess, I barely keep it going, not thriving, in a container in deep summer shade. It has lived there for several years and produced about three flowers. It does not like Florida summers. For best results sow seed in fall. Or start it indoors in August for a longer season, or any time to have it handy on the windowsill.

I may improve on growing this here, but I doubt if I will bother because I have found such an easy substitute in garlic chives.

Garlic Chives. Chinese chives, called *nire* in Japan.
Allium tuberosum, previously *A. odorum*
Lily family
Native to China and Japan
Uses: culinary, ornamental, garnish, crafts
Grows in N, C, and S through zone 10

These flat-leaved plants grow larger and bolder than common chives, with leaves up to 18 inches tall and white clusters of pretty, rose-scented flowers on 2 foot stems.

This thrives in full sun and survives the summers well with lots of bloom every year. I use the leaves extensively for both their dark green color and their mild flavor with just a hint of garlic.

Like most herbs, the more you use garlic chives, the better they grow. Cut and wash the leaves and snip them into potato or egg salad, tossed salad, soups, and stir-fry dishes. You can use the flowers in salad as well. All chives are high in vitamins A and C. An edging of them around your vegetables will deter pests. The flowers attract bees.

When garlic chives bloom, harvest several stems, flowers, and leaves and put into a decorative bottle of wine vinegar. This looks pretty and makes a good gift that adds a light garlic flavor to salad dressings.

Flowers and seedheads are attractive in dried arrangements and wreaths. Or use the green, knobby seedheads for rubbing the salad bowl for a trace of garlic taste. Cut off seed stalks before seeds fall to the ground and sprout all over. Store upside down in a paper bag until use.

Florida Culture: Start from seeds or divisions. For the latter, just take a trowel and separate several plants from the clump without disturbing the others, or dig a clump, divide it, and eat some, plant some, and give some away. Plant them in full sun (for best bloom) to partial shade. They respond well to enriched soil but are tolerant of a certain amount of neglect. Frequent watering will keep the leaf tips from yellowing.

OTHER ALLIUMS AND SIMILAR PLANTS
Onions. Gary Staley of Brandon, Florida grows thriving rows of Texas Granex red and white onions. "The best time to plant onions is when you plant strawberries, in early autumn," he says, although he has planted them as late as January with good results. "And in Florida you must plant only the alliums that form bulbs when the

days are short, or SHORT DAY onions. The long day kinds, including onions from sets, will never form bulbs here."

Shallots.
A. ascalonicum.
These produce clusters of bulbs. Use the scallions and bulbs, but they are sometimes strong-flavored in the heat and may be best for cooking or pickling. Save some to restart in autumn. Space 6 to 8 inches apart in enriched soil.

Bunching onions. *A. cepa viviparum.* A dependable perennial in the north, these tend to die out in Florida summers. Save some bulbs in the refrigerator to restart and use them as green onions. 'White Portugal,' 'Evergreen,' 'Beltsville Bunching,' and 'Perfecto Blanco' are good varieties for Florida. Bulblets can be pickled.

Leeks. *A. porrum.* These are mild-flavored vegetables you can plant in the fall. You can buy leeks in the grocery and plant 1 inch of root end for a start in the fall, or plant slow-growing seeds in October. Hill them up for a longer white section and use the entire stem. It will grow from pencil-size to an inch in diameter by spring. Good varieties are 'Titan' and 'American Flag' or 'Broad London.'

Garlic. James Steele (see chapter 6) sells garlic plants as a perennial herb and reports getting bulbs, as does Tom MacCubbin in Orlando. Tom plants the sections of fresh garlic from the grocery (break the bulb into many separate cloves) six inches apart in the fall, feeds frequently, removes seed heads in

February, and digs a harvest in May when the leaves yellow and collapse. Steele also says elephant garlic does well for him and he digs the bulbs after bloom in June or July. Garlic needs ample water and fertilizer to make bulbs. My own elephant garlic has not made bulbs but keeps growing year after year, and I use the leaves.

Society garlic. *Tulbaghia violacea.* This is not a true garlic, but it can be used the same way in soups and salads. It grows in grasslike clumps with decorative purple flowers in round clusters at the ends of 18 inch stems (this flower helps distinguish it from the similar mondo grass and liriope, which have flowers along a spike). This is a popular border, edging, and ground cover plant in Florida landscapes.

CILANTRO. See Coriander.

CINNAMON
Cinnamomum zeylanicum
(Cin-na-MO-mum)
Laurel family
Native to Asia and Australia
Uses: flavoring, teas, potpourri, perfume, medicines
Grows in S

Cinnamon grows into a handsome small evergreen tree or shrub outdoors from Melbourne south, or it can be grown in a container and moved to a warm place for winter in N and C. It likes a minimum temperature of 60 degrees. Dense, glossy green leaves have prominent veins. It has smooth pale bark and a round-headed habit. Leaves, bark, and fruit are fragrant.

The spice we use so lavishly is made from the bark, ground into a powder or shaved and curled into cinnamon sticks. A related species, *C. camphora*, the camphor tree (see entry on page 150) is hardy in zone 9 and below.

Florida Culture: Seed should be sown as soon as it is ripe in a shaded bed. Cuttings of half ripened wood root well in spring or summer. Or divide roots. Cinnamon prefers growing in sand, although it will tolerate heavier soils. Give it plenty of water and sun once established.

CITRUS FRUITS
Lemon, Lime, Orange
Citrus limon and other
species
Rue family
Native to southern Asia
Uses: culinary, medicinal, perfume, cosmetics, bee plant
Grows in N, C, and S

While many other herbs are treasured for their lemon or orange scent or flavor, we in Florida can grow real citrus trees. We do not often think of them as herbs, but lemon and lime especially, and all other types of citrus to some degree, have wonderful edible flowers that attract bees, and aromatic leaves and fruits used for many purposes.

Lemons have been treasured for centuries. A lemon-shaped earring from 2500 B.C. was found in the Indus Valley. Oranges were once considered the fruit of kings and grown only in walled gardens. Later their ability to fight scurvy facilitated the age of exploration and the discovery of America.

Juices and peels can be used as flavoring. Skins and leaves are great for both color and scent in potpourris and as a substitute for mothballs. All citrus flowers are edible and can be added to salads or soups. The scent of lemon is synonymous with "clean" and used in countless household products as well as soaps, perfumes, and cosmetics.

Lemon has been used to cool the body and treat fevers. The essential oil is a powerful germ fighter. Lemon has long been used in medicines. My mother was not a plant person, but honey and lemon was standard treatment for coughs and sore throats. Lemon is also effective in steam vapors. A slice on the drink glass is partly garnish and partly for flavor, but it was once used to disinfect doubtful drinking water. Its antihistamine properties decrease inflammation.

Florida Culture: These evergreen trees are beautiful in themselves except when a freeze damages them. Even then they have tremendous comeback power as long as the graft point is not destroyed, so protectively cover trunks above the graft juncture during winter cold. As a rule, citrus trees take a minimum of maintenance and are wonderfully fruitful in only one to three years.

Buy grafted citrus trees from local nurseries, selecting the hardier varieties like satsuma orange, kumquat, and limequat if you live in northern Florida. Calamondin and kumquat are small enough to fit in a herb garden or grow in containers. Other types need up to 25 feet of growing space unless you are willing to trim them to smaller sizes, but they will also bear in containers where they can be kept to about 12 feet. Protected sites like the south side of the house can reduce frost damage.

The more sun, the more fruit. All citrus is subject to root rot, so mulch is not recommended and the soil around the base of the trunk should be clear of other plants for good air circulation.

Water citrus well only every two weeks if rains do not provide. Feed young trees at least four times a year, every six weeks from March to September. Feed older trees in mid February, June, and early October. Pruning is only necessary to remove dead or crossing wood or for common-sense shaping.

CLOVE PINK
Gillyflower, Dianthus
Dianthus caryophyllus
(di-AN-thus)
Native to southern Europe
Uses: ornamental, culinary, potpourri
Grows in N and C

Pinks of various species are cousins of carnations. Some are annual and some perennial, and most do very well in Florida. Some have silvery foliage and make nice clumps which serve as ground covers. Some have stems long enough for cutting. The name 'dianthus' means divine flower from the Greek.

Also considered flowers of love, pinks were floated in the drinks of betrothed couples, and symbolize that committment in art. They attract bees to the garden.

After removing the bitter white heel from the petals of pinks and other kinds of dianthus, add them to sugars, vinegars, wine, or salads, or crystallize or candy them like violets (see recipe on page 59).

Florida Culture: Sow seeds almost any time in N and C, but only in the cooler months in S. Annuals take 5 to 10 days to germinate; perennials up to 3 weeks. Or buy plants and set them into the garden at any time of year. Cuttings or divisions will also thrive. Plant 12 to 18 inches apart, depending on the variety. They grow well in full sun to light shade. Give them enriched, well-drained soil and limestone, but not lime that contains magnesium (check the label). Shear off flower stalks after bloom ends and remove annual plants when they are past their prime.

COMFREY
Knit-Bone, Blackwort
Symphytum officinale
(Sym-FIE-tum)
Borage family
Native to Europe and Asia
Uses: ornamental, dye, bee
    plant, compost activator
Grows in N, C, and S

This was another of the plants I brought from Iowa. During our years on the farm it became an important source of medicine for people and animals alike and we have been using it ever since.

Nothing grew quite like it up north. In Russia it is cut back several times a year and used for livestock feed. It contains 35 per cent protein and produces great quantities of green material. As late as the 1970s it was hailed as the wonder food and cure-all medicine and it seemed so to us. We used it for animal feed, tea, poultices, medicine for any ailment or wound, and I put a few leaves in every batch of tomato juice I canned. I still do. Our children have always been healthy and we had at least one goat and one dairy heifer live because of comfrey who really should have died. The vet couldn't believe it.

When cancer producing alkaloids were first found in comfrey in 1978, we were glad we'd always used it in moderation, and we continue to do so.

Even if we didn't use comfrey, I'd keep some for the bees. It produces less growth in Florida and fewer of the bloom spikes that were bounteous in the Midwest. My only warning is that the poisonous leaf rosettes of foxglove (*Digitalis*) have been mistaken for comfrey, for the appearance and texture are similar. Be sure you have true comfrey before you eat any.

Florida Culture: Comfrey is an easy perennial. It will not die out in Florida's winters or its summers. It is drought resistant, but grows best in enriched, moist soil, and responds remarkably to the least attention. It has never been invasive for me anywhere. It only spreads if you dig and replant any piece of the root. Though you can grow it from seed, root divisions or cuttings are the easiest way to get a start. Cut back established plants in January to encourage new growth and put the old leaves on the compost pile or use them for mulch. Some people say it draws snails, of which we have plenty both near and far from the comfrey. But under this plant might be a good place to put a saucer of beer to drown them.

CORIANDER

Cilantro, Chinese Parsley
Coriandrum sativum
(cor-i-AN-drum)
Carrot family
Native to the Mediterranean
Uses: culinary, potpourri,
    soap, perfume
Grows in N, C, and S

Coriander is said to increase the appetite and the passions. One of the most widely used of all the herbs, it has one of the most powerful flavors, so experiment with small amounts.

Coriander is one of the bitter herbs used for Passover in the Bible. It is grown commercially in Argentina, Poland, and Morocco, and in Kentucky for the liquor industry. The Romans brought it to Britain where it grows wild. Chefs from many warm countries such as Thailand and Mexico consider the leaves essential to their cuisines.

Bees make delicious honey from the pink pollen. The flowers are in flat umbels and white to pale mauve with a reddish accent atop feathery plants up to 3 feet tall. The leaves look something like parsley, but become more finely cut higher

on the stem. Use with beets, eggs, cheese, onions, tomatoes, sausage, oysters, clams, pasta, salsa, guacamole, curries, and potatoes. Thai cooks also cook and chop the root. Add leaves near the end of cooking. The round green seeds may be used as a garnish, but the flavor differs from the mature ones.

Florida Culture: Sow seeds of this annual 1/4 inch deep in the fall where plants are to grow or in containers, being sure the seedbed does not dry out. Germination takes 7 to 14 days. Wash seeds in dish soap, then rinse before sowing to speed germination. Transplant early and carefully, for this has a taproot like parsley.

Florida's cold weather won't hurt cilantro. It actually stays leafier in the winter. Set plants in full sun to partial shade about 12 inches apart and begin to harvest leaves when 6 inches tall. If you want to use both seeds and leaves, cut one section of the row for leaves (cilantro) and let the other grow and flower for seed (coriander). The flowers make a pretty garnish. Do not overfeed or the plant will have less flavor. Seed maturity takes about three months and the plants may need staking.

CULANTRO

Eryngium foetidum
    (e-RIN-jee-um)
Carrot family
Native to southern Europe
Uses: culinary
Grows in N, C, and S

This herb is gaining popularity for its strong coriander flavor. It has a low-growing rosette of blue-gray, stiff, spiny leaves. When it dcides to go into reproductive growth, you can pick off but hardly stop the spiny buds that grow on stems a few inches above the ground. They look as if they are about to burst into exciting bloom, but actually the flowers are inconspicuous.

Culantro, to my surprise, is related to sea holly and rattlesnake master, the latter of which is a plant with medicinal properties. But culantro is a much smaller plant and grows well as a low ground cover, never getting more than 8 to 10 inches tall.

Florida Culture: Culantro is a perennial with high salt and drought tolerance, though it likes moist soil. It is hard to find: one source is Companion Plants. Set it into the garden any time of year.

CUMIN

Chili Herb, Comino
Cuminum cyminum
(KOO-mi-num)
Carrot family
Native to Egypt
Uses: culinary, flavoring
liqueurs, oil in some
perfumes
Grows in N, C, and S

This is a low growing, often sprawling annual that varies from its carrot cousins in that it likes hot weather. Leaves resemble fennel

but most types grow only about 6 inches tall. The flowers are pink or white in flat clusters followed by yellowish green-brown seedheads that weigh down the plants. The seed is the part used for flavoring and it takes four months of warm weather for them to ripen.

Cumin is one of the oldest of the cultivated herbs, grown by the Egyptians as far back as 2000 BC and found in King Tut's tomb in 1323 . The ancient Romans used it like we use pepper. It was once considered a treatment for obesity (!) and urinary and liver ailments. It is one of the herbs mentioned in the Bible (Isaiah 28:25,27 and Matthew 23:23) where the tithes were not money but herbs and spices.

Use the small, dainty plants to edge a flower bed. Seeds do not develop their full flavor until dried. Some cooks recommend parching them in the oven just before using them. Whole or as powder, they have a strong, spicy taste and are part of commercial curry powder. Use cumin carefully until you are sure of the taste. Although the flavor is different, cumin tastes good used in the same foods as caraway, including breads, cookies, soups, beans, and rice, in marinades and gravy, or with roasts. It is a major herb in Mexican and Indian cooking.

Florida Culture: Cumin seed must be fresh or it will not germinate, and it is sometimes hard to find. One source is J.L. Hudson. Plants will not stand frost; otherwise they are easy to grow. Sow in early spring in N and C, fall through spring in S, either directly in place in full sun or in containers for transplanting. Seeds take 10 to

14 days to germinate. Grow a row if you want to produce many seeds. Set plants 4 inches apart. Do not thin seedlings as they will support one another somewhat. Water during dry times. Gather the seeds by pulling up the entire plant and hanging them with the stems in a bag to collect seeds as they fall. Rub them between your hands and put the resulting mixture through a sieve to remove chaff from the tiny seeds.

CURRY LEAF
Murraya koenigii
(murr-REE-ah)
Rue family
Native to Asia
Uses: culinary
Grows in N, C, and S

This spice grows as a small tree with small leaflets that have a distinctive odor and flavor, actually quite different from curry powder. My neighbor has one that is 10 to 12 feet tall. If a branch breaks off, he takes it to an Indian food market in exchange for credit at the store. Another friend at the Rare Fruit Council says his wife uses the leaves like bay leaf to season dishes, then removes them. It is used like parsley in India and is a staple in curries, chutneys, and stews.

There is also *Murraya paniculata*, orange jasmine, which grows to 12 feet in S. This one is available from The Banana Tree. They were both named for Swedish botanist Johan Andreas Murray, a pupil of Linnaeus.

Florida Culture: Plants are often available at Rare Fruit council sales, but otherwise hard to find. They grow easily in partial shade to full sun. They spread with underground runners, and one grower reports shoots coming up 20 feet away from the parent, so you may want to plant this in a large, sunken container to keep it in bounds. If killed by a freeze, plants will usually come back from the roots.

CURRY PLANT
Helichrysum angustifolium
(hel-i-KRY-sum)
Daisy family
Native to the Mediterranean
Uses: ornamental, culinary
Grows in N, C, and S

This cousin of the strawflower is often used in northern herb gardens for its silvery, rosemary-like foliage that smells like good curry powder. However, the curry powder sold in spice cans is something else, actually a varied combination of East Indian herbs like cumin, fenugreek, coriander, tumeric, ginger, pepper, mustard, allspice, and such (recipe, p.43).

Curry plants are tender perennials and grow slowly to about 8 inches, with clusters of tiny yellow flowers. Though some books recommend adding them to recipes that call for curry, latest authorities do not recommend internal use. The leaves and dried flowers are good as insect repellent, in potpourris and sachets, and as strewing herbs.

Florida Culture: Start with purchased curry plants if possible or cuttings in fall in C and S, early spring in N. Starting curry plants from seeds takes skill and patience. They do best in well-drained, even dry soil. They like full sun and dry air, so Florida summers are difficult for them. Growing them in clay pots gives better results. Leaves may die back from light frosts if not covered. Plants die at about 22 degrees F, so bring in cuttings or plants if necessary.

DANDELION
Tell Time, Blowball
Taraxacum officinale
(ta-RAX-a-cum)
Daisy family
Native to Europe
Uses: salads, greens, wines, bee plant, dye, cosmetics
Grows in N and C

Transplanted gardeners remember this well as a weed that some loved and some hated. I loved it, partly because the bees did, but also because dandelions were the first flowers that little children could pick with wild abandon and I was presented many a bouquet crushed in little hands.

The settlers thought highly enough of dandelions to bring them across the ocean and Native Americans used them as a tea for tonic and medicine. Before WWI, dandelions were planted by the acre and the roots dried for a coffee substitute. During World War II, Russia got 80% of her rubber from *Taraxacum* plants. Children have blown the fluffy seeds off the stalk for centuries.

The dandelion grows with a rosette of long, narrow, deeply toothed dark green leaves, rich in vitamins. Then a hollow stem rises with an ugly bud that opens into a delightful bright yellow, mumlike flower, about 3/4 of an inch across. Whole yards turn gold with it in the spring up north and bees work wildly. My mother made wine from the blossoms.

Too bad it is only now I learn that a decoction of the flowers contains a rich emollient good for cleansing dry, mature skin. I made this with my granddaughters on my last visit north, found it at least as helpful as expensive products I've used, brought home a bit, and froze most of it in ice cubes I melt to use one at a time.

Alas, in Florida's heat, dandelion blossoms come and go literally overnight and the leaves always seem to have a bitter taste. I've seen them growing wild near Tampa and they lift my spirits, but their usefulness except in nothernmost Florida is questionable. All parts of dandelions are edible. In Iowa I used them in spring salads and cooked them with greens. It horrified some relatives when I dug some up to bring to Florida.

Florida Culture: While homeowners in the rest of the country are trying to get rid of dandelions, I still cherish my few plants. They made the car journey  and transplanted well one spring in spite of their deep tap roots. They are perennial and grow in full sun to light shade. They can be started from seed: try improved varieties for milder flavor. Blanching under an upside-down flowerpot with the hole covered or indoors in a bucket of moist sand inside a cupboard, as for Belgian endive, also gives milder flavor.

DIANTHUS. See p. 160.

DILL

Anethum graveolens
(ah-NEE-thum)
Carrot family
Native to the Old World
Uses: pickles, salads,
    garnish, cooking
Grows in N, C, and S

The settlers brought this herb over, too, and no wonder. Dill is a staple in gardens and kitchens. The leaves are often called dillweed and the seeds dill.

This and fennel were "meeting seeds" to chew during long sermons. The Greeks used it to cure hiccups. In the Middle Ages people infused it in wine to increase passion.

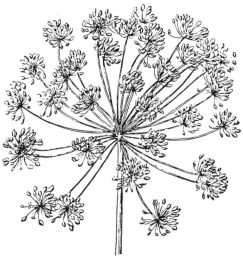

The plants have fernlike, blue or silvery green, threadlike foliage. Each plant sends up a single, long, hollow stem from which opens an umble of tiny yellow flowers. These flat clusters can reach 8 inches across on stems 3 feet tall. Most commercial dried dill is grown in India.

Florida Culture: This hardy annual grows easily from seed. Plant it from fall through late winter, for it likes cool weather and dies out in the heat. It self sows in some places.

Plant dill in a place protected from wind in full sun and improved soil. I've even grown it in pure mulch.

Like carrots, seeds take 1 to 3 weeks to germinate. When 4 inches tall, thin to 9 to 12 inches apart and try transplanting the thinnings or use them in cooking. Water and feed as needed. Pick umbels when the seeds are almost dry but before they scatter and place in paper bags. Dry or freeze the leaves. Make vinegar with the seeds and use it whenever you have the other vegetables for pickling. If you want to use mostly the leaves, keep cutting off stems or make successive plantings.

ELDERBERRY

American or European
    Elder, pipetree
Sambucus species
    (sam-BEU-kus)
Honeysuckle family
Native to Europe and N.
    America
Uses: large shrub, fruit,
    cosmetic, attracts birds
Grows in N, C, and S

These shrubs were thought to be endowed with spirits in earliest times. Farmers did not drive cattle with an elder switch or build a cradle with the wood lest the spirits bring harm. My elderberries have always had friendlier spirits who do not worry me when I pull seedlings out as weeds. I've valued the tree since I went through college with a bottle of elderberry "cough syrup" hidden in my drawer. It was made by my father's friend and we used it to toast great occasions.

The plants are usually tall shrubs with shiny green, opposite, compound leaves with toothed leaflets. The flowers are small and white in large, flat clusters, and when these grow heavy with ripe, usually purple-black berries, they hang down. Elderberries make fine jellies, jams, pies, cobblers, and syrups. The flowers are good in fresh or dried bouquets and so are the berries when green or just turning purple, before they get juicy. Flowers are also good in teas, baked goods, salads and in some cosmetics and medicinal teas and steam treatments good for stomach, sore throat, fever, and colds.

Warning: The scarlet elder, *S. pubens*, has inedible fruit, but the one that grows wild all over Florida and blooms on and off all year long is the American elder with edible flowers and fruits. Leaves, bark, and roots can be toxic and should not be used internally. Children have gotten sick from playing with elderberry whistles and blowguns.

Florida Culture: I was trying to root cuttings from elderberry shrubs I recognized from the blooms when I finally realized that some of the weeds I was pulling out were elderberries planted by the birds. Plant these or get named varieties for larger, better quality fruit. Pollination requires two plants, so if yours is isolated, plant another. Give them plenty of room and plenty of water. They like to grow beside streams or in low,

moist soil. They will root from cuttings, soft wood or hard. But if you only want them occasionally, you can pick flowers from wild plantings all year. Fruit is best in late spring or early summer. Pick it by the cluster and then watch a TV movie while you pick off enough berries with a fork to make a pie or a batch of jelly.

EUCALYPTUS
Blue Gum, Fever Tree,
  Silver Dollar
Eucalyptus species
  (yoo-ka-LIP-tus)
Myrtle family
Native to Australia
Uses: ornamental,
  aromatic, cosmetic, craft
Grows in N, C, and S,
  through zone 10

When I first visited Florida I was interested to see eucalyptus (*E. cineraria*) growing as a small evergreen shrub or tree with round, silvery leaves.

There are hundreds of fast-growing eucalyptus species in Australia, where they comprise 75 percent of all trees. Some of these grow as trees in Florida, but are not considered choice because they are weak-wooded and have thirsty roots, but I find them fascinating with their smooth or shaggy bark and silvery leaves. Different varieties have different scents, which can irritate some people.

They have been widely, though not always wisely, planted to dry up swamps. The trees provide timber, firewood, volatile oil that is used in cough drops, tannin, fiber, and dyes. The fragrant aroma is insecticidal. So is mulch made from this tree.

As an infusion for the vaporizer, eucalyptus helps ease bronchitis, asthma, colds, coughs, and congestion. Add tea of eucalyptus to bath water for a stimulating astringent, use it for dry skin, aftershave, or acne, or mix it with alcohol in liniments for rheumatism.

I add stems of eucalyptus to make any flower arrangement, fresh or dried, look more elegant, and save the lower or less attractive leaves for potpourri.

Florida Culture: This plant is difficult to start from cuttings, but is easy from seeds. Some kinds need cold treatment for 3 or 4 weeks. Sow in partial shade and transplant when 2 to 3 inches tall. They will grow about 12 inches the first year and faster once established. I just buy a new plant whenever the old one dies. A plant in a gallon size pot becomes a 10-foot tree in 2 or 3 years.

Plant in fairly rich soil in full sun and protect from frost. Eucalyptus prefers temperatures over 60 degrees and freezes at 27 degrees. Grow it in a container in N. Trim and use foliage often, for new growth has the best silvery-blue color. You may want to stake the plant to keep it from sprawling.

Silver dollar eucalyptus is shallow-rooted and needs constant support during the rainy season. It tolerates wet conditions, is drought resistant, and has low to medium salt tolerance. It can repel other plants as well as insects, but my eucalyptus does not bother the healthy fruit trees only 6 to 10 feet away.

FENNEL
Sweet Fennel
Foeniculum vulgare
(fo-NIK-cu-lum)
Carrot family
Native to the Mediterranean
Uses: cut flower, salads,
   soups, garnish, teas, as
   seed, dye, cosmetics,
   steam facials
Grows well in N, C, and S

The early Greek name for fennel means "to grow thin," and chewing the seeds is supposed to suppress the appetite. I must not have chewed enough seeds. These were used like dill as "meeting seeds." Chewing on the stalks or leaves is also supposed to reduce appetite. Early herbalists used fennel for eye problems, and the flowers and leaves make a yellow to brown dye.

The plant is attractive with tall feathery foliage, much like dill in bright green or bronze, in a clump that can be 3 to 5 feet tall. It will stay much smaller in containers or windowboxes. The flowers are similar to dill, growing in large flat umbels of yellow, attractive in the garden or in bouquets. Florence fennel grows only 2 to 3 feet tall and has a large blanched bulb called finocchio at the base of the stem. It can be cut into sticks like fresh celery or shredded for slaw. The entire plant has a sweet, mild flavor.

Fennel tastes less like licorice than it smells, somewhat like a nuttier anise. All of the licorice-flavored herbs add and enhance food flavors delightfully even for people who do not like licorice. The flavor resembles fresh tarragon, and the minced leaves make a good tarragon substitute with chicken or in salad dressing. All parts of fennel are edible. Leaves can be used from the moment the plant is large enough to spare them. If you have extra leaves, hang them in small bunches to dry, and then crumble them and store them in spice jars as a tarragon substitute.

Florida Culture: Grow fennel in full sun as a winter annual. The best time to start seeds is in the fall, and plants are somewhat frost tolerant. Be careful where you place it, for fennel can cross-pollinate with dill, thus altering the taste of the seeds and their off-spring. Fennel does not like growing near coriander or wormwood. Green beans, caraway, tomatoes, and kohlrabi do not like growing near it. My Florence fennel (*F. vulgare dulce*), is presently thriving near a healthy pepper plant.

For me, fennel usually dies out in summer, but comes back in the fall from the bulbs. Fennel may self sow, but it is more reliable to save seed or buy new seed. Start it as you would carrot seed, in place in the garden or in peat pellets. Gradually thin seedlings to stand 10 to 12 inches apart; you can use the thinnings in cooking. Protect from wind or stake if needed. Although plants are drought resistant, they respond well to occasional watering.

Cutting the leaves and seed-heads will increase fennel foliage but delay or eliminate the harvest of seeds. Seed heads must be carefully watched for the best time to cut. Since all parts of the seed head do not ripen at once, hold the head over a paper bag every few days and tap off the ripe seeds. Otherwise, cut the head when the first seeds begin to fall and hang it upside down in a bag.

Fennel likes alkaline soil and tolerates a wide range of moisture levels.

FEVERFEW
Wild Chamomile,
  Feverfew Daisy
Tanacetum parthenium, also known as *Chrysanthemum parthenium*
(ta-na-SEE-tum)
Daisy family
Native to SE Europe
Uses: garden flower, bouquets, medicines, crafts, dye
Grows in N, C, and S

Feverfew is sometimes offered as *Matricaria capensis* and there are many named varieties. Some are single, some double. It is really a good garden flower, similar to chamomile but more upright in habit, up to 3 feet tall, and more substantial in its dark green, strongly scented, alternated leaves. The flowers are small daisies, ususally with flat yellow centers but sometimes double and all white, and they bloom in sizeable flat clusters, while true chamomile is wispy looking with fewer flowers and threadlike leaves.

This plant with pungently fragrant, fernlike leaves gets its name from the traditional use of the leaves for tea to relieve fever. It has been said to help ease arthritis and migraine, using no more than two or three of the little leaves.

If you steep leaves in alcohol and dab this on the skin, it helps keep away small black flies when you work outside. Use flowers fresh or dried in arrangements or powder the dried blooms for a safe insecticide, since this plant is the source of pyrethrum.

Warning: Feverfew can produce mouth ulcers. The taste is very bitter and seldom used for flavoring. It should be avoided by pregnant women.

Florida Culture: This short-lived perennial is easy to root and grow and good in borders, rock gardens, and windowboxes as well as herb gardens in full sun to partial shade. It seems to keep harmful insects away, but beware: it also keeps bees away, so keep it far from plants that need bees for pollination or from plants grown especially to attract bees.

Divide clumps or start seeds in early spring in N, almost any time of year but preferably fall in C and S. Transplant to the garden to stand 9 to 12 inches apart. It needs occasional watering but thrives in dry places. It often self sows. Feverfew foliage is larger when grown in partial shade. Plants may not last more than a year, so keep cuttings and seedlings coming along.

FOXGLOVE
Thimbleflower
Digitalis purpurea
and other species
(dig-i-TAY-lis)
Figwort family
Native to Europe
Uses: medicinal,
ornamental, dye
Grows in N and C

Foxglove is an excellent example of an herb valued in ancient lore whose usefulness has been proven by modern medicine. It was used as long ago as 100 A.D., and some think Van Gogh may have taken it for his epilepsy, and that the rich yellow tones in his paintings may be the result of the yellow vision this drug induces.

In 1775, the English physician William Withering traced a remarkable cure to a woman who practiced herbal medicine with foxglove, and he experimented with extracts from the plant for the next 10 years. The herb is vital to drug companies today, for no one has yet found a way to synthesize the glycosides found in its leaves.

Warning: This is not a herb for home remedies. It can be fatal. Consider all parts poisonous.

The plant, where it thrives, is a lovely addition to any garden with its basal rosettes of large leaves, 6 to 12 inches long and 3 to 4 inches across, broadly lance shaped, toothed, fuzzy, wrinkled, and alternate along the stalk. The flowers are large, nodding bells with spotted markings on the inner lip. Spikes tower as tall as 4 to 8 feet in the north and bloom mostly on the sunny side of the stalk. But most types do not take well to Florida conditions.

Loretta Clements gave me starts of an unusual foxglove with no basal rosette or fuzz on the narrow leaves. After growing for a year, these produced my first Florida foxglove flowers, small, 1 1/2 inch bells of lavender and white. In February I found healthy self-sown seedlings, despite heavy frost. Loretta has a great clump of these plants, 3 feet tall, that blooms prolifically in late fall.

Florida Culture: A perennial or biennial farther north, foxglove is difficult to grow in Florida and does better the farther north you live.

Down as far as Tampa you can try it as an annual and sometimes get one batch of blooms per plant from a fast hybrid such as "Foxy" before the plants burn out in late spring heat. Plant fresh seeds in late summer or early fall. They take about 14 days to germinate. Set plants in enriched soil 15 to 24 inches apart. Put these in a well watered area, but do not overwater, for roots are prone to rot. They have the best chance in loamy soil in partial shade. I had some of the most beautiful clumps of foliage I'd ever seen, but got no bloom at all before summer wiped them out. Next year I will start at the beginning of fall and add some bloom booster fertilizer once the clumps seem large enough. I've had the same problem with Shasta daisies while others have had success.

GARLIC. See page 158.

GERANIUMS, SCENTED
Pelargonium species
(pe-lar-GOH-ni-um)
Geranium family
Native to South Africa
Uses: garden, tea, potpourri
Grows in N, C, and S

These are of the same genus as the common geranium but of different species. They were brought to England from the Cape of Good Hope in 1632, but gained little fame until discovered by the French perfume industry in 1847. The rose-scented leaves were used more than those with other scents. The essential oils are used today in cosmetics and aromatherapy.

The Victorians planted scented geraniums in pots indoors in winter and along paths in summer where they would be often brushed and could scent the room or the air.

Scented geraniums all do well in Florida. The leaves of different kinds vary in form and color as well as scents that include rose, apple, orange, ginger, lemon, coconut, strawberry, and peppermint. The scents may differ somewhat in our humid climate, for they do not seem quite the same to me. But I have one by the front door than smells like a sycamore tree at the right time of day or when it rains, and I love it. I grow it more for the leaves than for the flowers, but they are edible and good in salads or candied. Use the leaves, even ones that dry on the plant, in sachets, pillows, or potpourris. Some are good as seasonings or in teas. A leaf in a glass of clear jelly adds flavor and decoration. Use leaves also if you make cosmetics or perfume, infuse them for a mildly astringent cleanser, or add some to your bathwater.

Florida Culture: These are perennial and thrive in full sun or partial shade in slightly improved but well drained soil with occasional watering. They are hardy only to about 20 degrees, so grow some cuttings indoors in containers in winter in the north. Or add them to your list of cuttings to take when severe frost threatens. You can start them from seeds, but they are slow to germinate and can vary greatly from the parent plant. They usually root easily from cuttings, though they may rot in the rainy season. Many forms are sprawling, so give them ample room.

GERMANDER

Teucrium chamaedrys
  ((TOO-kri-um)
  Mint family
  Native to Europe, N. Africa,
    and W. Asia
  Uses: ornamental
  Grows in N, C, and S

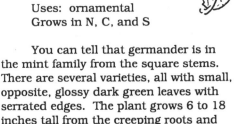

You can tell that germander is in the mint family from the square stems. There are several varieties, all with small, opposite, glossy dark green leaves with serrated edges. The plant grows 6 to 18 inches tall from the creeping roots and has a rich, piney fragrance. It prefers the dry climate of California, but some gardeners manage to grow it here. Use it as a strewing herb.

Florida Culture: Seeds take 30 days to germinate. It is easier to start with plants or with cuttings, layers, or divisions. Plant 1 foot apart. Shear back to encourage new growth. Mulch well and protect from summer sun and rains.

GINGER

Zingiber officinale
  and related species
  (ZING-i-ber)
  Ginger family
  Native to Southeast Asia
  Uses: cooking, ornamental
  Grows in N, C, and S

The Greeks used the root of this herbaceous tropical perennial

RECIPES FOR FRESH GINGER

Crystallized Ginger. You can make your own crystallized ginger with half a pound of fresh root from your plant or from the market. Scrape skin and trim off leaf bases. Cut into desired pieces, cover well in water, bring to a boil, lower heat, cover and simmer for about 3 hours. Add more water as needed or use a crock pot. Combine 1 1/2 cups of sugar with 1 tablespoon of light corn syrup with remaining water and boil this over medium heat for 2 minutes. Add to ginger pot and heat to boiling again for 1 minute. Then cool. Return to heat and simmer again for 1 to 3 hours until pieces are translucent and tender. Add hot water and stir occasionally as needed, cooking down to a spoonful of syrup. Let pieces dry on a wire rack, then roll in granulated sugar and store in a covered container. Considering all this cooking, maybe it is not overpriced ready made at the store!

Natural Homemade Ginger Ale. To make ginger ale, bring to boil 1 tablespoon of grated ginger root (or half as much ginger powder) in 6 cups of water, then simmer 5 minutes. Remove from heat, cover, and set to steep for 10 more minutes. Strain. Add 3 cups carbonated water and juice of up to 3 lemons just before serving over ice cubes. A pinch of cayenne powder adds the ultimate zing, and a fresh ginger stalk in flower is a knockout as a swizzle stick garnish.

spice, the source of flavoring for our gingerbread, over four thousand years ago. It is a staple in Chinese cooking; they make few stir fries without it. You can chop or grate the roots and brown the pieces in hot oil with onion before adding meat and vegetables. Use only half as much of the fresh as you would of the dried powder. Add one or two slices to taste for each pound of meat in marinades. The Japanese also use the tender new shoots.

While adding its spicy flavor, ginger also eases digestion. Ginger tea is considered a mild and safe stimulant as long as one drinks only a cup or two a day. Researchers have found it effective against motion sickness. The mature leaves are leathery, but can be added to flavor dishes and then removed like bay leaves. The leaves and conelike flowerheads can be used in flower arranging.

This is not the same plant as ornamental gingers of other species such as *Hedichium*, or butterfly ginger, and *Curcuma*, or hidden ginger, though their leaves may be similar. The roots of all gingers are edible, but they vary in flavor. When true ginger blooms, it looks like a smaller version of pinecone ginger, with conelike spires of yellow-green flowers with one purple lip.

The plant is easy to grow from the aromatic, tuberous root (rhizome), called a hand, which you can find in grocery stores and ethnic markets. It is knotty and branched and may be whitish or tan. It should be fleshy and thick, not withered. The leaves are grasslike, much like cardamon and the flowering gingers, and shoot up directly from the root to about 3 feet tall. As the plant grows, so will the rhizome – the part most used.

Florida Culture: Purchase a bit of plump ginger root with a strong ginger fragrance and well defined eyes at a nursery, grocery, or health food store. Early spring is the best time. Plant it whole or cut it into 1 1/2 inch pieces. Kaye Cude says to place these in a shallow tray of water until sprouts are an inch long. Then press these into the soil and cover with 2 inches of light, moist mulch, or into well-enriched, moist soil. Plant the pieces 12 inches apart in partial shade.

Feed as needed with a balanced fertilizer with major and minor elements; gingers are heavy feeders. Small bits of concrete block or stone under the mulch will supply the lime ginger needs. Gingers can take temperatures down to the low 20's.

You can cut and use small pieces of ginger from the rhizome of a thriving plant as soon as three months after planting without hurting the plant. The roots from younger shoots have the most flavor. Peeling is not necessary. Wash well.

Tops will die back 9 to 11 months after planting for a natural dormancy. For maximum production, dig the entire root before that with a spading fork. Keep small pieces of your best plants in a cool, shady place for replanting. Or you can just leave one big plant in the garden and dig as needed.

Store the partly used rhizomes by wrapping in paper towel and then in plastic, and then put into the refrigerator. You can freeze it but it may become stringy or tough.

Or slice the whole piece into a jar full of vinegar, wine, or brandy and keep it refrigerated. Add a few drops of the liquid to sauces for flavor.

Pinecone ginger or lanolin lily, *Zingiber zerumbet*, looks much the same as edible ginger, but is much larger, 5 or 6 feet tall. I bought one in the fall and saw no growth until the next spring. A year later it had a dozen leaf stalks, some as tall as I am, and the first green, pinecone flower on a low stalk near the base. Now established, it spreads quickly.

Already the flowerhead is full of sweet smelling lanolinlike liquid. A gentle squeeze and it overflows. This is great for washing, coating, and cooling face and hands while working in the garden or as a hair rinse or body lotion when you are finished. I thought this would only grow in S, but I've seen others growing well in C and blooming abundantly (a south-facing exposure is best). By Christmas the cones will be a deep red. There is also a highly decorative form with variegated green and ivory leaves.

Butterfly ginger lily (*Hedychium coronarium*) and **yellow butterfly ginger** (*Hedychium flavescens*) are both easy-to-grow perennials with gingerlike leaves from 3 to 6 feet tall, and are tipped with delicate, wonderfully fragrant flowers. The only problem with them is that some of the flowers in the clusters die and look messy,

but you can clean them up for cut flowers. The blooms are edible and delicious with a ginger-mint flavor. They like shade, rich, constantly moist soil, and will tolerate flooding. The reddish rhizomes are edible after much boiling and sweetening.

GINKGO
Maidenhair Tree
Ginkgo biloba
(JINK-go)
Ginkgo family
Native to China or Japan
Uses: ornamental, shade
tree, culinary, medicinal,
dye
Grows in N and C through
zone 9

The ginkgo, the world's oldest and one of its most beautiful trees, has been growing for 200 million years, but it is no longer found in the wild. It was held sacred by the Chinese monks who are probably responsible for its long history.

The botanical name comes from the Chinese word for silver apricot, and the common name, maidenhair tree, is the result of the uniquely fan-shaped leaves resembling those of that fern, except for being much larger.

There are several named cultivars with various shapes from columnar to pendulous, and with some variation in leaf color. Unless you don't mind the fruit, buy only named varieties (clones) because unnamed seedlings do not fruit for 20 years and you can't tell whether you have fruiting females until then. Since the sticky round fruits smell something like rancid butter, this is important, eventually.

This deciduous tree can grow to 70 feet tall with proper care. The two-inch, fan-shaped lobed leaves have a corduroy texture with their long, nearly parallel, raised, radiating veins. In autumn the leaves turn yellow and fall off almost all at once, in only a day or two. The bark is light brown with corky fissures. The inner bark makes a pale brown dye.

The Chinese sweeten the fruit and eat it as a delicacy. The nuts or inner kernels are sold in oriental markets and roasted for snacks and to help hangovers. Leaves and fruits are used to control aphids and grubs in China. Herbal qualities are strongest in autumn.

Modern studies are showing that ginkgo may have valuable uses to enhance memory, increase blood flow, and boost oxygen levels in the brain. It has also shown promise for treating Alzheimers and other mental disorders, resulting in less dizziness, fewer headaches, less ringing in the ears, depression, and hearing loss, and better short-term memory. Professionals use extracts for such treatments, but I don't advise home treatment. However, I would not hesitate to add a few well washed leaves to a herbal steam facial or vaporizer.

Florida Culture: Start from seeds or cuttings or buy well started plants from a nursery. Seeds take 21 days or more to germinate. Ginkgo likes full sun but will take a wide range of soils. It is pest free and pollution tolerant, but can cause a rash for some people. It grows slowly, has low salt tolerance, and medium drought tolerance. It will stay smaller if grown in a container.

GINSENG
> Chinese or Oriental Ginseng, Sang
> *Panax ginseng* or *P. quinquefolius*
> (PAN-ax)
> Aralia family
> Native to Eastern USA
> Uses: medicinal, ornamental curiosity
> Grows in N

I first saw this fascinating plant back in Iowa when a neighbor, then in his mid 90's, showed me the ginseng he had planted on all the shady sides of his house.

Ginseng has been considered almost magical in its healing powers since the beginning of Chinese history. Native Americans used and regarded ginseng highly and medicine men may have taken some secrets of its preparation to their graves.

The uses of the plant are still unclear, but interest remains intense. The Russians once fought wars with the Chinese over ginseng gathering grounds and a Russian ginseng is used in Olympic training diets and was reportedly taken into space by cosmonauts.

In Florida it grows only in the cooler parts of N. It can get 18 inches tall in its native hardwood shade. In the garden it is more a conversation piece than an imposing plant. A single stem separates after several years into whorled compound leaves with up to six finely toothed or lobed leaflets joined at a central point. These were edged in red on the ones I saw. Four to 40 flowers form a small cluster, rising from the main stem and blooming just above the center of the leaf umbrellas. Each green flower has five petals, five stamens, and two styles. Fruit is a showy cluster of bright red berries with white seeds inside.

Wrinkles around the neck of the root indicate the plant's age (like growth rings in trees) and some are extremely old. The most valuable roots, rarely found, are those in the shape of a man.

Sang gathering has been quite lucrative in the United States from early times until the present day, and it was exported by the boatload in centuries past. Today it is either a threatened or an endangered species in many places and hunters are required to plant the seed of any plant they dig for roots. Some ginseng is grown as a crop, mostly in Wisconsin under lath or black nylon shading, but it is a very tricky, expensive, and slow endeavor. Home grown or gathered roots can be used to flavor teas.

Warning: Perhaps women prone to fibrocystic breast disease should avoid ginseng because it contains an estrogenlike compound.

Florida Culture: If you live in a cool enough part of the state and are determined to try this, you can buy roots from herb growers or plant seeds or seedlings in a shady site, facing northeast if possible. Under oaks would be good. Ginseng likes well enriched, slightly acidic soil. Or plant in a container set in such shade for extra protection. Keep the soil mulched and moist

and be prepared to wait 5 to 7 years before digging roots of 3 to 4 inches.

GOLDENROD
Blue Mountain Tea
Solidago species (many)
(sol-i-DAY-go)
Daisy family
Native to North America
Uses: wildflower, crafts,
tea, dye
Grows in N, C, and S

This common wildflower, often scorned as a weed, is a rugged herbaceous perennial that grows in Florida as it does elsewhere, in golden masses by the roadside or in open fields. It reaches 3 to 7 feet tall with graceful, branching spires of mustard yellow flowers in late summer. They air-dry nicely in a well ventilated place if picked just before they open. The alternate, lance-shaped leaves have an anise- or tarragon-like aroma when crushed. Like tarragon, they numb the tongue when they are chewed.

Native American medicine men used goldenrod for many ailments. After the Boston Tea Party the colonists used it as a tea and it had such a pleasant taste that they exported it to China. In British folklore, the flowers were supposed to point to golden treasure and also to mark hidden springs. Goldenrod is wrongly blamed for hay fever while it is other plants (often ragweed) with windborne pollen that cause the trouble. The heavier pollen of goldenrod is carried by bees. A tea (infusion) of goldenrod leaves is said to help sufferers of hay fever, allergies, colic, stomach upset, measles, sore throat, and flu. Some people apply tea or crushed fresh leaves to sores, wounds, or insect bites. As a dye plant, goldenrod makes various shades of yellow. Use all parts of the plant for yellow-green, flowers for yellow-orange. Use the flower spikes in fresh or dried bouquets and the smaller sprigs in wreaths.

Florida Culture: Plant this at the back of the flower border or wildflower garden. There are many forms, including named cultivars (usually bred in Europe where the plant gets more respect). Seeds and plants are available from nurseries, divisions are dependable, and even cuttings from wild plants root easily. Goldenrods transplant easily and don't mind poor soil. Give them full sun to light shade. They have low salt but high drought tolerance The plant I brought home has now spread nicely. Goldenrod can be very invasive, but mine is not, even after several years.

GOTU KOLA
Indian Pennywort, Elephant
Plant, Marshpenny
Centella asiatica, formerly
Hydrocotyle asiatica
Carrot family
Native to India, Malaysia,
and South Africa
Uses: culinary, medicine,
ground cover
Grows in N, C, and S

This low, spreading herb has leaves that looked like violet leaves to me at first, until I planted them near the violets and lived with them for a while. Actually the leaves are rounder with small teeth on the edges, a different texture, lighter and more glossy in color.

Gotu kola is a perennial in Florida but can be grown as an annual in other states. It sends out runners like a strawberry plant and is already claiming more room than I allowed. Now I believe it when I read that it will spread a full yard each way from the original plant. My plant from a four-inch pot spread to cover 2 square feet in only one year. The flowers are small, reddish, and hidden under the leaves.

This herb is sold in health food stores with many claims that it prevents aging, expands intelligence, and aids overall health and healing. East Indians say it improves the memory and elephants eat it. I already know that nothing prevents aging, but we can try to make it a less painful process.

Warning: Gotu kola may be harmful in very large amounts. Worse yet, it may stimulate the appetite like a tonic. My parents gave me a tonic when I was too delicate at age five. It's effects are still apparent 50 years later in myself and my children. It is a family joke: "No matter what, never give them a tonic."

You can try small amount by adding young leaves to salads, rice dishes, or stews. It is used in Indian and Thai cooking. Use the leaves in a tea. Gotu kola tastes somewhat like parsley with a slight bitterness.

Florida Culture: Gotu kola starts easily from offsets and also from seeds. Germination takes 7 to 10 days. Give plants plenty of room. It does best in partial shade with ample water, and likes our humid summers. It makes an interesting container plant, and it's wise to treat it this way because it can be invasive.

HENNA

Mignonette Tree
Lawsonia inermis
(Law-SON-nee-ah)
Loosestrife family
Native to Asia
Uses: dye, cosmetics, ornamental
Grows in S (zones 10 and 11)

Henna is a spiny, evergreen shrub or small tree, 7 to 10 feet tall. Leaves are narrow and grayish green; flowers are small but fragrant, and may be cream or pink in color. They may bloom year round, and are followed by clusters of blue-black berries. The dried leaves have been used for centuries to make a red or orange dye to color hair, skin, and nails.

The leaves keep for years and also are astringent. A cold compress of them soothes fevers, headaches, stings, aching joints, and skin irritations.

Florida Culture: Grow plants from seed or cuttings. Plants prefer dry soil and full sun, and are killed by frost.

HOLLY

Ilex species (many)
(EYE-lex)
Waterleaf family
Native to North America
Uses: ornamental, medicinal, wood for walking sticks
Grows in N, C, and S

The root and bark of American holly, *Ilex opaca*, was used to treat coughs and colds. Leaves of Paraguay tea (*I. paraguariensis*), also called yerba mate, contain twice as much caffeine as coffee and are used for a commercial tea popular in South America. Yaupon holly, *I. vomitoria*, is sometimes called black drink. It too has leaves containing caffeine and was used by native Americans for a ceremonial drink, and also an everyday beverage and tonic for various disorders.

All the hollies have glossy, alternate, evergreen leaves, fragrant though sometimes inconspicuous flowers, and beautiful fruit following the female blooms.

Some but not all have separate sexes on separate plants, so check this with your nursery before you buy for fruit (holly berries). The yaupon is among several holly trees and shrubs that make good landscaping plants in Florida. It grows up to 20 feet tall, withstands drought and salt, and has white flowers in spring and summer followed by red or yellow fruits from the female plants only. There are many cultivars, some compact, some with new leaves colored red, and some weeping in form. For a nice scent, burn green branches with firewood.

Florida Culture: Start seeds (if you are very patient) or, for faster results and known cultivars, start with plants from the nursery or take cuttings. Give plants full sun or partial shade. Hollies transplant easily and have few pests or problems. Use them as screens, hedges, mass or specimen plantings, barrier plants, espaliers, or topiary.

HOREHOUND
Marrubium vulgare
(ma-ROO-bee-um)
Mint family
Native to Europe, Asia, and Africa
Uses: cough drops, candy, crafts, bee plant
Grows in N, C, and S

The common name of this herb comes from its use for dog bites. Horehound grows well in Florida as a perennial, 1 to 2 feet tall, and its silver-white, crinkled leaves add interesting texture when planted among flowers. When mature it has whorls or white flowers above each of the upper pairs of leaves. The barbed seeds latch onto clothes and animal fur for a ride to new territory, so seedlings can spring up anywhere.

Leaves have a menthol taste. Horehound was once popular in England for flavoring ales. Horehound drops, still available in many drug stores, were a standard cough remedy in my childhood, and I hated the strong taste. Use leaves in candies, teas, or steam treatments for colds or congestion.

Florida Culture: Horehound grows easily from seeds, cuttings, or divisions. Germination takes 8 to 12 days. Transplant while small to a site in full sun. Set plants one foot apart in the garden or sow seed directly outdoors. Cut off flowers before they set seeds. Trim plants back to keep them bushy.

HORSERADISH
Armoracia rusticana
(ar-mor-RAY-cee-ah)
Mustard family
Native to Southeastern Europe
Uses: condiment, medicine
Grows in N, C, and S

The plant I brought from Iowa survived the summer and spread fairly well over the first winter in Florida, but it never spread as far, grew as dark green, bloomed, or promised to stay forever as it did in Iowa. In fact, it disappeared the second summer. Nevertheless, it did well enough for a harvest and convinced me it is worth trying again.

Horseradish is thought to be one of the bitter Passover herbs. It was used medicinally to help in digestion, to treat congestion, and as a diuretic. Leaves applied in

HOMEMADE HORSERADISH

Dig, then scrub, scrape, or peel the roots to clean them. Dice into a blender with enough vinegar to moisten. Do not touch your face or anywhere near your eyes with this on your hands. Puree. Add sugar to taste, if desired. Fill clean glass jars with it, and store them in the refrigerator. This keeps for months, has more flavor than store-bought kinds, and makes a fine gift.

* Mix with mustard or spread alone on roast beef.

* Mix with grated raw beets and sour cream for a beet relish.

* Add to mayonnaise for spreading on sandwiches or use in salad dressing.

skin ailments. Leaves or a bit of root make an invigorating bath. The Germans and Scandinavians were the first known to use it as a condiment. The French sometimes slice the root and eat it with salt.

Horseradish has bold leaves, fairly coarse, about a foot long, and usually growing directly from the ground. When it blooms it sends up stalks bearing small, faintly scented, fairly showy, mustardlike white flowers, but seed almost never matures.

Florida Culture: Buy or bring home divisions of horseradish from your northern friends, or buy a root at the grocery store. You can use the bottom of the root for making the condiment and plant the top inch or two of root, with an inch of leaf stalks attached if they are present. Or start from any piece of root. Grow in full sun in moist, enriched soil. Containers such as half whisky barrels are large enough if you don't grow this in the ground. Set in plants or roots with the crowns about two in-

ches below the soil surface and 12 to 18 inches apart.

HYDRANGEA
> *Hydrangea* species
> (Hy-DRANE-gee-ah)
> Saxifrage family
> Native to Eastern U.S.
> Uses: ornamental, wreaths,
>   medicine, pH indicator
> Grows best in N and C

Only a few herbals list hydrangea, but its history as well as its present day uses qualify it as a herb. Native Americans called it seven bark for the layers of different colored bark. The Cherokee chewed the bark for stomach pain and put it on wounds, burns, or swellings. Early in this century dried root and leaves were used to help pass kidney and bladder stones. It is not a plant for home remedies though, for at least one case of food poisoning is reported from adding buds to a salad.

The papery flower clusters, which will dry and last for months on the plant, can be cut as they fade and hung to dry for wreaths and dried bouquets. On some varieties the cutting will bring on a second flush of bloom.

One of the most fascinating aspects of *H. macrophylla* or bigleaf hydrangea is the way some plants ('Nikko Blue' is one) can indicate soil acidity. Planted in soil acid enough to keep azaleas and camellias happy, they produce blue flowers. In soil closer to neutral or alkaline, from pH 6.0 and higher, the flowers are pink.

Hydrangeas are vigorous, deciduous shrubs growing 5 to 6 feet high and wide in Florida. The large, bright green leaves are opposite, ovate to elliptic. The showy part of the fragrant flowers are actually sepals, four to a floret. The bigleaf and oakleaf hydrangeas are thriving in our area of central Florida, though this is about their southern limit. Sargent, climbing, and panicle hydrangea do not thrive below zones 7 or 8.

Florida Culture: It amazes me that the hydrangea, the thirstiest and most sensitive plant in the flower shop we once had, now thrives in my yard. I did lose my first two, mostly because I planted them where they were too easily forgotten. The present success came from a cutting of *H. arborescens,* one of the easiest plants to root from softwood cuttings.

I planted it in improved soil and mulched it heavily, and later watered in Hydretain(TM), a water holding substance. The hydrangea bloomed through the dry spring with watering twice a week.

Hydrangeas do best here in light shade. They have low salt and drought tolerance, are hardy through summer heat or winter

cold, and can have scale or nematode problems.

HYPERICUM
St. John's Wort
Hypericum species
(hy-PER-i-cum)
Guttiferae family
Native to eastern N. America
Uses: ornamental,
   medicinal, dye

Hypericum got its common name from the legend that it began to bloom on the birthday of St. John the Baptist, June 24, and to bleed red from oil glands on its leaves on the day he was beheaded in August.

If you pinch the pretty yellow flower, the petals turn red, and leaves steeped in olive oil also turn red after a few weeks.

The astringent leaves were used on burns, bites, and bruises and to treat wounds, earaches, gout, coughs, and stomach disorders. But don't make home remedies, for it can be toxic in large or continuous doses.

Not all varieties of this plant will thrive in Florida. In northern Florida, James Steele sells *H. perforatum.* At least two others, *H. cristifolium* and *H. reductum,* grow as wild flowers in Florida. The first can be found in wet pinelands and on stream margins; the second in sandy woods, scrub, and dunes.

At least a dozen other species also grow here, and many can be found in nurseries. They are grown as small shrubs or short-lived perennials with opposite leaves with dots on the margins and a balsam or turpentine fragrance. The five-petaled, bright yellow flowers bloom mainly in spring and summer.

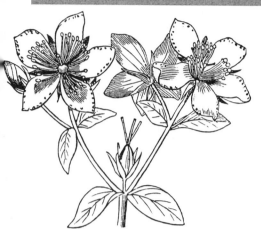

Florida Culture: Buy plants from local sources or start from seeds, cuttings, or divisions. Plant in sun or light shade. Remove old and weak wood in late winter or early spring.

HYSSOP
> *Hyssopus officinalis*
> (Hih-SOH-pus)
> Mint family
> Native to Europe, W. Asia
> Uses: tea, potpourri, bees
> Grows in N, C, and S

I have seen hyssop, a perennial, growing in several Florida gardens but never blooming. It does not last long in mine. Like many of the other summer sensitive herbs, it likes dry soil and lime. The tea is used for coughs.

JAMAICAN MINT BUSH
> *Micromeria viminea*
> and other species
> (mi-cro-MER-i-a)
> Mint family
> Native to Jamaica
> Uses: tea, flavoring
> Grows in S

This makes a tea with strong peppermint flavor that may be used to relieve indigestion. Most plants in this genus are tiny and thymelike, suitable for rock gardens, but *M. viminea* stands two feet tall and wide at Mounts Botanical Garden, although leaves and flowers are petite.

Florida Culture: Buy plants or grow from seeds or cuttings. Shelter low-growing types at the foot of a rock, in full sun. Protect from frost.

JIMSONWEED
> Angel Trumpet, moonflower
> *Datura* species
> (Dah-TYUR-ah)
> *Brugmansia* species
> Potato family
> Native to tropical America
> Uses: ornamental
> Grows in N, C, and S

Of easily grown plants, I think daturas have the largest and most beautiful flowers, lovely trumpets as much as 12 inches long and 6 inches across. Most types grow to the size of large shrubs in Florida.

For a while I avoided datura because of knowing it as a dangerous field weed, but I inadvertently grew some from "moonflower" seeds given by a friend. A garden visitor said, "I see you have angel's trumpet. Doesn't that smell wonderful!" Once I bent to sniff, I was hooked.

Now I have a pendulous white that blooms, as most do, only at night, but also an upright double lavender that blooms day and night. I've also seen the pendulous yellow and peach, but not the red.

Native Americans used datura as an anesthetic while setting bones, but this use was carefully controlled by the medicine man.

Other uses are recorded but should be rigidly avoided in light of the lethal dangers posed by this plant.

Warning: The entire plant is extremely poisonous, especially the seeds. It takes very little to kill a child, but there is not much about the plant to tempt a child to taste it. However, fatalities among adolescents or drug seekers have been all too common. We'd be wise to plant this in the back, not the front yard, out of sight of passers by.

Do plant these where you can enjoy the fragrance and beauty at night, at the edge of your back patio or near a walk where you'll pass them often. They spread widely and have soft, gray, alternate leaves. The flowers are followed by spiny round seedpods.

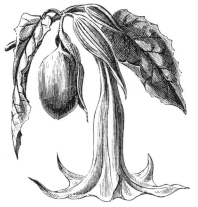

Florida Culture: Daturas are tomato cousins and grow in similar conditions, but have no serious pest or disease problems in Florida. They start easily from seed or cuttings, grow quickly, spread widely, and bloom abundantly. I recently moved one that was a good 2 feet tall without its even wilting.

Give them full sun for the most flowers. Frost will kill the tops, but the same plants have been blooming in our neighborhood since we arrived years ago, so they must come back from the roots or self sow. They do seed liberally, but I've never found them to be invasive. If you don't give them room, they won't grow.

JUNIPER
    Hackmatack, Horse savin
    Juniperus communis
        (ju-NIP-er-us)
    Cypress family
    Native to North America,
        Europe, and Asia
    Uses: ornamental, flavoring,
        cosmetic
    Grows in N, C, and S

Junipers are perhaps the toughest of evergreen landscape plants and will grow all over Florida, indeed all over the world. Their wood is good for paneling, novelties, fenceposts, fuel, pencils, and furniture. The fleshy berries are used in medicine, varnish, and as flavoring in gin, so the plant is definitely a herb.

Inconspicuous yellow male and green female flowers bloom, usually unnoticed, on separate plants. The 1/4 to 1/3 inch berries ripen over two year's time from green to blue or purple and are usually covered with white wax.

The Indians made a tea from the twigs to relieve colds and stomach ache. They wrapped sore limbs in steaming bundles of branches.

Put prunings on the outdoor grill to give meat a delicious smoky flavor. Use them for an invigorating bath that will ease aching muscles. They also make good strewing herbs or foliage for bouquets, freshening the air in either case.

Warning: Juniper can cause kidney damage, convulsions, or personality changes. Therefore I do not recommend that it be used as an edible.

Florida Culture: Junipers can be grown from seed, but may take up to 2 years to germinate, so most people start with nursery stock. Various named cultivars and varieties are available, with shapes that are low and spreading, midsize and bushy, or tall and narrow. The right ones in the right places are great landscaping solutions. Use them as ground covers, accents, screens, hedges, windbreaks, or foundation plantings.

Ground cover varieties, blue rug or blue carpet juniper, make excellent and spreading plantings. I have a low variety with gold edges. Some other outstanding junipers you will notice are the tall, narrow Italian cypress juniper and the twisty shaped torulosa juniper.

The shore juniper, *Juniperus conferta*, is salt tolerant. All junipers are drought tolerant, and prefer full sun although they tolerate light shade. They take heat, cold, and pollution in stride. Too much shade or poor drainage make them leggy and unattractive.

Because they are so sturdy, we sometimes forget that they are living plants and should be fed occasionally. They can suffer from twig blight, rust, and leaf spot. I notice my Italian cypress sometimes has brown foliage near the base from spider mite damage, but must have grown 10 feet in the 7 years we have lived here. Junipers will take heavy pruning but if you start with the right variety, little will be needed.

LAMB'S EARS

Betony, Hedge Nettle, Bishop's Wort
Stachys byzantina,
S. floridana, S. officianalis
(STAY-kis)
Mint family
Native to Europe
Uses: ornamental, medicinal, wildflower
Grows in N and C

An old Italian proverb says, "Sell your coat and buy betony." This genus has long been used as a tea for allergies, asthma, bronchitis, heartburn, headaches, and bladder and kidney problems. It has also been used as a poultice or natural bandage to stop bleeding, for ulcers, wounds, sprains, and swellings.

Any betonys that bloom are good bee plants. *S. Floridana* is a wildflower or weed in N and C. It has slender rhizomes with tubers on the end by which plants reproduce, narrow, textured green leaves, and strongly two-lipped small flowers in whorls.

The one James Steele gave me is the very wooly lamb's ears known in the North, though at first it seemed not quite as fuzzy. It spread from a 4-inch pot to cover a 2 by 2 foot space and was lovely with larkspur blooming beside it. It did well through the heat of April and May but perished quickly in the rains of June almost as if it were washed away.

Florida Culture: Start from seeds or plants. Grow in full sun or partial shade. Do not overwater. Protect from summer rains. Try growing it in a clay pot for improved drainage or move plants to a sunny indoor spot to keep from losing them in summer.

LAMB'S QUARTERS
Good King Henry, Goosefoot,
Wormseed, Mexican Tea,
Epazote, Fat Hen
Chenopodium alba, C.
ambrosiodes,
C. bonus henricus
(ken-o-POE-dee-um)
Chenopodium family
Native to Europe, Asia, and
America
Uses: culinary, medicinal,
crafts, forage
Grows in N, C, and S

This was a familiar weed in all
my northern gardens. Though it
grows wild in waste places and old
fields all over Florida, I have rarely
seen it here. The name comes from
Greek for goose and foot, which
 describes the
shape of the gray
green leaves.
There are annual
and perennial
kinds.
Leaves of the
annual types are
gathered and cooked as or with
greens, or shoots are cooked as a
substitute for asparagus. It is considered good with beans, corn, and
fish. Farmers once put branches in
the peas to repel weevils and used
it to fatten poultry. Dried, it can be
used as an air freshener. Its green
branches are cut and used as a
base for wreaths.
C. purpurascens is a vigorous
annual growing 3 feet tall with reddish stems and leaves. *C. capita-
tum* is a hardy annual, 18 inches
tall, with small flowers and bright
colored fruit like small strawberries. *C. quinoa* has seeds that
are used for food called quinoa in
Chile. *C. botrys* or ambrosia has

intensely aromatic foliage prized for
dried bouquets and wreaths. Used
in fresh bouquets, it keeps vase
water clean even with zinnias.
Atriplex hortensis or orach is a
close relative that looks much the
same but has decorative leaves with
cerise centers. There are several
ornamental cultivars. A red dust,
used as a natural rouge, rubs off the
leaves. Seedpods are attractive in
dried arrangements.
Native Americans made a tea
of goosefoot leaves to relieve stomachache. As a vegetable or condiment it is mildly laxative. In some
places a tea of the seeds is used
against worms and as a heart
stimulant. Plants are also used to
swab floors and porches to deter
insects in tropical countries.
Warning: In very large doses
or to sensitive people, lamb's quarters can be poisonous, so I do not
recommend taking it internally.

Florida Culture: Chenopodium species are easily grown from
seeds sown outdoors in fall or
spring. They germinate in 9 to 21
days, are very salt tolerant but like
arid regions, so try them in Florida
in fall. Thin to 10 inches apart.
They prefer full sun or part shade
and self seed easily. If they get
weedy, cut and dry seedheads for
wreaths before they can ripen.

LANTANA
Shrub verbena
Lantana camara, L.
montevidensis
(lan-TAN-a)
Verbena family
Native to tropical America
Uses: ornamental, fragrance,
medicinal, butterfly plant
Grows in N, C, and S

I always thought this should be considered a herb because of the aromatic leaves. I planted one beside the driveway on purpose to brush with the car and release such a cloud of fragrance that I can smell it even with the windows up. Then at Kanapaha Gardens I learned that the leaves are used as a tonic and stimulant. In Jamaica and Africa it is used for treating coughs, colds, and fevers and is applied externally to sores.

Lantana grows wild all over Florida, though special dwarf or specific varieties are sold in nurseries. It is being used more and more in landscaping because of its extreme drought resistance.

The stems are square and the opposite, evergreen leaves feel like fine-textured sandpaper. Both give off a fragrance that some call unpleasant but others like very much. The flowers come in small clusters, often with two colors of florets such as pink and yellow or orange and yellow on the same flowerhead. They also come in plain yellow, white, and lavender.

Florida Culture: Start lantana from plants, cuttings, layering, or from the large black seeds that take 6 to 8 weeks to germinate. Give plants full sun and moderately fertile soil. They are salt tolerant and recommended for seashore plantings. They are so drought tolerant, once established, that they survive on natural rainfall. Cut them back in late winter. They bloom in flushes almost all year, but less often in winter.

LAVENDER
English or true lavender
Lavandula angustifolia
(lah-VAN-due-lah)
Mint family
Native to the Mediterranean
Uses: ornamental, aromatic
Grows in N, C, and S

The name for this beloved herb comes from the Latin *lavare* which means "to wash." It was burned in hospitals to cleanse the air and used as a herbal bath. Just smelling it is said to cure headaches. In its native land and where it is grown commercially for a large perfume, soap, and scent market, one can smell the fields of lavender even out at sea. It has long been the favorite herb for scenting linens, stuffing sachets for drawers and closets, or strewing to repel insects and freshen rooms.

Lavender has slender blue-green to gray leaves and spikes of blue, pink, white, or lavender flowers. At the base of each individual flower is a small, shield-shaped yellow bract. Leaves are opposite. There are dozens of related species and varieties.

Florida Culture: Theoretically, lavender will grow in Florida through zone 10, but it isn't easy. I never could make it match in Iowa what we grew in Pennsylvania, and the loveliest I ever saw was blooming in Ireland, so it isn't the rain but the warmth that bothers it. But this is one herb I want badly enough to keep trying.

I have tried and killed many. The one that does best for me is

French lavender, *L. dentata*, with its less fuzzy gray green leaves that are finely toothed. This one has even bloomed for me with dainty, timid blue spires and has lasted the summers. This is definitely a herb to back up with cuttings, especially before summer. It is slow to start from seeds or cuttings, but not hard to root. It does well in full sun in winter but needs summer shade. Mulch it well and never forget to check it. It has medium drought tolerance and low salt tolerance.

LEMON BALM
Sweet Balm
Melissa officinalis
(me-LIS-ah)
Mint family
Native to southern Europe
Uses: ornamental, cooking, liqueurs, bee plant
Grows in N, C, and S

Lemon balm has a delightfully lemony scent and flavor in its mintlike leaves, and does indeed make the heart merry. I used it, when I had bees, to rub the inside of the hive to lure the swarms inside. This was the main ingredient of the original Carmelite water, made by nuns to treat nervous headache and neuralgia. Its main medicinal use was as a tranquilizer and the leaves are supposed to lower blood pressure. King Charles V of France drank lemon balm tea every day. Thomas Jefferson grew it at Monticello.

The opposite leaves are a dark, textured green with scalloped or toothed edges. The plant grows upright, loosely branched, to about 2 feet. It has small white flowers, but mine has not bloomed in Florida. There is a golden variety with variegated leaves, but it is not as tall or as hardy.

Lemon balm is good in wine or tea, chopped in salads or in salad dressings, and in recipes with chicken, yogurt, fruits, vegetables, fish, and rice. Use it in orange marmalade, too. Add it to canned pears. Chop leaves into cookies, custards, soups, and stews for a lemon-minty flavor. Rub on hands or hair for a fresh scent that will last for hours. Swish it in bath water or add it to potpourri.

Florida Culture: If starting from seed, sow sparingly in early fall in C and S, early spring in N. It may take lemon balm a while to grow to a good sized clump. Germination takes 12 to 15 days. Thin seedlings to 12 to 18 inches apart.

Lemon balm roots easily from cuttings. For me it needs deep shade to survive the summer and even then had spotted leaves and a sickly look. Back it up with cuttings in various places and don't forget to move most of them to more sun once summer is past.

LEMON GRASS
Cymbopogon citratus
(sim-bo-PO-gon)
Grass family
Native to South India and Sri Lanka
Uses: ornamental, cooking, tea, potpourri
Grows in N, C, and S, through zone 10

Lemon grass is an easy-to-grow tropical perennial grass that loves Florida's hot summers and takes well to much moisture although it has moderate drought tolerance. In very dry climates leaves turn brown and the plant goes dormant until the rains return. It forms a 3 to 5 foot tall clump of green flat blades about 3/4 inch wide. The inner, lower, white portion of the stem is tender, but the green blades are tough. Flowers are grasslike spikes but are seldom seen. If you plant it in a pasture, neither sheep, goats, nor horses will eat it.

Lemon grass produces one of the ten largest selling essential oils in the world. It is widely used in soaps and cosmetics. Related to citronella, *Cymbopogon nardus,* the plant is a natural repellent for flies, fleas, and mosquitoes. Studies show that it destroys many types of bacteria, fungi, and odors. Other uses abound.

The tender part of leaves is used fresh or dried, often minced for stir fries and curries. Soak dried pieces. Leaves are used for tea, to flavor coffee, and also in fish stock, and poultry sauces. Remove tough leaves before serving. Mix dried leaves with dried lemon and orange rinds for a delicately scented potpourri.

Florida Culture: Lemon grass is usually started from a side shoot. It will grow in poor soil with a pH anywhere from 4.3 to 8.4, acidic to alkaline, but res-

ponds well to additional nourishment. It will also survive in partial shade but prefers full sun. Water it occasionally, but do not overwater for that lowers the oil content of the leaves. Use it as a specimen or accent plant in the back of a planting or instead of shrubbery. Sometimes you can find bunches of lemon grass with some roots still attached. Look for them in markets that cater to Indonesian cuisine. Buy the bunch. Eat some. Grow some.

LEMON VERBENA
Aloysia triphylla, once called
Lippia citriodora
Verbena family
Native to South America
Uses: Ornamental, culinary,
   fragrance, crafts
Grows in N, C, and S

This deciduous woody plant with a light, lemony fragrance was taken to Europe by the Spanish and called Herb Louisa for the wife of King Charles IV of Spain. It was used to treat colds and fevers, stomach pains, and as a sedative. Leaves were added to finger bowls at Victorian banquets. As a sachet it was a favorite of Scarlett O'Hara's mother. It makes a delicious hot tea that was thought to lower fever. It is also used in soaps and cosmetics.

The light green leaves are lance shaped with margins either slightly toothed or fringed with hairs. Leaves are 2 to 4 inches long and borne in whorls of three or four. Flowers are tiny, tubular, and white to lavender in loose clusters at the branch tips. The plant has an airy silhouette. The leaves can be used fresh or dried with fish or poultry, with vegetables, in jams, marmalades, stir fries, cookies, and breads, or wherever you want a touch of lemon. Mince them well or remove them like bay leaves.

Florida Culture: Lemon verbena is not easy to grow, but is not impossible in Florida. Starting from either seed (4 to 6 weeks to germinate) or cuttings it is iffy, so it is best to buy started plants. Give full sun to partial shade. Train plants as standards for dramatic effect. Do not discard the plants or allow them to dry out when the leaves disappear. They will come back in spring at the end of dormancy. When buds swell, cut stems back to encourage new growth.

LOQUAT

Japanese plum
Eriobotrya japonica
(erio-BOT-rya)
Rose family
Native to Asia
Uses: ornamental,
    edible, medicinal
Grows in N, C, and S

I bought a tree that has never done well due to fire blight, but a bird dropped me a seedling that has grown taller than my house in six years and produced two crops of apricot-like fruit in March. The first was so-so, the second delicious.

I was fascinated to learn that loquat leaves were used in China as a remedy for coughs, stomachache, nausea, ulcer, and nosebleed. I do not suggest trying them, however. It is enough to have the small, evergreen tree (seldom over 15 to 20 feet tall) with its handsome, leatherlike leaves and small, fragrant flowers that stand in upright panicles throughout the winter.

Only the last flowers to appear are fertile. The yellow to orange fruits of apricot size ripen in March and April. They have one or more large brown seeds inside, but are easy to eat right off the tree and, like peaches, also good in relish, jam, or pie. I dried some in the oven for the ugliest looking, best tasting food I've ever eaten.

Florida Culture: If birds or friends don't provide seedlings (look under any loquat tree) and you must buy one, 'Oliver' and 'Wolfe' are supposed to be the best. Other grafted Japanese varieties are 'Early Red,' 'Champagne,' 'Pineapple,' and 'Premier.' Chinese varieties are 'Tanaka' and 'Thales.'

Plant where there has been no sign of fire blight, and if one plant fails, plant elsewhere, but not where fruit drop will be a problem. Give the tree full sun.

Related to photinia and pyracantha, loquat tolerates various soil types, moderate salt spray behind the dunes, and moderate drought. Water as needed until the tree is established. Mulch the root zone and feed once or twice a year. If you don't have room for your own tree, there are many around (planted for their landscape value) that no one picks. Ask, pick, and enjoy.

LOVAGE
Levisticum officinale
le-VIS-ti-cum
Carrot family
Native to Southern Europe
Uses: culinary, ornamental, medicinal
Grows in N,C, and S

This celery cousin never grows to be the giant in Florida that is does in northern states, but it does fairly well all winter and can grow 2 to 3 feet tall. It has celerylike leaves and flavor, a bit stronger with a hint of yeast. Stems are hollow and can be used as drinking straws to add zest to tomato juice or cold herbal teas. It grew in Charlemagne's garden, and monks and medieval innkeepers grew it to make beer and cordials and to help digestion, as a diuretic, and to ease migraines. It was also used as a love charm, hence the name.

The leaves, stems, and seeds can be used raw, added to salad, soup, stew, potato salad, rice, stuffing, and tomato sauce or juice, or cooked as a side dish like asparagus. The seeds are good, whole or ground, in pickling brines, biscuits, cheeses, salads, salts, butters, and salad dressings.

Lovage is particularly good in low-salt diets. Leaves and curls of the stem make a great garnish.

Florida Culture: Grow lovage as an annual in Florida. Start seeds in late summer and grow in good soil and high sunlight over the winter. Shade in late spring may help it last longer, but do not expect it to last over the summer.

MARIGOLD, FRENCH
Tagetes patula
(TAG-e-teez or ta-JEE-teez)
Daisy family
Native to Mexico
Uses: ornamental, insect repellant, food color
Grows in N, C, and S

This attractive bedding plant, used throughout Florida, has a long history as a herb. South American Incas planted marigolds with potatoes to repel insects centuries ago, an early example of companion planting. The Mexicans fed the petals to chickens to color their skin and eggs. Aztecs used marigolds to cure coughs and dysentery, the Chinese to treat whooping cough, mumps, and colds.

Recent research verifies the insect-repelling value. Flower petals are good for color as well as fragrance in potpourri, and can also be used in salads and as a garnish..

Florida Culture: Start from seed, covering the dark end 1/4 inch deep, or buy as bedding plants. Grow in full sun to light shade in fertile soil. Protect from frost. Varieties vary from 6 to 24 inches in height, and most spread one to two feet wide. These short-lived annuals bloom profusely, blooming themselves to death in 3 to 4 months, so be prepared to tear out and replant.

Cuttings will sometimes root in bouquets and I take cuttings from healthy looking shoots when I pull up an old plant. Marigolds spread and bloom best in full sun in a well-watered part of the garden, but also survive with only occasional watering.

MARJORAM
Origanum majorana
(or-RIG-ah-num)
Mint family
Native to Asia
Uses: cooking, crafts, dye
Grows in N, C, and S

Crowns of marjoram were once placed on the heads of bridal couples as a symbol of love and happiness. Plants were also put on graves to bring peace to the departed. In ancient Greece, marjoram signified honor and was worn by great leaders. The Greeks also used it for seasoning, tea, pain relief, and as a pomade for their hair and eyebrows.

By the Middle Ages, it was common as an antidote for narcotic poisons, a flavoring, a strewing herb, and a filler for sachets.

Marjoram can be either creeping (usually this is pot marjoram,

O. onites) or erect but low growing with opposite, ovate, fuzzy, pale gray-green leaves, 1/4 to 1 inch long. These have a sweet, pungent, sagey fragrance that may vary slightly (see oregano). The tiny white or pink blossoms come in spring in Florida and are attractive to bees. There are cultivars available with crinkled, yellow-to-white leaves, but these have less scent. A fairly new hybrid, *Origanum* x *marjoricum,* proves to be much hardier, especially in Florida, and equally good for flavor.

Florida Culture: Start marjoram from seeds, cuttings, or division of clumps in fall to early spring. Germination takes 1 to 2 weeks. Space plants 12 inches apart. Marjoram makes an attractive border for a flower garden and does well in containers or hanging baskets indoors or out.

Pot marjoram is sometimes used as a ground cover. It likes full sun in winter, some shade but good air circulation in late spring and summer. Use or cut it back often enough to keep it bushy and remove flower heads. Harvest leaves at any time.

Marjoram is winter hardy in most cases, but it may die off over summer in C and S. If so, treat it as you would any annual and start over in the fall.

MINT
Mentha species
(MEN-tha)
Mint family
Native to
    Europe, Asia,
    and Africa
Uses: tea, garnish,
    scent, crafts
Grows in N, C, and S

Mints of many species have been cultivated and used throughout the world since ancient times. Mint was used to keep milk from curdling and to pay tithes in Biblical times. The Roman poet Ovid mentions it as a symbol of hospitality and by the ninth century, one monk wrote that he'd rather count the sparks of Vulcan's furnace than the kinds of mint.

The mint family is characterized by square stems, opposite leaves, and whorls of tubular, two-lipped flowers.

I gathered wild mint from the roadside as a child in Ohio, and my father made mint juleps (page 54) that were the celebration of the adult world. I had mint in Iowa that tried to take over the earth and almost managed in my yard. I was horrified to see the same mint die in my Florida garden the first summer after we moved.

Since then, I have grown pineapple, apple, and orange mint, spearmint, curly mint, Costa Rican mint, creeping pennyroyal, and others. These differ in appearance, fragrance, and flavor.

Mints are ideal for garnish, for making mint tea or adding to any other tea, for settling the stomach, and for cleansing the breath.

Mint grows so abundantly that you can use it as a strewing herb. Add it to bathwater, potpourris, soaps, and cosmetics. Use it as foliage in bouquets. Rub it as you pass just for the scent.

Florida Culture: Plant mint where you can brush against it, walk on it, or pick it often. Mint is easy to grow in Florida from seeds, cuttings, or plant divisions. Seeds are small and germinate in 10 to 20 days. They like moist soil, full sun for the winter, and some shade in the summer. Trim the mature plants back frequently. The aroma is strongest before they start to bloom. More rampant kinds can be mown down occasionally.

In Florida summers, move some cuttings into the shade to be sure your choice kinds survive. Mint is one of several herbs that are best moved to new ground every four or five years.

MISTLETOE

Phoradendron serotinum
(Phor-a-DEN-dron)
Mistletoe family
Uses: Christmas decoration
Grows in N, C, and S

When the oak leaves thin out in late winter and you see clumps of green up in the tree branches, you are most likely looking at mistletoe. This small evergreen shrub grows in and on the trees as a parasite, usually planted by birds dropping the sticky seed that clings to the bark and sends out tiny roots within a few days.

The name comes from the Greek *phor* for "thief" and *dendron* for "tree" and this plant definitely saps strength and steals nutrients from the tree in which it grows. Mistletoe has been used medicinally, but can be toxic and should never be used for home remedies. Even the white berries should be hung high enough so children cannot reach them. Mistletoe grows all over Florida with brittle stems and thick, opposite leaves. Plants are dioecious, that is male or female on different plants. Only the females bloom and bear white berries.

Florida Culture: Mistletoe is to know but not necessarily to grow. You could place seeds in a low enough branch to reach if you want. I have seen children selling sprigs at Christmastime. But, in the best interest of your oak trees, remove what you can from their branches.

MONDO GRASS
Ophiopogon japonicus
(O-fi-o-PO-gon)
Lily family
Native to Asia
Uses: ornamental
Grows in N, C, and S

 This looks similar to liriope, though the grassy evergreen leaves may be shorter, more slender, and darker green. At Kanapaha Gardens there is a vast area with this rich, dark green carpet.

Ophiopogon is sometimes called dwarf lilyturf and is often confused with *Liriope*, which is also called lilyturf. *Ophiopogon*, hardy and adaptive, grows in sun to full shade. It has small lilac flowers on spires in summer, often hidden in the foliage. *Ophiopogon* and *Liriope* are both fine ground covers in the shade, ideal for edging formal beds or walks. *Liriope* is showier with flowers above the foliage. Both are salt and drought tolerant. There is also a black mondo grass with purple-black leaves and pink or purple-black flowers, and giant types with striped leaves.

In China the tubers of mondo grass are used to make a tonic to improve memory, for fertility, as an aphrodisiac, for lung and stomach problems, and for coughs and sore throat. They have shown anti-tumor activity in animals.

Florida Culture: Plants are usually started from divisions. Water moderately until established, then only during severe drought. Feed yearly in the spring.

MUSTARD
Brassica species
(BRASS-i-ka)
Cabbage family
Uses: vegetable, condiment, medicinal
Grows in N, C, and S

Many vegetables come from the same genus: broccoli, cauliflower, cabbage, collards, Chinese cabbage, kale, kohlrabi, turnip, rutabaga, Brussels sprouts, rape, and mustard greens. All thrive through Florida winters. Plant them from September through March.

Herbal mustards include white or yellow mustard, black mustard, and brown mustard, all of which are grown to make the condiment that coats our hot dogs. Mustard grows wild in Florida as elsewhere and colors the fields and roadsides yellow in early spring with four-petaled broccoli type blooms borne on large, wide-spreading branches. The plants grow 2 to 6 feet tall with bright green alternate leaves of various shapes, the lower ones pinnately lobed, coarsely toothed and up to 8 inches long. The upper ones are less lobed. Long slender pods begin to form on the lower stems while flowers still bloom above. The pods elongate and turn from green to brown when ripe. Each contains 4 to 6 seeds. The black mustard is hottest in taste, brown is easiest to harvest, and white is the most preservative.

In the garden, mustard is a good companion plant for beans, grapes, and fruit trees, according to growers. Research shows that wild mustard reduces cabbage aphids on collards and brussels sprouts and keeps flea beetles from collards. It also releases a chemical that inhibits cyst nematodes and prevents root rot.

My family will not eat mustard greens even in salad, but I make green noodles by blending the leaves with eggs until they are a puree, then adding enough flour to roll the noodles (recipe p. 58).

Mustard plasters are a time-honored treatment for congested chests, rheumatism, toothache, and soreness or stiffness. Our grandmothers mixed powdered mustard seeds with water, rye flour, and sometimes egg white, and spread this over a cloth, then applied it to the chest. An infusion of mustard seeds as a foot bath relieves sore and aching feet.

Florida Culture: Mustard grows easily from seed sown directly outdoors in any part of Florida from September through March. Thin to 9 inches apart. Plants will flower in the spring if you don't keep them cut for the greens. Feed and water as you would for any vegetable.

To harvest the seed, gather as the pods turn brown, before they split open. Spread on a screen or tray covered with cloth or hang them upside down in brown paper bags. Pound out the seeds after two weeks of ripening, winnow, and store whole or ground in airtight jars.

Since it takes many plants to grow much seed, you may want to gather in the wild or buy your seeds at the grocery. Mustard can become a weed if plants are left to go to seed unharvested, as in pastures and on roadsides, but this has never been a problem in my yard.

MYRTLE
Myrtus communis
Myrtle family
Native to Chile, Peru,
    New Zealand, Australia, and
    the Mediterranean
Uses: ornamental, culinary,
    strewing, potpourri, cosmetic
Grows in N, C, and S

This useful evergreen shrub is absent from most herb books because it is not cold hardy and can only be grown as a pot plant in northern states. It does very well in most of Florida and makes a handsome evergreen shrub 8 to 10 feet tall. The leaves vary from 3/4 to 1 1/4 inch long and are opposite, green and shiny on compact rather formal plants that look almost artificial. The flowers are white and showy with many stamens.

The Greek legend says that Venus turned her favorite priestess Myrrha into this fragrant evergreen to save her from too ardent a suitor. You don't have to believe that to appreciate that myrtle has always been associated with Venus and love and is therefore used in bridal bouquets. Shakespeare had Venus and Adonis meet in the shade of the myrtle.

myrtle

The leaves have a spicy, somewhat citrusy fragrance. You can flavor meat by putting them under the roast the last 10 minutes of cooking or on the barbecue. Myrtle is especially good for pork or lamb. The flowers are edible; remove the green part and add to fruit salads. Grind the berry for a mild juniperlike flavor. Sprigs are good for strewing or for decorating wreaths or gift packages. Add a decoction to furniture polish.

Infused, they are antiseptic and astringent. Myrtle tea has been used for psoriasis and sinus problems. Apply as a compress for hemorrhoids and bruises. Flowers and leaves can be dried or pulverized fresh to add to ointments for skin blemishes and the berry makes a good hair rinse for dark hair. All parts are good in potpourris and herb pillows.

Florida Culture: Myrtle is a cousin of guava and Surinam cherry. A mere slip I got a few years ago is now about three feet tall in spite of complete neglect, but has not yet bloomed. A dwarf variety I bought in its spring bloom is growing well, though slowly, and stands out for its perfection of leaf and form. A variegated one I planted in too much shade did not thrive until I moved it to the sun. Myrtles like full sun but some protection from wind. You may want to keep some in a pot in extreme N, but it will survive down to 25 degrees, though it needs at least 41 degrees to grow. The stems are almost all woody, so stem cuttings take a bit longer to root.

Myrtle is fine to trim or shape as topiary or to grow in containers in its own rather stiff form.

NASTURTIUM
Indian Cress
Tropaeolum majus
(tro-pee-O-lum)
Nasturtium family
Native to South America
Uses: ornamental, cut flowers, culinary
Grows in N, C, and S

This is one of the most delightful herbs to grow in Florida. Always one of my favorite flowers, it never did well in Iowa because the soil was too rich. Seeds planted in peat pellets before we moved sprouted under the seat of our van on our way south. They miraculously survived summer by the northwest wall of the house. Then fall came and they burst into growth and bloom. We had plenty of flowers, foliage, and even seeds to add to salads, to which they add flavor and eye appeal, and for constant bouquets. They are also a bright garnish, good on sandwiches, or the talk of the party if you stuff the flowers with herbed cream cheese.

The Spanish conquistadors discovered nasturtiums in Peru and took them home in the 16th century. Soon they gained favor as a culinary herb throughout Europe and were part of the tussie-mussies of the Victorian age. Botanist John Parkinson called them yellow lark's heel because the flowers have a spur at their base. They come in many shades of yellow, orange, red, cream, and mahogany, and have a brightness and translucence that makes them shine like jewels in a vase. Flat, alternate round leaves of soft green have smooth, slightly wavy edges and grow from 2 to 7 inches in diameter. Both have a unique fragrance that stays on the hands after picking and are edible with a peppery-sweet taste. Rounded, turban-shaped buds and seedpods can be pickled simply by pouring boiling cider vinegar over a jar full. Substitute them for capers.

Nasturtiums contain a natural antibiotic that has proven effective even against some microorganisms that have built a resistance to common antibiotics. The leaves, made into tea or eaten raw, are said to promote production of red blood cells. Rub the juice of the plant on itches. Large amounts of the seeds can be purgative.

Nasturtiums have been fed to chickens for prevention and cure of fowl pox. They have few pest problems. I hate to part with them

in late spring when they grow pale and leggy as the heat increases. But they pull out easily and come back soon. Volunteers can be transplanted and are excellent in hanging planters or cascading over a wall.

Florida Culture: Grow this as an annual, planting seed in August or September in C and S, early spring in N, in full sun to partial shade. A freeze can kill them but they come through a light frost with little setback. Use fresh seed and soak it overnight to improve germination, which requires darkness and takes 7 to 10 days. Nasturtiums have no seed leaves. Place them about a foot apart in enriched soil. They like poor soil, but not as poor as most of Florida has.

Climbing varieties often reach the roof. They won't hurt trees or shrubs they use for support, or the porch screen. Feed lightly as needed. They tolerate drought but need occasional watering.

Nasturtiums are easy to propagate from cuttings. Root some and put them in deeper shade to keep them over the summer. Mine now self seed abundantly, but color variety and flower size decrease somewhat, so I plant new colors every few years.

NEEM TREE
Azadirachta indica
(a-za-di-RACH-ta)
Mahogany family
Native to India
Uses: medicinal,
insecticide, oil
Grows in C and S

This may be the ultimate herb! Although Indian farmers have been using this tree as the village pharmacy for 4,500 years, only very recent and ongoing research is confirming its extensive value. The name comes from *aristha*, the Sanskrit word for reliever of sickness. It is greatly used in the tropics, where it grows quickly to produce shade, firewood, and a safe and simple insecticide for third world farmers who could never afford commercial insecticides. Leaves placed in books, beds, or grain bins repel insects. Commercial insecticides made from neem extract are being marketed under various trade names such as Martosan. They are so far very expensive, but are proving effective against a remarkably wide variety of pests.

This is because the tree's most active compound, azadirachtin, somewhat resembles steroids and seems to either repel pests or interrupt their stages of development. Since neem has a complex makeup of more than 20 compounds, insects are less likely to develop resistance.

A tea made from neem leaves has been used as an antidote for malaria for centuries. Asians use the twigs to clean their teeth and there are commercial neem toothpastes in some countries. Neem is said to be antiseptic, antibacterial, antiviral, antipyretec (reduces fever) and anti-inflammatory.

The oil is used medicinally as well as for lamp oil and as a lubricant. The leaves have a bitter taste and the oil is said to taste worse than castor oil.

Neem has a compound leaf with pinnate leaflets. Small white flowers appear in spring, with a sweet, jasmine-like scent. Edible fruit ripens about July. Children in Aftica love to eat the fruit, which is about 3/4 of an inch long and is rich in vitamin C. A tree begins bearing fruit at 3 to 5 years.

A closely related species, *A. siamensis*, grows in Thailand, and is known as sweet neem. Leaves and seeds are used as additions to many foods as spices. Medicinal uses are similar. Compounds are similar to those of Indian neem but the leaves are about twice as large and less bitter. The seeds are large and have a spicy, hot tinge.

Florida Culture: Neem grows quickly as long as it is not touched by frost. In the Tampa area, Vickie and Mac Parsons are growing five acres of neem trees, the largest plantation known in this country, so far. In the northern part of the state or for anyone who doesn't want to take a chance on frost, neem grows well in containers with about the same care as you would give a ficus. The larger the pot, the larger the tree will grow, so eventually give it 10 gallons of soil if possible.

Neem makes an ideal indoor plant because it grows well with a minimum of maintenance or humidity. Keep it near a sunny window.

Indoors or out, neem trees must have well-drained soil. They are relatively heavy feeders, responding well to organic fertilizer such as fish emulsion, bone meal, and kelp. However, if leaves turn yellow, it may mean the trees have been given too much fertilizer or water. Although evergreen, neem trees may lose leaves in dry periods or after frost. They will revive quickly with watering or the onset of warm days. In severe frost they may die back to the ground, but usually regrow from the roots. Several fungal diseases and slugs can also be problems.

Although two trees are needed for cross pollination to get seed, one tree will give you leaves and flowers. Seed is said to be hard to grow in Florida, although the Parsons have had seed form on the trees in their Tampa plantation after only three years.

Seed may be purchased from ECHO farms, 17430 Durrance Rd., N. Ft. Myers, FL 33917.

NIGHTSHADE
Marriage Vine, Violet-Bloom, Fair Lady
Solanum dulcamara,
Atropha belladonna
(so-LA-num) (ah-TROH-fa)
Potato family

Native to tropical America, Europe and Asia
Pull from garden: poisonous

These two dangerous plants grow as weeds in Florida, not as often or as robustly as in my other gardens, but with just as much potential danger. I take most poisonous plants in stride, but I've seen these growing among the shrubbery in public parks, laden with just the kind of red berries that are tempting to small children. They are toxic enough to kill a colt.

Deadly nightshade can be viney once it passes the regular weed size, and can continue to climb up to 8 feet. Leaves are oval, usually with two earlike segments at the base of each leaf. Flowers are star-shaped with white to purple petals and a yellow-orange point of stamens in the center. These are followed by not quite pea-size dark green berries that ripen red.

Fair lady is more shrublike, 3 to 6 feet tall. Alternate upper leaves each have a smaller leaf at the base. These flowers are shaped like bells or hip hugging skirts, dull purple, drooping, and about 1 1/4 inch long. Fruits are berries set in a star-shaped calyx and turn from green to deep purple or black.

Learn to identify these, show them with dire warnings to your children, neighbors, or grandchildren, and then weed them out ruthlessly. Birds must both survive and drop them. Children have died from eating only three berries. Some people absorb the poison through their skin, but I've pulled out dozens with no ill effects.

However, no plant is all bad. Recent research showed that nightshade contains a tumor-inhibiting agent which could prove useful in

treating cancer. Belladonna, the source of atropine, once used by Italian ladies as eye makeup, is used today by eye doctors to dilate the pupils for eye examinations. There are several other uses in medicine, past, present, and possibly future, but none is safe for home application.

OREGANO
Wild marjoram
Origanum species
(or-RIG-ah-num)
Mint family
Native from Europe through the Middle East
Uses: culinary, ground cover, ornamental
Grows in N, C, and S

The name for this herb comes from the Greek and means joy of the mountain. In Greece, meat from goats who graze on wild oregano is a delicacy. The recent popularity here of the flavor we know and use so lavishly stems from soldiers returning from WWII with a taste for Italian food.

Oregano is good with cheese, eggs, breads, meat, shellfish, and vegetables, especially eggplant, beans, zucchini, and potatoes. As a medicine, the tea is said to help coughs and asthma. A drop of oil rubbed on an aching tooth or gum eases the pain. In baths, it relieves aches and sprains.

There is much confusion of names among the 25 or more *Origanum* species and other plants that contain the same fragrance or oils. Most have small, round, opposite leaves and a low, spreading habit, though a few are erect and as much as 2-3 feet tall. Flowers are small, white to pink, in 1 inch spikes. My first oregano (probably *O. vulgare*, wild or bastard marjoram) flourished and bloomed with pink flowers, but had hardly any fragrance or flavor at all. It is a nice Florida ground cover, though.

If you are buying oregano for culinary use, try to get *O. heracleoticum*, but even these vary in flavor, so taste a leaf before you purchase.

Florida Culture: Start seeds in fall or early spring. Germination takes 5 to 10 days. Or start from cuttings or root divisions. Set plants where they have room to creep. For best flavor, cut just as bloom begins. Take a few cuttings

in containers to the shade in early summer. This lives over well for some people and perishes in the dampness for others.

OREGANO-FLAVORED SUBSTITUTES

Coleus amboinicus

This oregano taste-alike is called tropical oregano, Spanish thyme, or Cuban borage. It grows easily to a sturdy and delightful  plant that does well in Florida summers or winters. It may need some protection from frosts in N, and even in C. I take cuttings before a freeze warning, but I have not lost it to winter yet. It has thick, slightly fuzzy leaves that look like a coleus, though not quite as large and much more fleshy and substantial. Mine has yet to bloom but may someday have purple flowers. It gets almost two feet tall for me before it sprawls.

Give it some lime, sun or light shade, and plenty of room. The only ones I've lost have been from crowding. It responds so well to water that mere cuttings in spring become large clumps by the end of summer. Tropical oregano roots best when barely pushed into the moist medium. I've seen plain green varieties, but the variegated is vastly superior as an ornamental. Both have robust flavor, a much better oregano flavor than any oregano I've come across. One leaf, chopped or pureed, will flavor a pot of spaghetti sauce.

Lippia or *Phyla graveolens*

Called Mexican or Puerto Rican oregano, this member of the verbena family is a 3 to 4 foot shrub with cream colored flowers and ovate leaves. It is a tender perennial that likes sun and a neutral pH, the same as true oregano, but needs fairly constant moisture. Namewise, this one is confusing, I have *Lippia dulcis,* called Aztec sweet herb or shrub, that fits this description except that the opposite leaves are toothed and the fragrance is different, sweeter, more minty than oregano and perhaps closer to *Lippia citriodora* (also called *Aloysia triphylla*), lemon verbena. It has grown well all summer as a ground cover in partial shade.

Poliomintha longiflora,

Also called Mexican oregano, this one is native to the dry parts of Texas and Mexico, but reportedly does well in the damper Houston area as well. This woody shrub grows to three feet with bright green, finely cut leaves and tubular white to lavender flowers, 1 1/2 inches long, with an oregano fragrance and a strong appeal to hummingbirds.

ORRIS ROOT
German or Florentine Iris
Iris germanica florentina

Although hardy from zones 3
to 10, this iris, like most bearded
iris, is extremely difficult to grow in
Florida because of the state's over-
plentiful moisture. Try keeping it in
a clay pot under a patio roof where
it gets sun but no rain.

OSAGE ORANGE
Hedge Apples, *Bois D'arc*
Maclura pomifera

This was always my favorite
roach and water bug repellent. It is
a shrub native to Oklahoma and
hardy in   zones 5 to 9.
Plants   have lived in
my   Florida yard
for seven   years now
and hard-   ly grown an
inch, let   alone borne
fruit. So   save yourself
the time and space and use
eucalyptus, feverfew, lavender, pennyroyal, or boric acid to keep the
palmetto bugs at bay.

PARSLEY
Petroselinum crispum
(pe-tro-SEL-i-num)
Carrot family
Native to Europe and
Western Asia
Uses: culinary, garnish,
container plant
Grows in N, C, and S

Parsley is the best known and
most commonly used herb. Pliny
said every sauce should contain it.
The Romans spread parsley and
soft cheese on bread and the
Greeks fed it to chariot horses to
give them the stamina to win races.
Charlemagne planted it in his gardens and herbalist Gerard said the
seeds helped the light-headed to
resist drink better.

There are three kinds of parsley.
The curled is the most common and
a very attractive as well as useful
plant. The flat-leaved Italian has
superior flavor, according to some
cooks, and also seems to survive the
summer better in Florida. There is
also Hamburg or Dutch parsley with
a parsniplike root that can flavor
soups and stews or be cooked as a
vegetable. Its foliage does not have
the flavor of either of the others.

Parsley not only adds color that
changes plain dishes to gourmet,
but it packs a wallop of vitamins,
especially A, B, C, calcium, and
iron. If you add it to any dish with
garlic, it takes away the problem of
garlic breath.

Parsley root has laxative
properties. It was used to treat urinary infections and help pass kidney stones, but do not use large
quantities because it can irritate the
kidneys. An infusion of the leaves
and stems is claimed to be soothing
and cleansing in the bath. The oil is
used in perfume, soap, shampoo,
skin creams, and lotions, though
this is not mentioned by Madison
Avenue as aloe is.

Florida Culture: Plant seeds
in February or March in N, from
September to January in C and S.
Seeds can take as long as five weeks
to germinate. I pour boiling water
over seeds right after planting and
they sprout in as little as ten days.
You can also hurry the sprouting by
presoaking in warm water for 24
hour, or freezing in ice cubes for a
few days, two or three seeds per
cube. Let the cube melt in the
planting place, then press seeds into
the soil.

You can buy plants at most nurseries and many grocery stores. Transplant them only when small, for parsley has a taproot that resents it. Cut the entire plant back to 2 inches above the ground and it will regrow. Or use the outer leaves and let the center grow. Feed plants every three weeks and keep soil moist. Mulch plants well and provide a bit of shade and they may come through summer, though it is not uncommon for the root to rot and the top to die suddenly.

The anise swallowtail butterfly lays its eggs on parsley, dill, and fennel. If you wish, you can pick off the lime-green, black, and cream-colored caterpillars and put them on a catch plant, but they usually go into their next stage before they eat too much. I'll gladly share my parsley with butterflies anytime.

If you allow parsley to bloom, you can collect the seeds in a paper bag, but the plant will die thereafter, so if you don't want seeds and it isn't nearly summer, you may want to cut off bloom stalks to prolong the plant's life.

PASSION FLOWERS

Passion Fruit, Maypop,
Passiflora species
(pass-i-FLOR-a)
Passion flower family
Native to Australia and
southeast U.S.
Uses: ornamental, fruit,
butterfly plant
Grows in N, C, and S

The name comes from the Spanish priests and explorers who first found passion flowers in South America. They saw in the bloom the story of the crucifixion of Christ. The fringed corona represents the crown of thorns, the three stigmas the nails, the five stamens the wounds of His hands and feet and side. The ten sepals and petals are for the faithful apostles, Peter and Judas excluded. The tendrils are the whips that beat Him. The three- to five-lobed leaves are the hands of the persecutors.

Plants flower from spring through summer and fruit from summer into early winter. Blooms vary with species from purple to blue to white with maroon marking for the giant granadilla. One species has scarlet recurved petals and looks like a completely different plant, but when you count the parts, you see it is still a *Passiflora*.

Native Americans used leaves for poultices to heal bruises and the leaves and flowers for a sedative and painkiller. A tea made from the flowers is supposedly calming. Use the same infusion for a bath to relieve tension.

Warning: Very large amounts can cause nausea and vomiting.

Flowers can be floated in bowls of water for table decorations. Dry them in sand to decorate wreaths. *Passiflora* is the state flower of Tennessee.

There are many species of these perennial woody vines. They climb with tendrils and can grow 30 feet a year. All have edible fruits, but many need hand pollination and are therefore mostly ornamental. They are greatly favored for butterfly gardens as a host or larvae feeding plant.

I couldn't wait to grow these and planted seeds and cuttings with minor success. They will die to the ground at about 30 degrees, sometimes to come back from the roots and sometimes not. Mine died the first three winters. Then birds began to plant them for me and I've been plagued with passion vines as weeds ever since. Still, I can't help but love them. Be advised that they can and will take over if given a chance.

Florida Culture: Passion flower seeds take 10 days to 2 years to germinate. Plants grow rapidly and should flower and fruit the first year from cuttings, but may take two years from seed. Some of my fruit friends have gallons of juice in their freezers and this is the main ingredient in commercial Hawaiian Punch. For fruit production, you must plant the right kind like the yellow or the giant granadilla, and the frost sensitivity relegates these to protected places in C and to S. The wild maypop grows from C north and has a small edible fruit, but it can be a serious weed.

Fruits change color as they ripen. Let your first ones ripen until they drop. Soon you'll learn the right time. Then gather daily or else animals will do it for you.

Passion flowers bloom best in full sun and tolerate a wide range of soils, especially if you supply minor elements and fertilizer. Support is essential. This is one of the few vines that will cover a wooden fence with a little guidance at the start. A red one is covering my peach tree

and a white is trying to swallow a mature banana planting.

Do not hesitate to prune back drastically as the vine grows, for a shrub size plant can produce plenty of fruit. When plants are dormant in the winter, prune out all dead and weak growth, cutting back to vigorous shoots with many fruit buds. Take cuttings when frost threatens and expect to start over every several years in C. Even in S plants usually give only three to five years of productivity.

Feed lightly but frequently, 4 to 6 ounces per vine, every four to six weeks during active growth. Passion flowers are sensitive to nematodes, the purple one so much so that it is best grafted onto a yellow rootstock. Otherwise they are mostly pest free except for the caterpillars of the zebra and gulf fritillary butterflies, whose pruning does them more good than harm.

PATCHOULI
Pogostemon patchouli
(Po-go-STE-mon)
Mint family
Native to India, S.E.Asia
Uses: potpourri, ink, perfume, cosmetics
Grows in N, C, and S

The oil of patchouli has a subtle musky fragrance and antiseptic, antidepressant, and sedative properties. Leaves are dried and used primarily as a fixative in sachets and potpourris. The commercial fixative of this name is blended from several species of *Pogostemon*, sometimes with leaves of other plants with similar fragrances as well. The essential oil is also used to repel moths, as a bath, facial or massage oil, or as a deodorant. Mixed with oils of citronella, vetiver, and sweet almond, it is a safe insecticide to apply to the skin. In fact, it is rejuvenating to the skin. Unlike most oils, it improves with age.

The leaves are opposite, fairly thick, an elongated diamond shape with scalloped edges toward the tip, smooth ones at the stem end. Tiny white flowers come in a cluster of spikes 2 to 3 inches long.

Florida Culture: Patchouli thrives as a perennial in Florida gardens AS LONG AS you give it what it needs. It will die quickly if allowed to dry out or freeze, so you may want to grow in it containers in N. Give it ample room.

Patchouli is a heavy feeder, so if leaves are mottled, it is hungry. For best results, give it loamy, neutral soil. A specimen at Selby Gardens in Sarasota is almost 4 feet tall, not quite as wide. My much smaller one has bloomed throughout the winter. It will take full sun to partial shade.

PEPPER

Hot or Chili Pepper, Cayenne
Capsicum species
(KAP-si-kum)
Potato family
Native to subtropical
America
Uses: ornamental, culinary,
insecticidal
Grows in N, C, and S

When I moved to Florida and read that peppers would sometimes keep growing and bearing for 3 or 4 years, I was elated. Then came reality. The bell peppers I

was used to growing may do that for others, but not for me, though I see them growing commercially nearby in Plant City.

However, there are all sorts of other peppers, many that I'd never heard of before, that grow here for me with wild abandon and have lasted and borne for years. My latest experiments with peppers include one from Costa Rica that is 2 feet tall and has been bending under its load of small, sweet, heart-shaped red peppers for a year and a half. Another, 'Aurora,' a shorter-lived plant for me, is a smaller plant with purple tones to the foliage and hot little pointed fruits that turn from purple to yellowish white to red.

As early as 5000 BC, South American natives noticed that food seasoned with peppers did not spoil as quickly and was easier to digest. The fruits contain capsaicin, a substance that reddens human skin by increasing blood circulation wherever it touches. It is an important ingredient in liniments for treating bursitis, rheumatism, and similar ailments. Extracts are antibacterial.

Cayenne pepper is not related to black pepper. Paprika is the mildest form of the powdered cayenne and highest in vitamin C. Tabasco is one of the hottest. Chili powder is a combination of peppers, herbs, and spices.

Some of Florida's peppers become shrubs or small trees, others grow as annuals. Leaves are pointed, oval, and alternate with a 1 to 3 small leaves at the base of each larger leaf. Flowers are dainty white to purplish with veinlike markings, star-shaped, about 1/2 inch across, followed by the fruit which can vary in color, shape,

KINDS OF PEPPERS

SWEET PEPPERS

Banana peppers ripen early and have a high yield of long, narrow fruit, up to 2 inches across the shoulders, 8 inches long, tapering to a point They start out green and ripen from yellow to red. 'Sweet Banana' is recommended for Florida.

Bell Peppers are the kind usually seen in the grocery store. Blocky fruits start out green, then turn yellow, red, orange, brown, or purple as they ripen, and increase in sweetness and nourishment as they do in color, especially in vitamins A and C. 'Early Calwonder,' 'Yolo Wonder,' and elongated 'Big Bertha' are recommended for Florida.

Pimento Peppers take longer to mature and have heart-shaped fruits about 4 1/2 inches long on dwarf but strong plants.

Costa Rican peppes grow as small shrubs and have many small (2-inch) but sweet peppers that ripen to a bright red.

Giant Anaconda, the other extreme, has oblong fruits up to 11 inches and 12 ounces that are as sweet as apples and best picked in the light green stage.

HOT PEPPERS

Anaheims, also called New Mexican chiles, vary from mild to medium hot and are used for chili powder and paprika. 'Hungarian Wax' is recommended for Florida. Ancho is a Mexican pepper used for chiles and chili powder.

'Mexi Bell,' a hybrid recommended for Florida, is a bell shaped pepper with a hot chili flavor in fruit that changes from green to chocolate to red. 'SuperChiliHybrid' is also recommended. Its 2 1/2 inch, cone-shaped peppers go from green to orange to red and are good fresh or dried. For milder taste, remove the core and ribs.

Jalapenos are small, hot, thick-skinned, and popular. The dark green peppers ripen to red and are used in salsa.

Cayenne peppers grow 4 to 12 inches long. They are narrow and cone shaped with a curl on the end. Even hotter are Thai peppers, narrow, waxy, and red, about 2 inches long. They make attractive plants that reach several feet or more in height. Wear gloves when you chop cayenne or Thai peppers and watch out for the burning capsaicin in the membrane and seeds.

Habaneros are the most potent of the peppers and grow well in Florida. Pumpkin shaped fruits may be green, red, orange, or yellow. They look fascinating but handle with care.

habanero

Many pepper varieties are listed in seed catalogs. Some offer a packet of mixed hot pepper types. You can also grow seeds from within the hot fresh peppers you buy, but results are less certain.

size, and sizzle. Those that are too hot to eat can still be ornamental and make a fine insecticide spray because few insects like them either. Put fresh or dried hot peppers into the blender, add water, blend, strain and use as a safe and effective bug spray or squirrel repellant on vegetables and flowers. Add a little salad oil to make it stick.

Freeze peppers in halves or chopped for use in cooked dishes. They loose their crunch, so they are not as good raw. Pickle small peppers by packing in jars and then filling with boiling white wine vinegar. After cooling, store in the refrigerator. You can dry chiles by stringing pods on heavy thread and hanging in a cool, dry place.

Warning: People with ulcers, bowel disease, or other intestinal problems should check with a doctor before using hot peppers. Never touch the eyes after handling them. If you bite into a hot

one, milk or beer may be better than water to put out the fire.

Florida Culture: Start with seeds or plants in early spring in N, fall or spring in C and S. Sow seeds 6 to 8 weeks before transplants are wanted. Germination takes from 5 to 25 days and seedlings look like their tomato cousins at first. Unlike tomatoes, transplanted peppers like to stand high in the hole. Don't cover them as deeply as you would tomatoes. Set them 12 to 24 inches apart in enriched soil with even moisture and full sun. Feed every 3 to 4 weeks.

Branches break easily, so you may need to stake tall or heavily laden plants. Mulch to keep soil moist and fruit clean. Harvest by snapping off fruit with a twist or clipping it off. Protect plants from frost in N and C.

PEPPER, BLACK. See p. 145.

PERILLA
Summer Coleus, Beefsteak
    Plant, Shiso
Perilla frutescens
    (pe-RILL-a)
Mint family
Native to China and Japan
Uses: ornamental, culinary
Grows in N, C, and S

One of the Asian members of our Rare Fruit Council International brought this to the plant raffle several years ago, and it has popped up here and there in my garden ever since, looking like purple basil or coleus. It self sows prodigiously. The Japanese use a green-leaved perilla, shiso, for cooking and

flavoring. Use fresh or pickled leaves or seeds of perilla with fish, tempura, and cucumbers. Add leaves or seeds to pickled plums or beets. Add leaves to white wine vinegar for a bright pink vinegar, excellent in salad dressings, or add it to the wine in which you store ginger and use this in Oriental dishes.

Perilla is lovely in the herb or flower garden or among shrubs. It is especially striking with silver-leaved plants like wormwood and salvia. I often use the foliage in bouquets with pentas, cordyline leaves, and roses. Save dried seed heads for wreaths.

Perilla is an annual, but grows most of the year in Florida and self seeds easily. It is usually 2 to 4 feet tall, though I have one now that is nearer to 5 feet. Leaves are opposite, 2 to 4 inches long, a purplish red with fringed edges, white hairs on top and purple ones underneath. Stems are square. Perilla blooms with spikes of pinkish green flowers unless these are cut off to encourage leaf growth and bushiness. Leaves and small round seeds have a spicy fragrance much like cinnamon.

Florida Culture: Perilla is easy to grow in Florida from seeds or cuttings. For better germination, mix the seeds with moist peat moss in a plastic bag and store this in the refrigerator for a week, then plant outdoors. Seeds germinate in 10 days and transplant easily. Set them at least 12 inches apart. Pinch plants at 6 inch growth intervals to keep them bushy. Unpinched, they tend to be leggy. Perilla loves Florida but you may want to take cuttings, which are so easy they root in water, when frost is predicted.

PLANTAIN

Plantago species
(plan-TA-go)
Plantain family
Native to Europe
Uses: insect bite relief, dye
Grows in N, C, and S

Like dandelion, this is not nearly as common a lawn weed in Florida as it is in northern states. Nevertheless, it appears throughout the state in lawns, cleared areas and along roadsides. The settlers brought it from Europe and the natives soon adopted their medicinal uses of the plant and added a few of their own.

Plantain grows with a rosette of wide, oval, deeply veined, long-stalked leaves with smooth edges. Pretzel-thin spikes of greenish white flowers that look like scales rise up in spring and summer.

Crush a leaf, soak it if possible, and apply it to wounds or to bee stings after you scrape, never squeeze, the stinger out. Young, tender leaves can also be added to salads or cooked greens but they do have a mild laxative effect, so use them sparingly.

Plantain has mucilaginous, cleansing, and stimulating properties for a skin or hair lotion. The entire plant makes dull gold or camel colored dye for wool.

Florida Culture: Don't grow, just know and gather as needed.

POKEWEED
   Pokeberry, Inkberry,
      Cancer Root
   Phytolacca americana
      (fye-to-LA-ka)
   Pokeweed family
   Native from Maine to Florida
   Uses: dye, bird and wildlife
      gardening
   Grows in N, C, and S

In her book Cross Creek, Marjorie Kinnan Rawlings told how she gathered pokeweed shoots in her groves after spring rains, cut the tender shoots from 6 to 10 inches long, removed the leaves and thin skin, cooked them like asparagus, and served them on toast with cream sauce.

Warning: Mature leaves, berries, and especially roots are poisonous and eating them can cause death. Pick only very young leaves and eat only after boiling in at least two changes of water to remove the bitter taste. Birds relish the berries and seem to come to no harm, but warn children and grandchildren not to touch.

Thoreau favored a purple poke stalk as a cane. Native Americans used the berries to color their baskets a dark blue and the settlers used the juice as a natural ink that still hasn't faded on some museum documents.

This is a plant to know, not to grow. It gets 4 to 12 feet tall and spreads widely with a few, thick, succulent, hollow stems. Leaves are long, glossy, and pointed with an unpleasant scent. Terminal spires of round white or purplish flowers are followed by berries, green at first but turning dark purple when ripe. The stems and veins of mature leaves tend toward reddish purple.

Florida Culture: Learn to recognize pokeweed, as the birds will sooner or later plant it in your yard. Pull out the roots, otherwise it comes back no matter how often you cut it to the ground. I wouldn't advise planting any more than Florida has, but J.L. Hudson offers seeds of two species.

POPPY, CALIFORNIA
Eschscholzia californica
(esh-SHOLT-zee-a)
Poppy family
Native to W. North America
Uses: ornamental, bouquets,
  hair tonic
Grows in N, C, and S

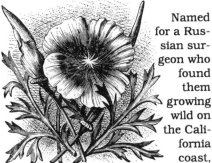

Named for a Russian surgeon who found them growing wild on the California coast, these were used by the Indians as a painkiller for toothache, a poultice for sores and ulcers, and to ease headaches and insomnia. Indian women knew how to use them in a potion to lure lovers, but this was a crime for which they could be expelled from the tribe. The Spanish cooked them in olive oil for a hair tonic supposed to make hair grow thick and shiny.

Lovely, chalicelike flowers of bright yellow, deep orange, soft cream to mahogany red each have four petals and many stamens and can be 2 to 4 inches across on neat plants, 6 to 24 inches tall. Buds have trim, pointed caps that pop off in the morning when the flowers are ready to open. Blooms close at night and on dark days. The foliage is fernlike and blue green, the seedpod a long, slender capsule which splits when ripe. Remove seedpods to stimulate more flower growth, being careful not to cut off the similar looking buds. I've cut off a promise instead of a past more than once.

Florida Culture: California poppies are easily grown hardy annuals. Improve soil with plenty of humus. Then start from seed sown in place in full sun in early spring or fall. Or sow in peat pellets or pots for they resent transplanting. Thin so plants are 8 to 10 inches apart. Remove faded flowers to prolong bloom until summer heat and humidity end the cycle. These can self sow.

POPPY, PRICKLY
Argemone mexicana
  (Ar-ge-MON-ee)
Poppy family
Native to Tropical America
Uses: Medicinal, wildflower
Grows in N and C

This annual grows to 3 feet tall, although height is variable. It has spiny, gray-green leaves and milky sap or latex. The showy flower, with 7 large creamy white or yellow petals with yellow centers, blooms from spring to fall along roadsides and in waste places. The juice of the plant is used to treat skin disorders and was once used for cataracts. The name comes from *argema* for cataract.

POPPY, SHIRLEY
Papaver rhoeas
  (pa-PAV-er)
Poppy family
Native to Europe and Asia
Uses: ornamental flowers
Grows in N and C

This is a beautiful cut flower, although short-lived in Florida. In spring, eye-catching blooms up to 4 inches wide have tissue-thin petals of white, rose, or red. Single poppy flowers can be made into dolls by turning the petals down for a skirt,

using the seed capsule for the head, and tying them around the stems with grass. Push a dried stalk through the capsule head for arms.

Florida Culture: Plant the seeds right in the ground between October 25 and November 25 each year. Keep the seedbed moist and thin plants to a foot apart. Seedlings are difficult to transplant but some people have good luck planting them in multicelled market packs to minimize root disturbance. Transplant them to the garden when they are 2 to 3 inches tall.

Like so many hardy annual flowers, poppies grow slowly over the winter, and then grow quickly in the spring. They begin to bloom by April and continue for up to two months. For bouquets, pick them in the morning and singe stem ends with a flame, then put flowers into cool water.

Gather the seedheads, which are striking in dried bouquets, after they dry on the plant.

Seeds from *Papaver rhoeas* are small yet easy to collect by shaking the pods over a small bowl. They add a nutty flavor and texture when sprinkled on bread, cake and biscuits, and thicken and add texture to curry. They can also be put out in feeders for the birds.

PORTULACA

Portulaca oleracea
(por-tew-LAK-a)
Portulaca family
Native to India, China, and
    Greece

Uses: culinary, medicine,
    ornamental
Grows in N, C, and S

This cousin of the bedding plant, rose moss, grows wild in Florida, even in my St. Augustine grass lawn. Given garden care, it forms a carpet of color all summer long. Some think the name comes from the Latin *porto* (to carry) and *lac* (milk) for the juice in the stems. The *oleracea* is Latin for potherb, for the plant was grown as food in Europe in the 16th to 18th centuries. The crushed leaves and stems soothe burns, stings, swellings, and sore gums. High in vitamin C, it was once used to cure scurvy.

Dr. Artemin P. Simopoulos, a former chairwoman of the U.S. National Institute of Health, noticed that purslane, which she cooked in her native Greece, looked much like fish oil. Laboratory investigation showed that it is the richest known plant source of Omega-3 acids otherwise found mostly in fish oils. These are thought to help reduce cholesterol and blood pressure and may strengthen the immune system.

The stems and leaves are soft and fleshy, often reddish. Leaves are alternate, and small: spoon shaped on the purslane; almost needlelike on the garden portulaca. The flowers are showy with five petals, a clear bright yellow in the species, soft pastel shades of yellow, orange, pink, red, and purple in cultivars. All parts and species are edible and I add purslane to salads no matter what stage it is in. The tiny black seeds are good, too. Leaves and seed add texture and vitamins without changing the taste much, though some say leaves have a vinegary flavor and others compare it to asparagus. Purslane can be steamed, added to soups or casseroles, mixed with eggs, or pickled for winter.

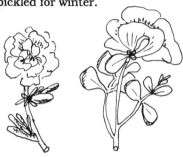

Florida Culture: Portulacas are easy to grow from seeds, plants, or cuttings. Germination takes 7 to 15 days. Plants bloom best in the heat of summer in full sun. Set starts from 6 to 10 inches apart. Once established, they are drought resistant, but are killed by frost. Start harvesting in 6 to 8 weeks.

They have only two faults. Flowers close in the afternoon and the stems are too short, only about 6 inches, for any but the smallest bouquet. After they have been blooming awhile and don't seem so colorful, shear off the seedheads to start new growth. Portulaca roots easily from cuttings and self seeds easily, too.

PURPLE CONEFLOWER
Echinacea angustifolia
(e-ki-NAY-she-a)
Daisy family
Native to central and
  southeastern U.S.
Uses: ornamental, medicinal
Grows in N and C

This herb has lately found new favor among herbalists. Native Americans used the thick roots for a panacea to help restore general health, cure snakebite, alleviate stings, toothache, and mumps, and as a blood purifier. It was one of the plants used most by drug companies until antibiotics came on the scene. So many articles have been written about it that there is now concern about overharvesting of the wild plants, as studies show it activates the immune system and therefore helps fight off almost any disease. It is also nontoxic.

But for most Florida growers, coneflower is strictly an ornamental herb with its showy, slightly fragrant large daisy blooms. The rose colored ray flowers are often recurving rather than flat and centers can be purple to brownish-orange. Leaves are long and hairy with three distinct veins along their length. Plants grow 1 to 5 feet tall, depending on climate and variety.

Improved varieties include some with white flowers and flatter petals. Echinaceas bloom for two months, usually in the fall, sometimes in the spring as well.

Florida Culture: Purple coneflowers grow wild on Midwestern prairies but need a bit of special attention in Florida. They start easily from seed that takes 10 to 20 days to germinate and does best if either planted or mixed with damp peat moss and put in the refrigerator for 4 weeks (stratified.) Set plants 18 to 24 inches apart and mulch well. Purchased plants seem vulnerable to insects and snails when first planted. Several of mine disappeared within a few days, so protect them with insecticidal soap, pepper spray, or a canning jar shield until established. Many growers in the Tampa area have thriving, abundantly blooming plants if they give them plenty of space, full sun, slightly enriched soil, and moderate watering. The flowers last over a week in arrangements and the centers are good in fresh or dried bouquets.

REDBUD
> Judas Tree
> *Cercis canadensis*
> (SIR-sis)
> Pea family
> Native to North
> America and Florida
> Uses: ornamental,
> medicinal, summer shade
> Grows in N and C

This is a good tree for the center or edges of a herb garden because it is deciduous and lets in all the winter sun, then shades the other herbs in summer. It grows (slowly for me) with dark green heart shaped alternate leaves and small purplish pink flowers close to the branches before the leaves come out in early spring. Seedpods 3 1/2 inches long turn brown in the fall. There is a seldom-seen white-flowered form and several named, im-

proved cultivars, one with pink foliage that turns green when mature.

The bark of the redbud was used by Native Americans to treat diarrhea and dysentery and a closely related species is used in China to treat bladder disease and hemorrhoids.

Florida Culture: Trees are sold in nurseries in N and seem to do better the farther north you live. Tampa foresters use redbud as a street tree.

Plant in fertile soil. Wrap the trunk to protect against borers. Mulch the root zone and feed twice a year. Redbuds have low salt tolerance but high drought tolerance and need full sun to partial shade.

RICE PAPER PLANT

> *Tetrapanax papyriferus*
> (tet-tra-PAN-ax)
> Aralia family
> Native to China
> Uses: ornamental,
> medicinal
> Grows in N, C, and S

The name comes from Greek *tetra* for four (the parts of the flowers come in fours), *panax* for all-healing, and *papyriferis* for paper-bearing. It grows as a tropical shrub to 10 feet and can be rather treelike. It has large, palmately lobed, gray-green leaves a foot across with velvety whiteness underneath and in new growth. You can see the resemblance to its relatives, aralia and ginseng. The flowers are small, yellowish-white, fuzzy balls produced in great profusion above the foliage. Though coarse in texture, it gives a tropical feeling to the landscape.

The Chinese use the stem pith as a source of rice paper, also as a liver stimulant and a diuretic and to increase milk production. Plant extracts have shown anticancer activity in animals. It can be an irritant to some people.

Florida Culture: Rice paper plant grows easily in full sun but prefers partial shade. Start it from seeds, stem or root cuttings, air layering, or from suckers growing around or even a great distance from another plant. In fact, it can become invasive and you may want to grow it in a container for control. It is not salt tolerant but has medium drought tolerance. It will die to the ground in a freeze but usually comes back. Use insecticidal soap if mealybugs are a problem.

ROSE

Rosa species
Rose family
Native to Asia Minor
Uses: ornamental, culinary,
    potpourri, cosmetic
Grows in N, C, and S

Many people are surprised to realize that roses are herbs, and have many practical uses. Roses have symbolized love and beauty throughout history and in many legends. The Romans and the native Americans used roses in bridal crowns. Rose water was used as early as the tenth century and attar of roses has been an important industry in France since the 16th century.

William Penn brought roses to the colonies in 1699 and John Adams planted the first bushes around the White House where the Rose Garden often is the scene of today's news. Recently, the rose became the official flower of the United States.

The hardy shrub damask and French roses are traditional for

herbal use. They are the ancestors of many modern hybrids, and any rose can be used as a herb today. New, improved kinds bloom throughout the year in Florida with a minimum of care. There are roses for every garden use, for accent, background, hedges, miniatures, climbers, ground covers, and for erosion control on banks.

Florida Culture: Roses need full sun to partial shade in Florida, regular feeding, and regular to occasional watering. They have low salt tolerance and can have some pest or disease problems, but as a rule they grow well here and make very good backgrounds or centerpieces for Florida herb gardens. They provide color in their flowers and the red of the new leaves. They grow large enough to provide summer shade for other herbs.

The only drawback to using roses in a herb garden would be the necessity to keep pesticides away from any herbs you cut and use regularly in cooking. This is no problem for me because I use very few pesticides, even on roses, and those applications would be so few and far between that I could work around them. But for people who are using pesticides to raise perfect roses, any food plant would be best placed well away.

In Florida, roses should have special rootstocks such as Fortuniana and Dr. Huey that are resistant to nematodes. Ask your local nurseryman for the best types for your area. This is a good reason to buy locally or from Florida sources rather than from northern mail order growers.

I have one lovely rose that I started from a cutting. It's small flowers are extremely fragrant and excellent in potpourri. So far it seems to have no problems and be very pest resistant. So there are some exceptions to the rootstock rule, but it stands in most cases.

ROSEMARY
Rosmarinus officinalis
(ro-ma-RI-nis)
Mint family
Native to the Mediterranean
Uses: ornamental,
culinary, crafts
Grows in N, C, and S

Rub or hug a rosemary, and the next few hours of whatever you are doing will be more pleasant. During the harvest season where it grows wild in the salt spray along the Mediterranean coast, the fragrance carries 20 miles out to sea. Rosemary means dew of the sea, and the Spanish say the flowers turned from white to blue when touched by Mary's cloak when it sheltered Mary and the Christ Child on their flight to Egypt. This is possible since it thrives in desert conditions. What is more surprising is that it thrives in Florida despite and during our muggy summers.

St. Thomas More let it run all over his garden wall, both for the bees and as a symbol of remembrance and therefore of friendship. There are many varieties listed in any herb catalog. They vary in height from 2 to 4 feet indoors, can grow up to 5 feet outdoors. There are both upright and prostrate forms. The latter are lovely cascading over walls, in hanging baskets, or in bonsai or topiary work. All have tiny, gray-green leaves from needle thin to the width of a pencil and their strong, delightfully piney fragrance when crushed will stay on the fingers for hours. Varieties with pink, white, or blue flowers are available.

Rosemary supposedly increases the rate of blood flow and therefore is good for the memory and the brain. In ancient Greece students wore garlands in their hair while studying. Add it to the steam facial or tea for students in stress. Add it also to any meat, fish, or game dish, especially to roasts. Use it with vegetables, cheese, eggs, and dry beans. Combine it with bay, chives, chervil, parsley, and thyme. Use flowers and leaves as a garnish. Freeze sprigs whole or dry leaves for a more intense flavor. Use rosemary as a strewing herb, in potpourris, baths, or as a hair rinse or spray, especially for brunettes.

Florida Culture: Rosemary starts from seeds that take 15 to 20 days to germinate, or more quickly and easily from cuttings, or by layering. Set plants 2 to 3 feet apart in well drained soil.

I had one sprawling in the shade for years and an offspring now grows upright and blooms in full sun by the pool. Neither summer heat nor winter cold seemed to hurt them. My old one finally died. The only ones I'd lost before were those that dried out in the pot. They seem more drought tolerant in the ground.

Bury a piece of concrete near the roots of rosemary to add a bit of lime from every rain. I use the same piece to hold down the current layer until it roots. Use rosemary often or prune as needed to keep the plant bushy.

RUE

Ruta graveolens
(ROO-ta)
Citrus family
Native to southern Europe
Uses: ornamental,
    everlasting flower, dye
Grows in N, C, and S

Bunches of rue were used in churches to sprinkle holy water, so it was called the herb of grace. Leonardo da Vinci and Michelangelo ate it to preserve their eyesight and their creative inner vision. It was also used to increase appetite. The leaves of rue inspired the suit of clubs on playing cards. As a symbol of grief and regret, it has filtered into our language in such phrases as "rue the day..."

Nothing looks quite like rue with its upright stems of finely cut, lacy blue-green foliage. It can grow 2 to 3 feet tall. Each round leaflet is widest at the top. There are extra blue, dwarf, variegated, golden, and dark green varieties. Flowers are a bright cluster of mustard yellow, very pretty against the blue-green foliage. Mine bloomed in Iowa but not yet in Florida. Seeds resemble miniature oranges. Tiny glands over the entire plant release a volatile oil that bears the musky fragrance and bitter taste.

Rue causes a rash much like poison ivy to some people, especially when it is wet or in hot sun. It can be toxic in large amounts and should never be taken internally.

Rue is an interesting plant in the garden or in containers with crimson thyme, golden sage, or silver-leaved herbs like wormwood. Some say it should not be planted near basil, sage, or cabbage, but improves the growth of figs. I tried the latter, but it did not thrive with the same degree of neglect as the figs. Some people hang branches to repel flies or make a decoction for fleas.

Florida Culture: You can grow the common varieties of rue from seeds, but for the named varieties you'll need to buy plants or grow it from cuttings or divisions. Seeds take 10 to 14 days to germinate. Set plants one foot apart. They like full sun to partial shade through the winter. Fertilize moderately for the best color.

Rue is sensitive to root disease, like citrus. My rue plants usually die out in summer, but a survivor often shows up in some strange place, which is remarkable  since I've seen no flowers or seeds. For insurance, carry cuttings over in containers in shade for the summer or be prepared to start over again in the fall.

SAGE
    Garden, Clary, Muscatel,
        Pineapple, or Mexican Sage
    Salvia species
        (SAL-vee-a)
    Mint family
    Native to the
        Mediterranean region
    Uses: ornamental, culinary,
        aromatic
    Grows in N, C, and S

The common culinary herbal sage, *S. officinalis*, with its pebbled, gray-green leaves, grows easily in Florida only over winter. Yet it was one of the few summer survivors for my chef friend, Rick Munroe, and I started over with cuttings of his weathered plants.

There are other sages that grow wonderfully here, even in summer. *S. elegans,* pineapple sage, grows year round as easily as a weed but is much more useful. It's pineapple-scented leaves and dark red edible flowers are good as a garnish, in drinks, in fruit salads, chopped into cream cheese, or as a fragrant addition to bouquets. Freeze the flowers in ice cubes for drinks. Grow this one in

partial shade and prune woody
stems often enough to keep it in
shape. It attracts hummingbirds
and butterflies.

I have a new grapefruit sage,
which is similar. It
seems even hardier
with larger, citrusy-
smelling, velvety
leaves that suffered
stress and insect
damage over summer
but recovered for a
long, pleasant winter
season, and bloomed
bright pink in spring. It is now
four feet tall.

I grew lovely plants of clary
sage, *S. sclaria*, but summer came
and took them before they could
bloom. This biennial is also a
fixative and I aim to try again,
starting earlier in late summer,
and harvest some of the leaves
before the next summer comes.

Mexican sage, *S. leucantha*,
is a fixture in my garden and I use
the lavender and white spires to
make lavender wands (see page
21) as well as for fresh or dried
bouquets throughout the year.
Its long, narrow, gray-green
leaves are not considered safe by
some experts, but I have to confess we ate and gave away some
before we knew this. It does not
have the fragrance or flavor of
culinary sage.

Among the purely ornamental
sages, I have *S. uliginosa*, or bog
salvia, with its large clumps of
sky-blue spires growing in full
sun in dry places. I have forsythia sage, *S. madrensis,* with
beautiful yellow flowers above
large, coarse leaves, and a constantly blooming red, *S. coccinea*,
brought to me by the birds. It is
such an endearing weed that I will

always have room for it. You can
trim it as a hedge.

Companion Plants (Sources)
offers a wide collection of salvias,
and Floridians should explore this
amazing genus further.

Culinary sages are the base of
poultry seasoning, essential to
Thanksgiving stuffing and sausage
seasoning. Add young leaves to
salads, soups, omelets, fritters,
breads, marinades, meats, or vegetables. For a treat, dip the leaves in
batter, and fry. Drain them before
serving as an appetizer.

Dried sage leaves are stronger
but somewhat different in flavor
from the fresh. Foliage can also be
frozen. Sage leaf tea is supposed to
promote longevity, increase wisdom, and improve memory. Add
extra tea to the bath or use it as a
rinse on gray hair. Add dried
flowers to wreaths and both leaves
and flowers to potpourri.

Florida Culture: Start sages
from seed, cuttings, or divisions.
Germination takes 2 to 3 weeks.
Cuttings root easily. Set plants 1
1/2 to 3 feet apart, depending on
kind, in full sun to partial shade.
Prune to keep plants in shape.
Take cuttings of sensitive species to
get them through the summer or
replace them as necessary.

SANTOLINA
Lavender Cotton
Santolina chamaecyparisus
(San-toh-LYE-na)
Daisy family
Native to the Mediterranean
Grows in N, C, and S
Uses: ornamental, insect
repellent, potpourri

This small, shrubby peren-
nial with hairlike, tiny leaves forms

a silvery mound. It is difficult to grow in Florida, especially in summer, but it can be done by providing excellent drainage and shelter from hard rains. Don't give up if you really want this plant. If not, use the more reliable wormwoods for the touch of silver in your garden. In the past, santolina was used for worms, snakebite, insect bites, and as an eye wash. The aromatic leaves are good in sachets used for moth repellent.

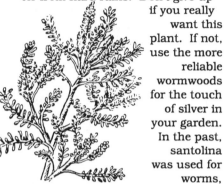

Florida Culture: Start with seeds, cuttings, divisions, or purchased plants in the fall. Guard from frosts. Give them full sun to partial shade, as little as 5 hours of sun per day. Mound up the soil around the base to encourage layering. Trim lightly.

SAVORY
    Summer Savory
    Satureja hortensis
    Winter Savory
    S. montana
    (Sa-tu-REE-ja)
    Mint family
    Native to dry Mediterranean
      hillsides
    Grows in N, C, and S
    Uses: culinary

Though these are among the most popular of the culinary herbs, they are difficult in Florida summers. I managed to keep a nice clump of summer savory alive through summer in a clay pot, set where it gets morning sun, afternoon shade, and protection from driving rains. The leaves are gray-green and linear. I must try the same conditions for winter savory, whose stems are more upright.

Legend has it that summer savory increases sexual drive but winter savory cools it, so plant whichever you need. Both have a peppery taste, similar to but milder than thyme.

Florida Culture: Start seeds, take cuttings, or buy plants in late summer or early fall. Be sure they get at least 5 hours of sunlight. Once established, allow the soil to dry out between waterings. Use often or clip back. Mulch well and give shade in summer.

SESAME
    Sesamum indicum
    (SES-a-mum)
    Pedalium family
    Native to Asia and Africa
    Uses: culinary, medicinal
    Grows in N, C, and S

This tropical annual grows two feet tall with lance shaped leaves and drooping, one-inch pinkish purple to white flowers. The long seed capsules are filled with many seeds, which are well known for use on bread and rolls as well as in Asian and Middle Eastern dishes and for cooking oil.

Florida Culture: Grow this in sun from seeds started in the spring. It responds well to manure and lime.

SHOO FLY PLANT
  Nicandra, Apple of Peru
  Nicandra physaloides
  (nye-KAN-dra)
  Potato family
  Native to Peru
  Uses: ornamental, fly
    repellent, crafts
  Grows in N, C, and S

I read about the fly chasing properties of nicandra long ago in *Organic Gardening* magazine but it took me four years to find seeds. Then they germinated strangely.

I've since learned that it is not unusual for one plant to come up, grow two feet, and then finally have many other seeds sprout at its base. Park Seed stopped selling the seed for this reason, but when I offered to share my seeds (a bagful from one plant) in my Iowa newspaper column, I got 250 requests. One article I wrote about shoofly was in the Louisville Courier on Derby Day and resulted in 1000 requests to J.L. Hudson, a source of seed. He thinks I wield a powerful pen, but actually it is the peskiness of flies that brings such results.

Flies are not much of a problem in Florida. My spouse jokes that the palmetto bugs eat them. Still, nicandra is an interesting, ornamental, and preventative plant, especially around animals or compost piles. It has quietly followed me to every garden ever since I first planted it, but it is not rampant.

The plant is named in honor of Kiknader of Colophon, a writer on medicine and botany in the second century. One Iowa lady, who was born in 1890, wrote me to say she remembered her grandmother raving about the benefits of shoo fly. This may be how people survived for all those centuries before the invention of window screens.

Nicandra looks like a tomato as a seedling, but soon develops oval, deeply lobed leaves of light green that eventually grow 4 or 5 inches long. Blooming begins when the plants are only a foot tall, but they soon grow to 4 or 5 feet in Florida, with a branch spread equally wide. The flowers are a lovely, delicate lavender-blue with white centers, cup shaped and more than an inch across. But they stay open only part of each day. You may hardly see them before you notice green, five-sided, winged, round seedpods that grow to about an inch in diameter and turn tan and papery as the seeds inside ripen. The plant is slightly coarse in leaf and habit. Seedpods are excellent in dried bouquets or wreaths.

Florida Culture: Send away for your first seeds (J.L. Hudson or Companion Plants) and don't give up if they germinate erratically. Start them indoors or in containers to be sure to recognize them, but once started, they should self seed reliably, even in Florida, without becoming invasive. I've transplanted them as large as two feet. They are annuals and take the same care as their tomato cousins. They, too, may disappear in summer.

SORREL

French Sorrel
Rumex scutatus, R. acetosa
    (ROO-mex)
Buckwheat family
Native to Europe
Uses: culinary
Grows in N, C, and S

Sorrel grows well in Florida in winter and usually survives the summer. In chicken broth it makes a classic soup, but is also good cooked with greens, added to salad, or chewed while you work in the garden. It is high in vitamins A and C. Saute chopped leaves in butter and add lemon juice for delicious fish, or use with meats. Chop into avocado salad.

Like spinach, sorrel is high in oxalic acid, so use it lightly if you have rheumatic or kidney problems, gout, or are pregnant. Parboiling and pouring away water reduces the content considerably.

Sorrel grows with a large rosette of bright green, arrow-shaped leaves and has branching flower stalks. The Egyptians used it in 3000 B.C., and the name means sour. Gerard said it made one pleasant and agreeable and should never be left out of salad.

Florida Culture: Start from seeds, plants, or divisions in fall. Give it high shade and rich, moist soil. Cut flower stalks back for best flavor in leaves.

Note: Wood sorrel or *Oxalis* is a completely different, shamrock-like plant that grows wild all over Florida. Its leaves close up at night and its small flowers are decorative, but it can be invasive. Children often chew these leaves to satisfy thirst and they can be added in small quantities to salads. These also contain oxalic acid.

There is also a sorrel vine or marine vine, *Cissus trifoliata*, that grows wild in C and S but has no known herbal properties.

SUNFLOWER

Helianthus annuus
    (hee-lee-AN-thus)
Daisy family
Native to North America
Uses: ornamental, culinary,
    bird food, oil
Grows in N, C, and S

Sunflowers were probably first used by Native Americans, and anthropologists have found seeds in clay containers that date back 3,000 years. The unmarried Hopi Indian maidens made a face powder from the petals. Seeds arrived in Europe by 1510 and were soon grown in many royal gardens, but it was the Russians who took them most to heart and seemed to grow them best. Today Russian doctors use a decoction of the seeds for treatment of jaundice, malaria, heart conditions, and diarrhea. The nutritious seeds contain up to 30%

protein, the relatively uncommon Vitamin D, copper, and all the amino acids we need. All sunflower parts are useful: the petals for dye; the buds cooked as a vegetable; the pith and stems as fiber for making textiles, rope, and cloth and for use in laboratories; and the seeds pressed for oil or eaten whole. The seeds are also prized by wildlife.

Florida Culture: Annual sunflowers bloom 9 to 11 weeks from planting. Susan Bishop of *My Mother's Garden* in Ruskin, Florida, grows sunflowers commercially. For a time she was planting 1000 transplants a week and getting more orders than she could fill. She found it was possible to grow sunflowers all year, but the best production with fewest problems came from plants growing when the days were getting long, between the winter and summer solstice, January to June. By August plants tended to be puny and also suffered from a fungal disease.

"Of all the plants I've grown," says Susan, "these showed the most marked difference between those planted in the waxing and the waning of the moon. If possible, plant them like above ground crops when the moon is getting fuller [waxing]."

Susan did best with ornamental pollenless varieties, especially 'Sunbright.' She started seeds in trays and transplanted to a foot apart in rows, and pinched off all side shoots for a 4 to 5 inch single flower for the market. She dried some of the flowers in silica gel, and they were even more valuable to florists.

For the home garden, plant seeds farther apart, and pinch off the top inch of the plant when it is about a foot tall, to force many side shoots to grow. This gives a bushy, branched plant with many flowers.

Sunflowers need plenty of water and enriched soil with ample nitrogen. They are sensitive to nemotodes but soil fungicide (see page 17) solved that problem for *My Mother's Garden*. The plants sometimes survive light frost.

TARRAGON, TRUE
   See Artemisia entry.

TARRAGON, MEXICAN OR WINTER
   Sweet Mace, Mint- or Anise-
      Scented Marigold
   Tagetes lucida
      (ta-GEE-tez)
   Daisy family
   Native to tropical America
   Uses: culinary, ornamental
   Grows in N, C, and S

This marigold has a flavor between licorice and chocolate, slightly like sweet anise. Though somewhat coarser in taste, it is a very suitable Florida substitute for true tarragon. It even makes a good bearnaise sauce. It is widely used in Latin America as a condiment. Sacred to the Aztecs, it was thrown in the faces of sacrificial victims, hopefully to deaden their senses.

With its green, slender, lance-like leaves and erect stems 1 to 2 feet tall, and especially its profusion of yellow-orange single flowers, 1/2-3/4 inch across, it is very decorative in the garden. Chop the tender young leaves for egg, cheese, and poultry dishes and add just before the end of cooking. Use it fresh when you can and use sparingly until you determine your family's taste. It makes a good vinegar.

Florida Culture: This perennial plant is easy to grow anywhere in Florida. Start from seeds or cuttings or divide clumps as you would mums. Give it high shade to full sun and add humus to the soil. It spreads easily, blooms continuously, and best of all, it likes our summers.

THYME

Thymus species
(TI-mus or THY-mus)
Mint family
Native to dry, rocky western
Mediterranean
Uses: culinary, ornamental,
crafts
Grows in N, C, and S

Florida's summer heat and humidity can keep some thyme from becoming the lovely, fragrant, blooming ground cover that it is farther north, but not necessarily. Experienced herb growers have mats of it that bloom for months in early summer. Even some of these patches look a bit battered by the end of the summer rainy season, but they come back quickly. Anyone can easily grow and enjoy it through the cooler months.

This most useful culinary herb (used to flavor Benedictine liqueur as well as many meats and vegetables) has a history as rich as its fragrance. The ancient Greeks believed it gave them fortitude and strength. As a symbol of courage, scarves embroidered with sprigs of thyme were given to the departing Crusaders. Thyme has been used for relieving coughs and spasms. It contains a disinfectant, thymol.

Thyme grows in many forms, but all have tiny leaves in opposite pairs, the green ones dark red on the underside. Some are creeping, some woody shrubs up to a foot tall. Flowers can be white, pink, or lavender to purplish red. In the garden, thyme is a good companion to potatoes, tomatoes, eggplant, and peppers. It also is supposed to repel cabbage worms and whiteflies, but my best plant ever did not deter clouds of whiteflies on orange tree branches 3 feet away last spring. Infestations, like sunshine and heat, can be more intense in Florida.

Use thyme while you have it. The plant seems to thrive on trimming as long as you leave at least 1/3 to 1/2 of the foliage. There are few foods or teas that are not improved by a bit of thyme. Use it also as a strewing herb or in potpourris and sachets.

Florida Culture: Through the cooler months, give the plant a sunny, dry spot. Rocks as mulch seem to help. Some growers I know keep thyme alive over the summer in containers or growing in elevated drain pipes where the drainage is perfect, but this also means watering more carefully through the winter. See chapters 6 and 7 on growers who have good growth and blooms, both in the ground and in containers. Varieties that seem to do best here include silver thyme, lemon thyme, and creeping thyme.

TI PLANT

Cordyline terminalis
(core-dee-LINE-ee)
Agave family
Native to Hawaii
Uses: ornamental, flower
arrangements, medicinal
Grows in N, C, and S

This plant with its beautiful leaves is an ornamental shrub in most of Florida, and a relative of both dracena and Spanish bayonet. The plant was considered sacred in ancient days and leaves were worn around the neck to ward off evil spirits and dipped in cold water and worn around the head to cure headaches, so it is growing in the medicinal herb garden at Kanapaha.

There are several cultivars, one with long pointed leaves and bright pink to burgundy color, one with more rounded leaves, not so bright overall, but often with pink edges. Colors tend to vary with the seasons and also with the amount of sun and shade each plant gets.

'Baby Doll' is dwarf with pink and purple foliage, 'Kiwi' has yellow and green striped leaves and pink margins, 'Black Magic' has nearly black leaves, 'Tricolor' has green, cream, and red foliage, and 'Red Sister' is much like 'Baby Doll' but with larger leaves. The flowers of some may be inconspicuous, but the ones I've seen have been quite showy in a lavender pink shade and covered with ecstatic bees. Globose berries will follow in some abundance where it does not get too cold. The leaves are excellent in flower arrangements. We used to import them from Florida when we had a flower shop in Ohio.

Florida Culture: Ti plants may die to the ground in a hard freeze in C or need further protection in N. They grow slowly to about five feet tall and almost as wide at best, here in the Tampa area, in full sun to considerable shade. The only one I've seen blooming was in full sun. But they grow somewhat larger at Cypress Gardens with all its heaters, and at points further south. They are not salt tolerant but have medium drought tolerance. They may be bothered by nematodes, leaf-spot, or mites. Mine have not had problems. I bought only one in 1987 and multiplied it with cuttings, which root easily. Layering also works.

TURMERIC
> *Curcuma longa, C. zedoary*
> (kur-KA-ma)
> Ginger family
> Native to India
> Uses: culinary, medicinal,
>   ornamental
> Grows in C and S

Last spring my friend George Riegler dug these in full, magnificent bloom and they transplanted without a qualm to my garden where the lavender pink bracts were lovely for two to three more weeks. They look like short banana plants with leaves coming from the ground.

Leaves can be from 2 to 5 feet tall. Mine are about 3. The flowers are yellow but showy bracts can vary from magenta to pink to waxy white. Some species bloom in early spring before the leaves appear, others in midsummer. Thanks to herbalist Kaye Cude, who has grown them longer, I can tell you that the plants begin dormancy when temperatures drop below 64 to 87 degrees (depending on the species) and resumes at 70 to 87 degrees.

Kaye says to wrap leaves around meats, fish, or vegetables before cooking for turmeric's strong, pleasantly bitter flavor. Young leaf shoots are good in salad or added to cooked foods for a ginger/lemon grass flavor.

Turmeric, a popular spice, is usually sold as a yellow powder which is made from the dried roots of the plants. It is used to color and flavor many foods including rice, mustard, and liqueurs, as well as to keep pickles crisp. It was once used to dye cloth. It was rubbed on women's stomachs after childbirth. Marco Polo considered turmeric flavor and color as good as that of true saffron.

Florida Culture: Soil should be mulched in winter. Buy plants or start from division of the fleshy rhizomes, best done in autumn. These must be lifted and planted higher occasionally for additional blooms. Grow in rich, loamy soil in full sun to partial shade. To harvest, lift the rhizomes carefully with a spading fork before they go dormant in late fall and become woody. Then boil, sun dry, and grind to use as turmeric flavoring.

VANILLA
Vanilla planifolia
(Va-NEL-ah)
Orchid family
Uses: flavoring
Grows in N and C with
protection, easily in S

Vanilla is a frost-tender, tropical, climbing orchid with leathery, oval leaves on stout stems. Vanilla beans are used for flavoring, but also as a coloring agent and in perfumes, cosmetics, and potpourris.

Florida Culture: Yellow or orange flowers bloom after the third year. Pollinate them by hand and they will develop into long, aromatic pods. In Palm Beach, Chef Hubert grows his up a fruit tree, for these stout jungle vines prefer moist shade. Vanilla is reliably hardy only in zones 10 and 11, but elsewhere can be grown in greenhouses or brought indoors for winter.

VETIVER
Khus-Khus
Vetiveria zizanoides
previously *Andropogon
zizaknioides*
(Ve-ti-VER-i-ah)
Grass family
Native to Tropical Asia
Uses: ornamental, hedges,
medicinal, aromatherapy,
crafts
Grows in N, C, and S

This grassy plant has been in several of the herb gardens I've seen and looks a bit like overgrown lemon grass. Its humble appearance belies its value for incense, perfume, cosmetics, soaps, and for flavoring sorbets and fruit drinks.

It is one of the main crops in India for its essential oil containing 29 compounds. The long roots are woven into floor mats and window blinds, which are wetted down on hot days so the wind releases their exotic odor, similar to sandalwood. Vetiver also protects clothes from insects. In Haiti it has been used to make fans, baskets, and thatched roofs. It is a fine addition to potpourris or sachets.

In tropical countries a tea from the spongy roots is used as a tonic to treat indigestion, fevers, flu, rheumatism, and parasites.

The plant grows in a bushy clump that can get 7 to 8 feet tall but is usually shorter with a pleasant, fountainlike habit. Leaves are long, thin, rough-edged, and pointed, up to 5/8 inch wide, with sharp edges. They bloom with plumes like their cousin, pampas grass. Roots go deep and are difficult to harvest but dry for long-lasting fragrance.

Florida Culture: This is a perennial in zone 9. It could die to the ground in N in a severe winter but will come back from the roots. It does well in dry, poor soil as long as it is well drained. Start from clump divisions and give 2 to 3 feet of growing space. Give it full sun and ample water. Be sure to apply enough phosphorus and potash if you want high oil yield.

VICK'S SALVE PLANT
Plectranthus species
    (plec-TRAN-thus)
    Mint family
    Native to Australia and
        Pacific Islands
    Uses: ground cover,
        cold remedy
    Grows in N, C, and S

Plectranthus is a large genus of tropical and subtropical perennials and shrubs. The name comes from *plectron*, a spur, and *anthos*, a flower, and indicates the swollen base of the flower tube. I had never seen this plant before and find it mentioned in few books. I started mine from a cutting given me by Bette Smith, garden writer for the St. Pete Times, several years ago and it has been thriving ever since.

Mine, *Plectranthus amboinicus*, is also called Spanish thyme or Cuban oregano. It is a tender perennial that has grayish green, velvety, opposite leaves, almost diamond shaped, about an inch long and wide, with the bottom half smooth-edged and the top scalloped. At the base of each large leaf is a pair of tiny leaves. I have seen *Plectranthus madagascariensis*, called Swedish ivy, growing as a low ground cover in Kanapaha Gardens. It has smaller leaves and a different scent from my Vick's salve plant, which has not done well there.

The fragrance of both species is strong if rubbed or brushed, but not noticeable otherwise. My plants have short spires of blue flowers occasionally, but not often enough to grow this for the flower. They spread over the ground and new shoots may stand erect to about 18 inches. So far I have used it only as a conversation piece and in steam treatments for colds and congestion. Just a whiff of the leaves will clear the head.

Florida Culture: Vick's salve plant grows easily from seeds or cuttings, likes sandy soil with some peat moss or leaf mold, and spreads without being rampant. Either plain or variegated kinds are ornamental in hanging baskets. Partial shade is recommended. My plants are doing well in several exposures, with both nearly full sun and with light shade summer and winter. Pinching will make a bushier plant.

VIOLET
> Pansy, Johnny-Jump-Up
> *Viola* species
> Violet family
> Native to Europe, Africa,
>   North America, and Asia
> Uses: ornamental, culinary,
>   medicinal
> Grows in N, C, and S

The violet family includes many favorite garden and woodland plants. Pansies and violas, commonly used as winter bedding plants, are sold in garden centers throughout Florida. Nature dropped me a few plants of Johnny-jump-up which I enjoyed.

V. floridana

But I am discovering new violets now, some that grow as wildflowers throughout the state: the purple-flowered Florida violet, *V. floridana*, which is found in open woods and clearings, the long-leaf violet, *V. lanceolata*, which is common in moist, sandy open areas and has longer, narrow leaves, and white flowers, the halberd leaf violet or *V. hastata*, each

plant of which produces yellow flowers and only 2 or 3 leaves each year, with silver gray markings, and the field pansy, *V. rafinesquii,* which often blooms in lawns or fields in the Panhandle with white to pale blue flowers. I favor an Australian violet, *V. hedera*, that spreads quickly with round, scalloped leaves. It blooms all year despite summer heat.

Violet leaves and flowers are edible and rich in vitamins and I use them in salads when they are plentiful. The flowers of pansies and violas make exquisite garnishes in a rainbow of colors. Chill them in the refrigerator to keep them looking fresh.

Viola species are low growing perennials with basal rosettes of dark green leaves. Wild violet flowers are mostly lavender or white, with a few yellows, nodding on delicate stems. The plants spread on creeping runners.

Florida Culture: Try to get the violet varieties that do well here. Our hot wet summers are too intense for pansies, so you should buy new ones for bedding each fall or in winter, and remove them when they start to look tired. Plant them in moist, humus-rich soil. Most like some shade, but pansies and Johnny-jump-ups like full winter sun. Feed with a blossom booster fertilizer, high in phosphorus and potassium.

WATERCRESS
Nasturtium officinale
(Nas-TUR-shum)
Mustard family
Native to Europe and Asia
Uses: culinary, garnish
Grows in N, C, and S

The plants we call nasturtiums are botanically of the genus *Tropaeolum*. Watercress is the best known member of the true *Nasturtium* genus and grows wild all over Florida as a perennial. It has dark green, alternate, slightly scalloped round leaves . Each leaf stem has one thumbnail size leaf at the end and two tiny ones beneath.

Watercress blooms in spring and summer. Terminal clusters of four-petaled flowers, usually white, sometimes yellow, are followed by slender pods. In water and even in moist air, it quickly forms roots at each node.

Watercress is high in vitamin C, iron, and iodine, and has a tangy taste and crunchy texture. Store it in the refrigerator in a plastic bag with stems in water and use it within a few days.

It is the third most popular herb for commercial growers. Add the leaves to soups, salads, sandwiches, pastas, potatoes, fish, poultry, and stir fries. It is best eaten raw or added at the last moment of cooking. For a tasty dip, combine it with arugula, grated onion, lemon juice, a dash of Tabasco, and sour cream.

Florida Culture: When I was a child we had watercress growing so thickly in the stream in Hawkins' field that it almost held us up when we went wading. For years I tried to duplicate that creek, to no avail.

James Steele assured me that watercress will grow just fine in a pot or hanging basket of humusy soil watered often. The plant I brought home from his place grew   several inches in every direction in just three weeks. You can start cuttings with sprigs from the grocery store or a restaurant, even in a glass of water. The tiny seeds germinate in 5 days and eventually should be thinned to 6 inches apart. The plants grow to eating size in two months. They like soil slightly on the alkaline side.

MAILORDER & RESOURCE DIRECTORY

Brown's Edgewood Gardens
2611 Corrine Drive, Orlando, FL
32803. Expanded catalog, seminars.

Brudy's Exotics, P.O. Box 820874,
Houston, TX 77282-0874. Catalog $2.
Exotic gingers, butterfly plants,
butterfly eggs.

Companion Plants, 7247 N.
Coolville Ridge Road, Athens, OH
45701. Many herbs, catalog $2.

ECHO (See p. 229, right). Send $2 for
their unique seed list.

Gardens Alive! 5100 Schenley Place,
Lawrenceburg, IN 47025. Natural
controls and organic soil amendments.

Hartley's Herbs & Everlastings
6391 NW 150th Street, Chiefland, FL
32626. $1, plants, seeds, supplies.

Hartman's Herb Farm, Old Dana
Road, Barre, MA 01005. Good source
of dried flowers, craft supplies, plants,
essential oils.

Hearthstone House, 1600 Hilltop
Road, Xenia OH 45385. Handpainted
slate markers and garden art,
wholesale and retail. SASE.

J.L. Hudson, Star Route 2, Box 337,
La Honda, CA 94020. One of my
favorite catalogs for unusual seeds
and information, $1.

Le Jardin du Gourmet, Box 75C, St.
Johnsbury Ctr., VT 05863. Many
international vegetables and herbs,
famous 25 cent seed packets.

Johnny's Selected Seeds, Foss Hill
Road, Box 2580, Albion, ME 04910.
Herbs, cover crop seeds, and more.

L.E.R., 16245 SW 304th St.,
Homestead, FL 33033. Rare herb
seeds and plants. Catalog $2.

Mellinger's Inc., 2310 W. South
Range, North Lima, OH 44452-9731.
Good catalog for gardening supplies.

Nichols Garden Nursery, 1190
North Pacific Highway, Albany, OR
97321-4598. Herbs and rare seeds,
teas, and oils.

O'Toole's Herb Farm, see p. 229.

Pinecrest Farms, P.O. Box 9205,
Winter Haven, FL 33883-9205.
Herbs, workshops, crafts.

Richters, Canada's Herb Specialists,
Goodwood, Ontario, Canada LOC
1AO. Exceptional catalog with
unusual varieties, supplies, beneficial
insects, and complete list of herb
books. Free.

St. Fiacre's Garden Gifts, 1807 N.
16th St., Tampa, FL 33605. Herbs,
books, essential oils, gifts.

Sandy Mush Herb Nursery, 316
Surrett Cove Road, Leicester, NC
28748-9622. Herbs, books, and
supplies. Catalog $6, plant list free.

Shepherds Garden Seeds, 30 Irene
St., Torrington, CT 06790. 108 pg.
herbs, vegetables, and flowers. Free.

Sweet William Herb Farm (Billy
Daniel),18810 U.S. Hwy 41
Lutz, FL 33549

Thompson & Morgan, Inc., Box
1308, Jackson, NJ 08527. Many
specific colors and varieties of
flowering plants, good herb list. Free.

Territorial Seed Co., P.O. Box 157,
Cottage Grove, OR 97424. Herbs,
information, mortar & pestle, seeds,
essential oils, supplies.

Urban Farmer's Source Book,
3151 South Hwy. 446, Bloomington,
IN 47401-9111. Catalog $3. Beneficial
insects, drip irrigation, supplies.

Winstead Farm, 105 Romanshorn,
Interlachen, FL 32148. Culinary,
medicinal, ornamental herb plants.

PLACES TO VISIT

Check with your local County Cooperative Extension Service. Many have demonstration gardens on the grounds. At the Pinellas County Extension Office you can tour an excellent herb garden designed and maintained by the Florida Herb Society. Offices provide information sheets and agents can direct you to other local herb gardens. The ones near you show what can be grown under conditions like yours.

ECHO, Inc. (Educational Concerns for Hunger Organization)
1730 Durrance Road
North Fort Myers, FL 33917
941-543-3246

Kanapaha Botanical Gardens
4625 SW 63rd Blvd.
Gainesville, FL 32608
904-372-4931 (See chapter 6)

Mounts Botanical Garden
531 North Military Trail
West Palm Beach, FL 33415-1358
407-233-1749 (See chapter 8)

University of S.FL. Botanical Gardens (SW corner of campus)
4202 E. Fowler Avenue
Tampa, FL 33620-5300
813-974-2329 (See chapter 7)

O'Toole's Herb Farm
P.O. Box 268
Madison, FL 32340
904-973-3629 (See pages 110-111)

Maggie's Herb Farm
11400 C.R. 13
St. Augustine, FL 32092
904-829-0722

The Herb Garden
Route 1, Box 1307-X
Melrose, FL 32666
904-475-5475 (See chapter 6)
(Take SR 26 east of Melrose

**Chef's Herb and Citrus Garden
Four Seasons Ocean Grand Hotel**
2800 South Ocean Boulevard
Palm Beach, FL 33480

PERIODICALS FOR FLORIDA HERB GROWERS

The Herb Quarterly
P.O. Box 689
San Anselmo, CA 94979-0689

The Herb Companion
201 East Fourth Street
Loveland, CO 80538

Florida Gardening Magazine
P.O. Box 500678
Malabar, FL 32950

HERB SOCIETIES

The Herb Society of America (HSA)
9018 Kirtland Chardon Road
Kirtland, OH 44060

Tampa Bay Unit, HSA
405 Desiree Drive
Brandon, FL 33511
813-689-3025

Manatee Herb Society
Manatee County Extension Office
1303 17th Street
Palmetto, FL 33561

Florida Herb Society
Pinellas County Extension Office
12175 125th Street N.
Largo, FL 33544

Seaside Herb Society
River Bridge Meeting House
Beach Street and Granada
or Highway 40
Ormond Beach, FL 32174

**The Evening Herb Society
of the Palm Beaches**
Mounts Botanical Gardens
531 North Military Trail
West Palm Beach, FL 33415-1358
407-835-6724

International Herb Growers and Marketers Association
1202 Allanson Road
Mundelein, IL 60060

Bibliography

Bell, C. Ritchie, and Taylor, Bryan J. *Florida Wild Flowers and Roadside Plants*, Laurel Hill Press, Chapel Hill, NC, 1982.

Brandies, Monica Moran. *Florida Gardening: the Newcomer's Survival Manual*, B.B. Mackey Books,Wayne, PA, 1993.

Brandies, Monica Moran. *Xeriscaping for Florida Homes*, Great Outdoors Publishing, St. Petersburg, FL, 1994.

Bremnes, Lesley. *The Complete Book of Herbs*, Viking Penguin, New York, 1988.

Conrick, John. *Neem: The Ultimate Herb*, The Neem Association, Inc., 1511 Oneco Avenue, Winter Park, FL 32789, 1995.

Cude, Kaye. *Spice and Herb Arts Newsletter*, 5091 Muddy Lane, Buckingham, Florida 33905, 1987-1993.

DeFreitas, Stan. *The Complete Guide to Florida Gardening*, Taylor, Dallas, 1987.

The Herb Companion Wishbook and Resource Guide, Interweave Press, 1992, $16.95, 303-669-7672.

The Herb Garden of Kanapaha Botanical Gardens. Kanapaha Botanical Gardens, 4625 SW 63rd Blvd., Gainesville, FL 32608, $4.

Herbs in South Florida, Evening Herb Society of the Palm Beaches, Box 17318, W. Palm Beach, FL, 33416

Hill, Madeline, and Barclay, Gwen. *Southern Herb Growing*, Shearer Publishing, Fredericksburg, TX, 1987.

Hylander, Clarence J. *Flowers of Field and Forest*, Macmillan, New York, 1967.

Kelville, Kathi. *The Illustrated Herb Encyclopedia*, Mallard Press, New York, 1991.

Kruger, Anna. *Herbs*, American Nature Guides, Smithmark, New York, 1992.

MacCubbin, Tom. *Florida Home Grown 2: The Edible Landscape*, Sentinel Communications, Orlando, FL 32801, 1989.

Mackey, Betty Barr, and Brandies, Monica Moran. *A Cutting Garden for Florida*, B.B. Mackey Books, Wayne, PA, 1992.

Ortiz, Elizabeth Lambert. *The Encyclopedia of Herbs, Spices, and Flavorings*, Dorling Kindersley, London and New York, 1992

Oster, Maggie. *Flowering Herbs*, Longmeadow Press, New York, 1991.

Reppert, Bertha. *Growing Your Herb Business*, Garden Way, Pownal, VT, 1995.

Rodale's Illustrated Encyclopedia of Herbs, Emmaus, PA, 1987.

Shaudys, Phyllis. *The Pleasure of Herbs*, Garden Way, Pownal, VT, 1988.

Shaudys, Phyllis. *Herbal Treasures*, Garden Way, Pownal, VT, 1990.

Stout, Ruth. *Gardening Without Work*, New York: Cornerstone Library/Simon & Shuster, 1974.

Stout, Ruth. *How to Have a Green Thumb Without An Aching Back*, New York: Cornerstone Library/Simon & Shuster, 1968.

Tourles, Stephanie. *The Herbal Body Book*, Garden Way, Pownal, VT. 1994.

Van Atta, Marian. *Growing and Using Exotic Foods*, Pineapple Press, Sarasota, FL, 1991.

Wilson, Jim. *Landscaping with Herbs*, Houghton Mifflin, New York, 1994.

Wilson, Jim. *Master List of Herbs*, P.O. Box 305, Donalds, SC, 29638. $6 ppd.

Common Name/Botanic Name Cross Reference

Herbs in this book are usually called by their most common name, but botanic names, in italics, are added throughout the plant-by-plant section and elsewhere for clarification. The index listings include both common and botanic names.

Botanic (scientific) names such as *Aloe vera* include a genus name which comes first and is capitalized (*Aloe*). It is followed by the species name which is not (*vera*). There can be hundreds or just a few species within the genus. These species may or may not look similar even though they are closely related.

Look up the common name in this cross reference to get the botanic name. If you have the botanic name but want the common name, refer to the index (page 237).

Achiote
  Bixa orellana
African moth plant
  Ibosa riparia
Ajuga
  Ajuga reptans
Aloe, burn plant
  Aloe vera or
  Aloe barbadensis
Allspice, Carolina
  Calycanthus species
Allspice, true
  Pimenta officinalis
Alyssum
  Lobularia maritima
Anise
  Pimpinella anisum
Anise, Florida
  Illicium floridanum
Anise, star (Chinese)
  Illicium verum
Angel trumpet
  Datura species and
  Brugmansia species
Anise hyssop
  Agastache foeniculum
Annato
  Bixa orellana

Artemisia
  Artemisia species
Artemisia 'Silver King'
  A. ludoviciana
Artemisia 'Silver Mound'
  A. schmidtiana
Arugula, roquette
  Eruca vesicaria sativa
Aztec Sweet Shrub
  Lippia dulcis
Basil
  Ocimum species
Bay
  Laurus nobilis
Bay, California
  Umbellularia californica
Bay, red
  Persea borbonia
Bay, Sweet
  Magnolia virginiana
Bayberry
  Myrica species
Bay laurel
  Laurus nobilis
Beach wormwood
  Artemisia stellerana
Beebalm
  Monarda species
Bergamot
  Monarda species
Betony
  Stachys species
Bixa or Bixia
  Bixa orellana
Black pepper
  Piper nigrum
Borage
  Borago officinalis
Borage, Cuban
  Coleus amboinicus
Boxwood
  Buxus sempervirens
Bugleweed
  Ajuga reptans
Burnet, salad
  Sanguisorba minor or
  Poterium sanquisorba
Butterfly weed
  Asclepias species

Calendula
  Calendula officinalis
California poppy
  Eschscholzia californica
Camphor tree
  Cinnamomum camphora
Cardamon
  Elettaria cardamomum
Carpenter's herb
  Ajuga reptans
Castor bean
  Ricinus communis
Catnip, catmint
  Nepeta cataria
Cedronella
  Agastache cana
Chamomile, German
  Matricaria chamomilla
Chamomile, Roman
  Chamaemelum nobile
Chamomile, true
  Chamaemelum nobile or
  Anthemis nobilis
Chervil
  Anthriscus cerefolium
Chickweed
  Stellaria media
Chicory
  Cichorium intybus
Chive
  Allium schoenoprasum
Chive, garlic
  Allium tuberosum
Cilantro
  Coriandrum sativum
Clove, wild
  Pimenta acris
Clove pink
  Dianthus caryophyllus
Comfrey
  Symphytum officinale
Comino
  Cuminum ciminum
Coneflower, purple
  Echinacea angustifolia
Coriander
  Coriandrum sativum
Costmary
  Chrysanthemum balsamita
Culantro
  Eryngium foetidum
Cumin
  Cuminum cyminum

Curry leaf
  Murraya koenigii
Curry plant
  Helichrysum angustifolium
Dandelion
  Taraxacum officinale
Dill
  Anethum graveolens
Dianthus
  Dianthus species
Elder, scarlet
  Sambucus pubens
Elderberry
  Sambucus species
Elephant plant
  Centella asiatica
Eucalpytus
  Eucalyptus species
Fat hen
  Chenopodium alba
  Chenopodium ambrosioides
Fennel
  Foeniculum vulgare
Feverfew
  Tanacetum parthenium, formerly
  Chrysanthemum parthenium
Foxglove
  Digitalis purpurea and
  other *Digitalis* species
French marigold
  Tagetes patula
French parsley
  Anthriscus cerefolium
Garlic
  Allium sativum
Garlic, society
  Tulbaghia violacea
Geranium, scented
  Pelargonium species
Germander
  Teucrium fruticans
Ginger
  Zingiber officinale
Ginger, butterfly
  Hedychium species
Ginger, hidden
  Curcuma species
Ginger, pinecone
  Zingiber zerumbet
Ginkgo
  Ginkgo biloba
Ginseng
  Panax ginseng or
  Panax quinquefolius

Goldenrod
Solidago species
Good King Henry
Chenopodium bonus-henricus
Goosefoot
Chenopodium species
Gotu kola
Centella asiatica
Hackmatack
Juniperus communis
Hedge apple
Maclura pomifera
Henna
Lawsonia inermis
Holly
Ilex species
Horehound
Marrubium vulgare
Horseradish
Armoracia rusticana
Hortensia
Hydrangea species
Hydrangea
Hydrangea species
Indian cress
Tropaeolum majus
Indian pennywort
Centella asiatica
Inkberry
Phytolacca americana
Isabella wood
Persea borbonia
Japanese plum
Eriobotrya japonica
Jamaican mint bush
Micromeria viminea
Jimsonweed
Datura species
Johnny-jump-up
Viola species
Judas tree
Cercis canadensis
Juniper
Juniperus communis
Juniper, shore
Juniperus conferta
Khus-Khus
Vetiveria zizanoides
Lamb's ears
Stachys species
Lamb's quarters
Chenopodium species
Lanolin lily
Zingiber zerumbet

Lantana
Lantana camara
Lantana montevidensis
Lavender, English or true
Lavandula angustifolia
Lavender, French
Lavandula dentata
Lavender cotton
Santolina chamaecyparisus
Leek
Allium porrum
Lemon
Citrus species
Lemon balm
Melissa officinalis
Lemon grass
Cymbopogon citratus
Lemon verbena
Lippia citriodora or
Aloysia triphylla
Lime
Citrus species
Lion's ear
Leonotis nepetaefolia
Lipstick tree
Bixa orellana
Loquat
Eriobotrya japonica
Lovage
Levisticum officinale
Marigold, French
Tagetes patula
Marjoram
Origanum majorana
Marjoram, wild
Origanum species
Marshpenny
Centella asiatica
Mignonette tree
Lawsonia inermis
Mint
Mentha species
Mistletoe
Phoradendron serotinum
Mojean or Moujean tea
Nashia inaguensis
Mondo grass
Ophiopogon japonicus
Mosquito bush
Agastache cana
Mosquito Shoo geranium
Pelargonium citrosum
var. *Van Leeni*

Mustard
  Brassica species
Myrtle
  Myrtus communis
Nasturtium
  Tropaeolum majus
Neem
  Azadirachta indica
Nightshade
  Solanum dulcamara
  Atropha belladonna
Old Man's Beard
  Artemisia arbrotanum
  var. *Tangerine*
Onions, bunching
  Allium cepa viviparum
Orach
  Atriplex hortensis
Oregano
  Origanum species
Oregano, tropical
  Coleus amboinicus
Oregano, Mexican or Puerto Rican
  Lippia or *Phyla graveolens*
Oregano, Mexican
  Poliomintha longiflora
Orris root
  Iris germanica florentina
Osage orange
  Maclura pomifera
Oswego tea
  Monarda species
Palma Christi
  Ricinus communis
Pansy
  Viola species
Parsley
  Petroselinum crispum
Passion flower
  Passiflora species
Patchouli
  Pogostemon patchouli
Pepper, black
  Piper nigrum
Pepper, hot
  Capsicum species
Perilla
  Perilla frutescens
Periwinkle, Madagascar
  Catharanthus roseus
Pimpernelle
  Sanquisorba minor
Pipetree
  Sambucus species

Plantain, common
  Plantago species
Pokeweed
  Phytolacca americana
Poppies
  Papaver species
Poppy, California
  Eschscholzia californica
Portulaca
  Portulaca oleracea
Pot marigold
  Calendula officinalis
Prickly poppy
  Argemone mexicana
Purple coneflower
  Echinacea angustifolia
Purslane
  Portulaca oleracea
Red bay
  Persea borbonia
Redbud
  Cercis canadensis
Rice paper plant
  Tetrapanax papyriferus
Rose
  Rosa species
Rosemary
  Rosemarinus officinalis
Rue
  Ruta graveolens
St. John's wort
  Hypericum species
Salad burnet
  Sanquisorba minor
Sage
  Salvia species
Sage, bog
  salvia uliginosa
Sage, clary
  Salvia sclaria
Sage, forsythia
  Salvia madrensis
Sage, Mexican
  Salvia leucantha
Sage, wild red
  Salvia coccinea
Santolina
  Santolina chamaecyparisus
Savory, summer
  Satureja hortensis
Savory, winter
  Satureja montana
Saw myrtle
  Myrica cerifera

Sea holly
  Eryngium species
Sesame
  Sesamum indicum
Shallot
  Allium ascalonicum
Shiso
  Perilla frutescens
Shoo fly plant
  Nicandra physaloides
Sorrel
  Rumex scutatus or
  Rumex acetosa
Southernwood
  Artemisia arbrotanum
Star anise
  Illicium verum
Sunflower
  Helianthus annuus
Sweet Annie
  Artemisia annua
Sweet balm
  Melissa officinalis
Sweet Herb of Paraguay
  Lippia dulcis
Sweet mace
  Tagetes lucida
Sweetbay
  Magnolia virbiniana
Sweetgale
  Myrica species
Tansy
  Tanacetum vulgare
Tarragon, Mexican or winter
  Tagetes lucida
Tarragon, true
  Artemisia dracunculus
Thyme
  Thymus species

Ti plant
  Cordyline terminalis
Turmeric
  Curcuma longa
Uruca
  Bixa orellana
Valerian
  Valeriana officinalis
Vanilla
  Vanilla planifolia
Yarrow
  Achillea millefolium
Young Lad's Love
  Artemisia arbrotanum
Vetiver
  Vetiveria zizanoides
Vick's salve plant
  Plectranthus species
Violet
  Viola species
Walnut
  Juglans honorei
Watercress
  Nasturtium officinale
Wax myrtle
  Myrica cerifera
Wild clove
  Pimennta acris
Willow
  Salix species
Wormwood
  Artemisia absinthium
Wormwood, beach
  Artemisia stellerana
Wormwood, Roman
  Artemisia pontica
Young lad's love
  Artemisia arbrotanum

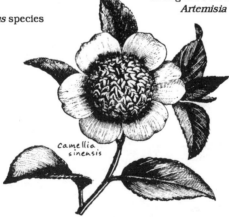

camellia
sinensis

Index

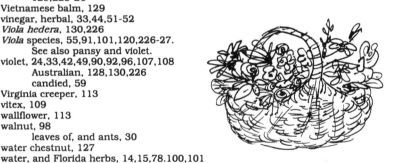

ABOUT THE AUTHOR

Monica Moran Brandies lives in Tampa and enjoys growing herbs, fruits, vegetables, and ornamentals in her half-acre yard. One of Florida's most popular garden writers, she is a fine lecturer and workshop leader, but is just as happy interviewing other gardeners to find out how they grow the marvelous array of plants that Floridians can choose.

Monica has been writing about her garden adventures since college days at the Pennsylvania School of Horticulture (now part of Temple University). She studied floral design under Bill Hixson in her greenhouse days in Ohio. She has been learning about growing plants in Florida since moving there in 1987 from Iowa (where she fed a family of ten with 90 percent homegrown food). She is the author of *Florida Gardening: The Newcomer's Survival Manual* and coauthor of *A Cutting Garden for Florida,* both from B.B. Mackey Books, *Sprouts and Saplings* (Strawberry Hill Press), *Ortho's Guide to Herbs* (Ortho Books), and *Xeriscaping for Florida Homes,* from Great Outdoors Publishing. Her most recent book, *Bless You For the Gifts* (B.B. Mackey Books), is a collection of autobiographical stories.

Monica's articles appear in many garden magazines such as Flower and Garden and Florida Gardening, and she writes a popular newspaper column for Central Florida. She contributed to *Better Homes' New Garden Book* and to Ortho's books on trees and groundcovers. In preparation for this book, Monica added to her longtime experience with herbs by testing Florida herbs and spices in her own landscape for several years and by visiting many expert herb growers in northern, central, and southern Florida.

 **B.B. MACKEY BOOKS**
P.O. Box 475
Wayne, Pennsylvania   19087
Booklist

Bless You For the Gifts. Monica Moran Brandies. From the Forties to the Nineties, evocative stories of real life in a large, rural, Midwestern Catholic family. 1997. $10.95, paperbound. ISBN 9616338-7-5.

Herbs and Spices for Florida Gardens. Monica Moran Brandies. Growing herbs for flavor, health, beauty, crafts, scent, and garden color. 1996. $15.50, paperbound. ISBN 9616338-6-7.

Florida Gardening: The Newcomer's Survival Manual. Monica Moran Brandies. How to laugh off the garden perils of Florida and grow a wonderful new landscape. 1993. $9.95, paperbound. ISBN 9616338-3-2.

A Cutting Garden for Florida, Second Edition. Betty Mackey and Monica Moran Brandies. 1992. Revised 1997. How to grow flowers for bouquets in your Florida landscape. $9.95, paperbound. ISBN 9616338-2-4.

Garden Notes Through the Years. A four-year blank journal for tracking garden events and accomplishments. Designed and illustrated by Betty Mackey, 1994. $10.95, paperbound, plastic cover protectors. ISBN 9616338-4-0.

The Plant Collector's Notebook. Blank notebook for tracking garden plants, designed by Betty Mackey, 1994. $7.95, paperbound, plastic cover protectors. ISBN 9616338-5-9.

A Cutting Garden for California. Pat Kite and Betty Mackey. 1990. How to grow flowers for bouquets at home in your California landscape. $8.00, paperbound. ISBN 9616338-1-6.

<u>All books are printed on recycled paper.</u>

Postage free on any two or more books. Add $1.25 on single orders. Pennsylvania residents, please add 6% state sales tax.

If you are interested in visiting Florida gardens to see how to deal with conditions similar to yours, there are opportunities in all parts of the state. Check with your local Cooperative Extension Service, usually listed under county numbers in the phone book. You can also call the Extension Office of the University of Florida in Gainesville (904-392-1781).

Many local extension offices have display gardens that are both inspiration and explanation. Visit them often to see how plants change and seasons vary. Also watch for notices on the garden page of your newspaper for classes, garden tours, special displays, sales, and other events. Consider joining a local garden club or plant society of your special interest. Ask about them at the extension office or the reference desk of your library.